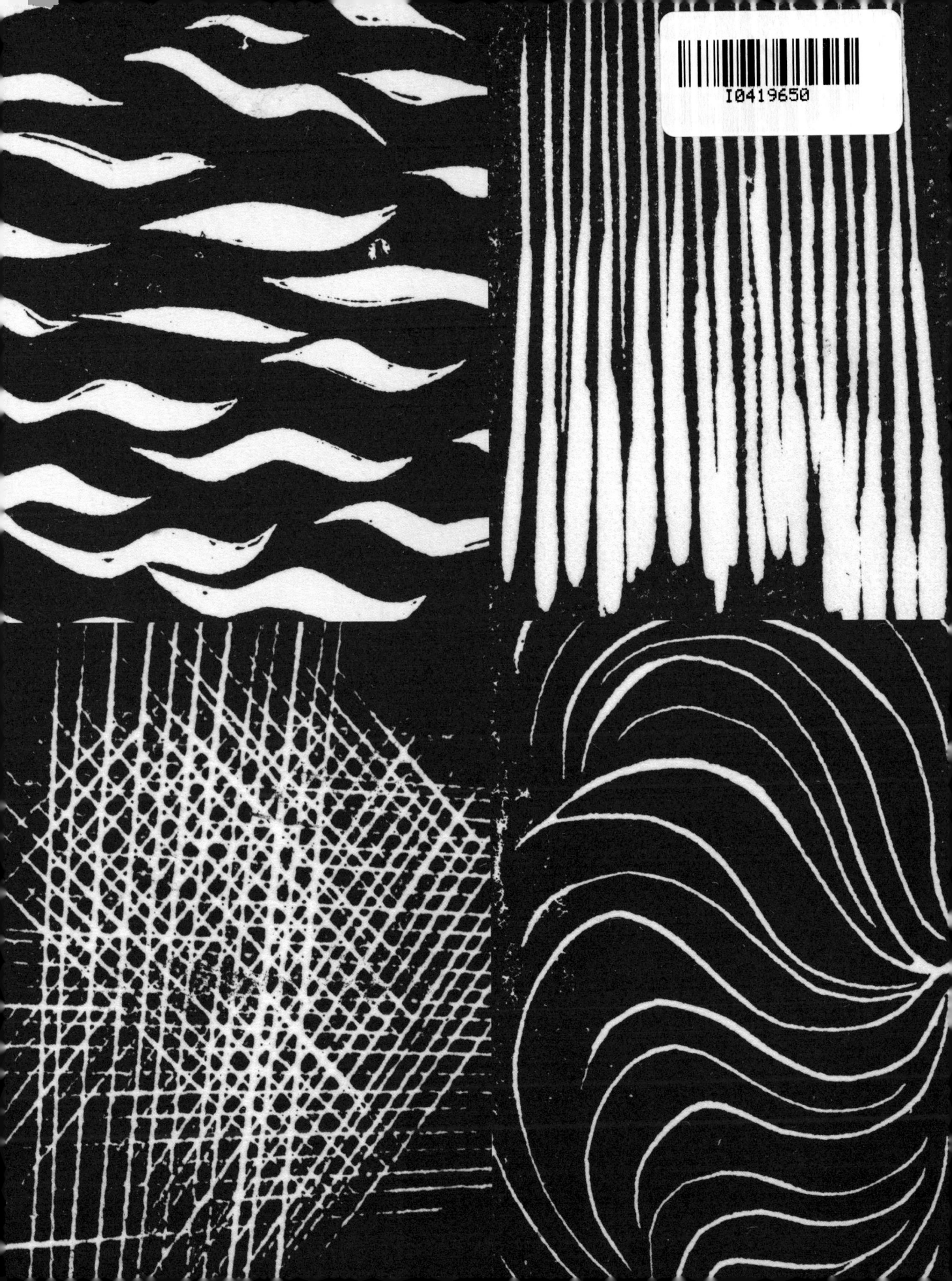

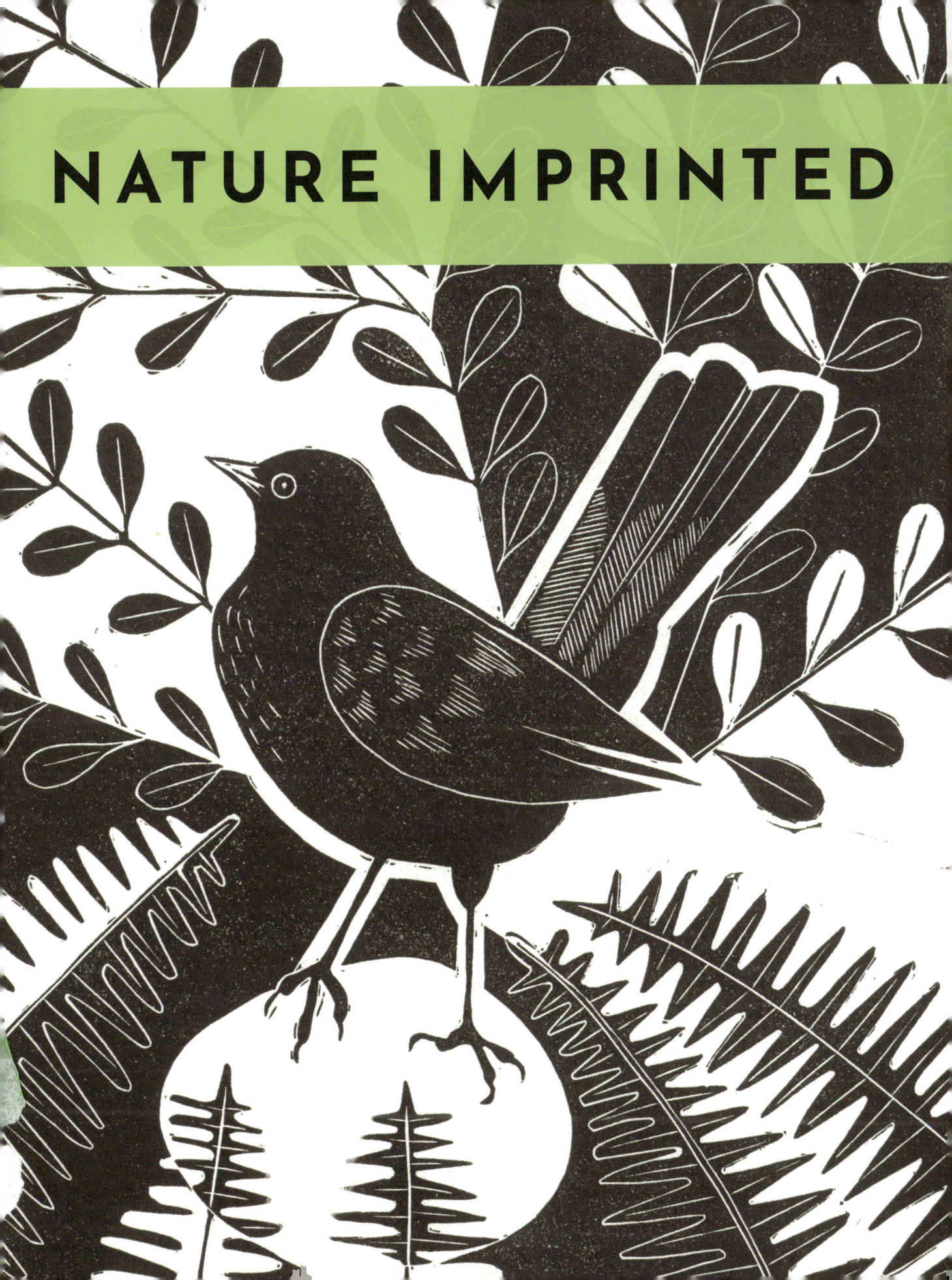

NATURE IMPRINTED

NATURE

First published in 2024

Search Press Limited
Wellwood, North Farm Road,
Tunbridge Wells, Kent TN2 3DR

Reprinted 2024, 2025

Text and templates copyright © Jane Spink, 2024

Cover design: Adam Constable

Book design copyright © Search Press Ltd., 2024

ISBN: 978-1-80092-097-2
ebook ISBN: 978-1-80093-088-9

GPSR information can be found at www.searchpress.com

SUPPLIERS
If you have difficulty in obtaining any of the materials and equipment mentioned in this book, then please visit the Search Press website for details of suppliers: www.searchpress.com

BOOKMARKED
Extra copies of the templates on pages 152–160 are also available to download free from the Bookmarked Hub. Search for this book by title or ISBN: the files can be found under 'Book Extras'. Membership of the Bookmarked online community is free. www.bookmarkedhub.com

DEDICATION
To Paul, Luke, Adam and Ben –
for your unending support of me
doing what I love to do.

ABOUT THE AUTHOR
You are invited to visit Jane's website:
www.inkydogstudio.com

Also visit her Instagram page, @inkydogstudio

PHOTOGRAPHS & ARTWORKS
Top artwork on page 11:
Hokusai, Katsushika. 'Under the Wave off Kanagawa' ('*Kanagawa oki nami ura*'), also known as 'The Great Wave', from the series Thirty-Six Views of Mount Fuji (*Fugaku sanjūrokkei*), c. 1830/33. From Clarence Buckingham Collection, via the Art Institute Chicago

Pine-cone image on page 76:
Jean Rivas via Unsplash

Photographs on pages 7, 26, 29, 51, 65, 66, 69, 67 (T), 68, 69, 82 (in image), 98 (T), 104 (T), 111 (in image), 118 (TL), 121 (TR) and 150:
copyright © Jane Spink, 2024

All remaining photographs:
Mark Davison (www.markdavison.com) for Search Press at Search Press Studios. Copyright © Search Press Ltd. 2024

MIX
Paper | Supporting
responsible forestry
FSC® C016973

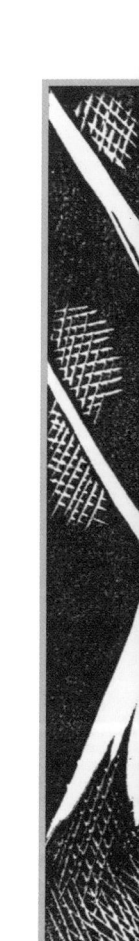

IMPRINTED

A complete guide to lino printing,
with 10 designs inspired by the natural world

JANE SPINK

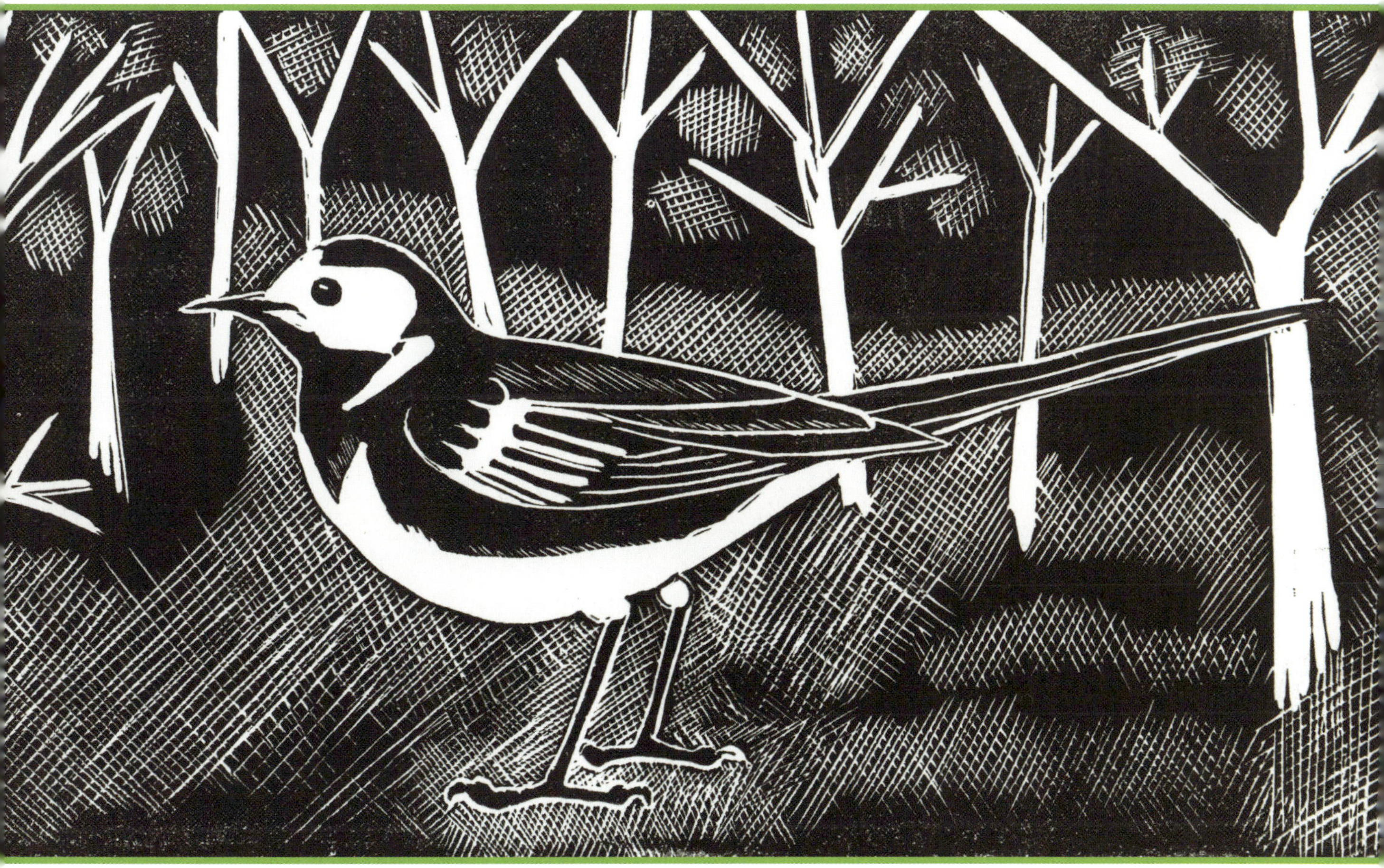

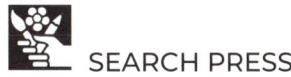

SEARCH PRESS

CONTENTS

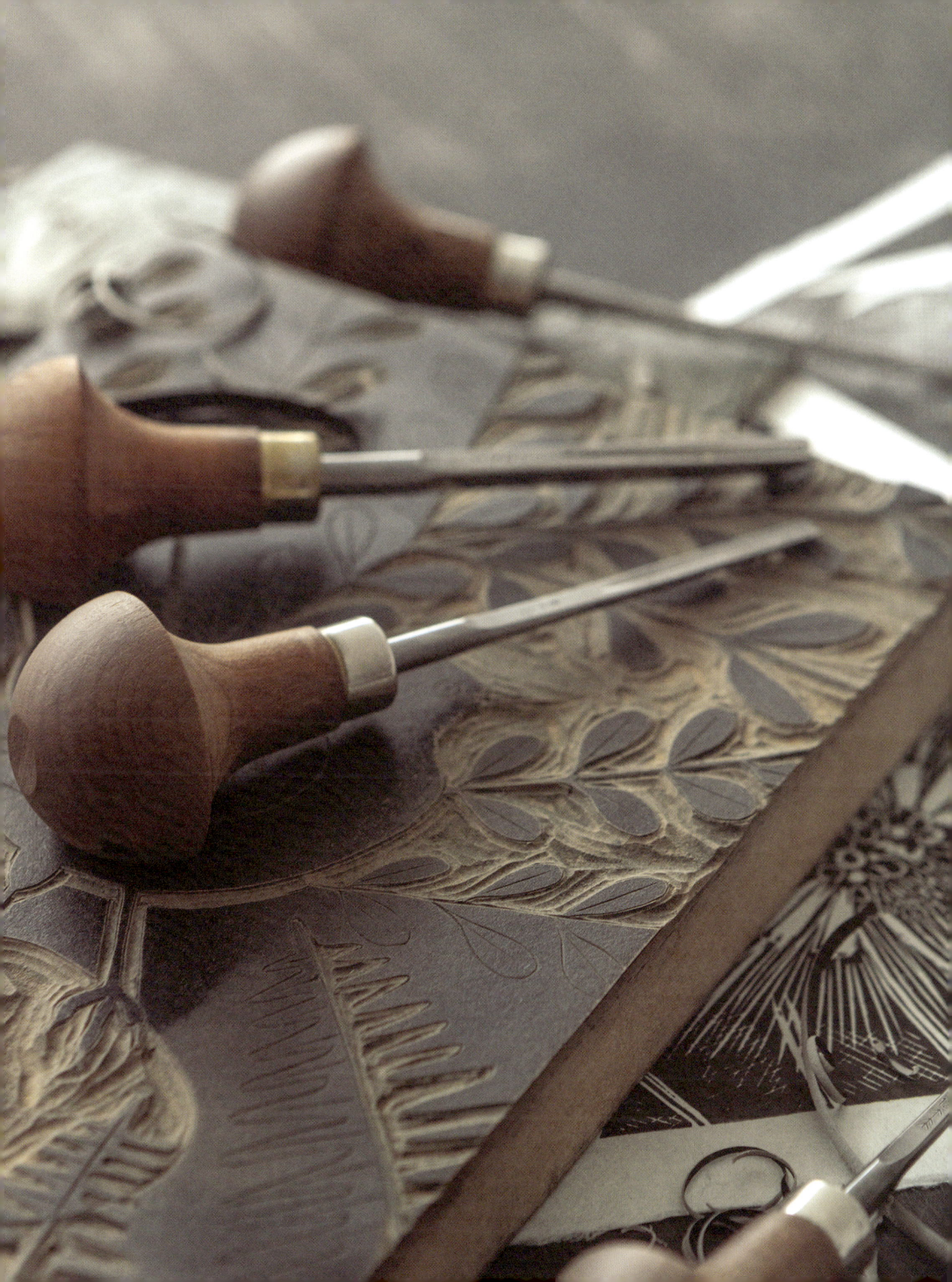

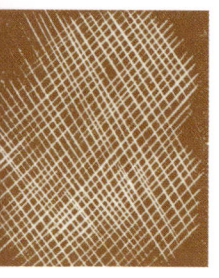

INTRODUCTION

As an artist who uses predominantly printmaking processes, my love affair with linocut printing has become far more than a brief fling! The range of marks and colours that's possible to achieve with this technique has made it one of my go-to methods for making artwork. I will never stop being amazed at the potential this process offers, to create new ideas. From strong, simple and graphic, to the capacity for achieving the finest details, linocut printing is a wonderful technique for creating many, many different styles of artwork.

Opposite
'Amongst the Autumn Brambles'
This design is a colour variation of my 'Amongst the Brambles' print, described later in this book (see page 66). I carved the design into a PVC linoleum substitute then printed it onto hand-made Thai mulberry paper. To achieve the colour gradient in this piece, I created a 'rainbow roll' with my brayer – I blended three different ink colours together while rolling out the inks, before applying them to the block.

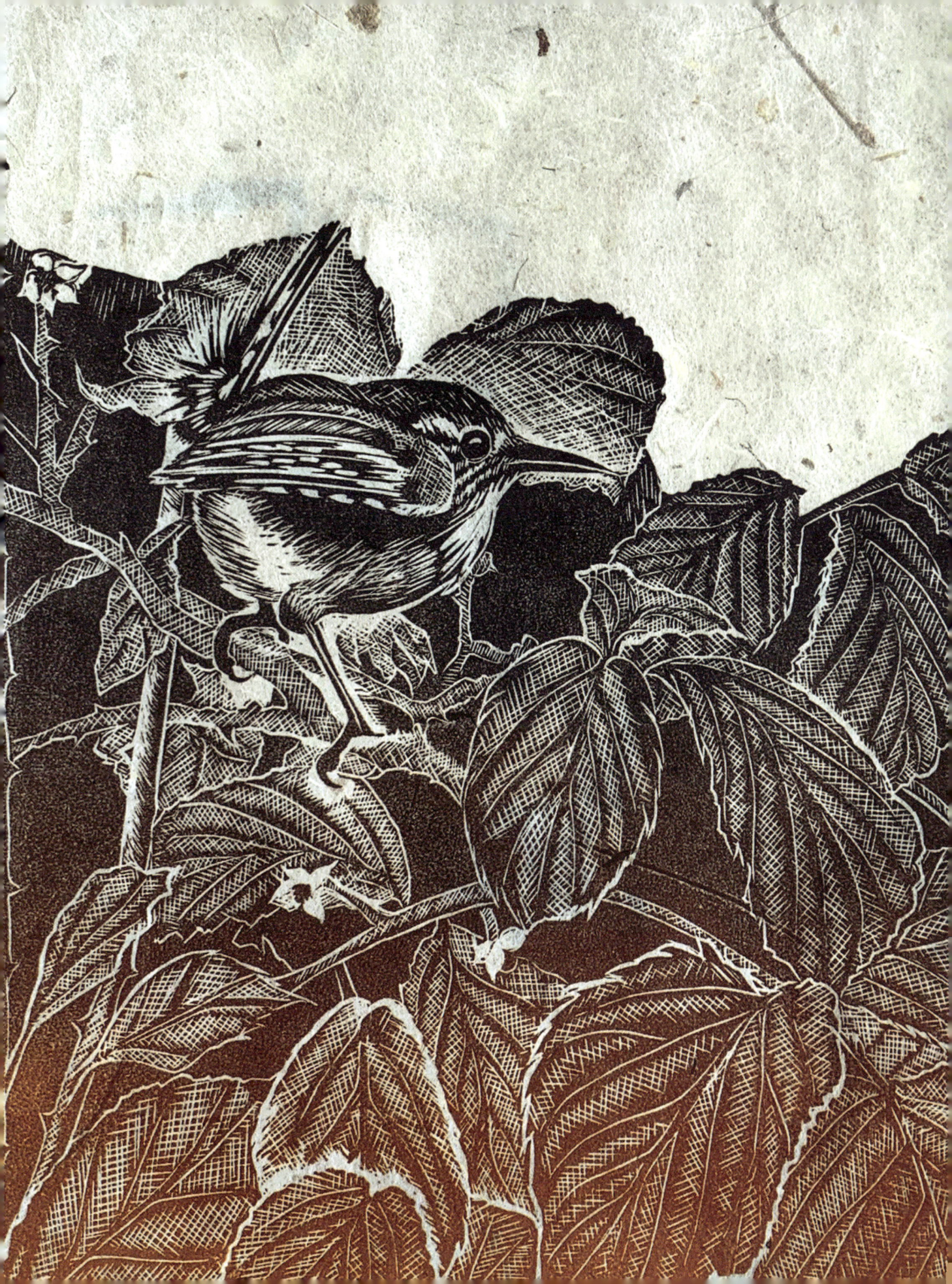

A number of people I have spoken to about my work remember learning some simple linocutting when they were at school. From my own experience of teaching art to children in secondary/high schools, it's clear to see that there is something comforting and reassuring about following a process that ends with such a satisfying result!

One of the great things about linocut printing is how accessible it is to everyone. Although linocut printing requires the artist to build up their skills over time, in order to create the type of work he or she desires, the concept of linocutting is simple. Fortunately, you really don't need to spend a lot to get started with this wonderfully versatile printmaking technique either – which you will discover as you read on! I find that the range of marks and textures achievable with linocut is very often a perfect way to realize my ideas for a piece of work – either as a stand-alone process, or in combination with other printmaking techniques.

I've been obsessed with nature since early childhood, so my own work is often populated with a selection of birds, insects, mammals and botanical subjects. In a similar way to how my love of birds and nature brings me comfort and inspiration, I find using printmaking processes for creating art to be absorbing and strangely reassuring in their own ways. Following a specific process to make a piece of artwork offers a structure to work within, a predictability which is never boring – mainly because following the same (or similar) paths when printmaking will rarely lead to the same result.

I confess unashamedly to being a purely visual learner and, personally, detest being confronted with wordy instruction manuals – which is something this book is definitely not intended to be! My other main aim for this book was to give people some starting points to inspire their own work. Creating artwork of any kind is infinitely more satisfying when it's a product of your own ideas, passions and experiences.

In the chapter 'What is linocutting?' (see pages 10 and 11), I have included a brief description of relief printmaking, and mentioned some artists who have used relief processes to make wonderful work. There is so much inspiration to be found by exploring the work of artists you admire and I would strongly recommend this.

Before you reach the 'Projects' section of this book, you will find chapters in which I discuss a variety of tools, equipment and materials used in linocut printing, followed by chapters on papers and inks (see pages 12–43).

In the all-important 'Techniques' chapter (see pages 44–63), there is a walkthrough on how to hold your tools correctly when carving. There are also some mark-making ideas, which will hopefully be a

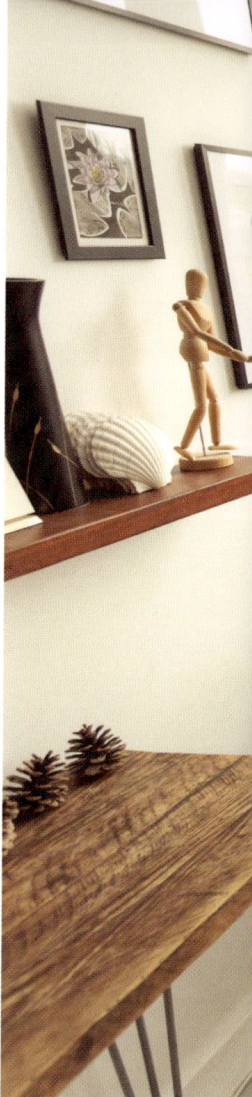

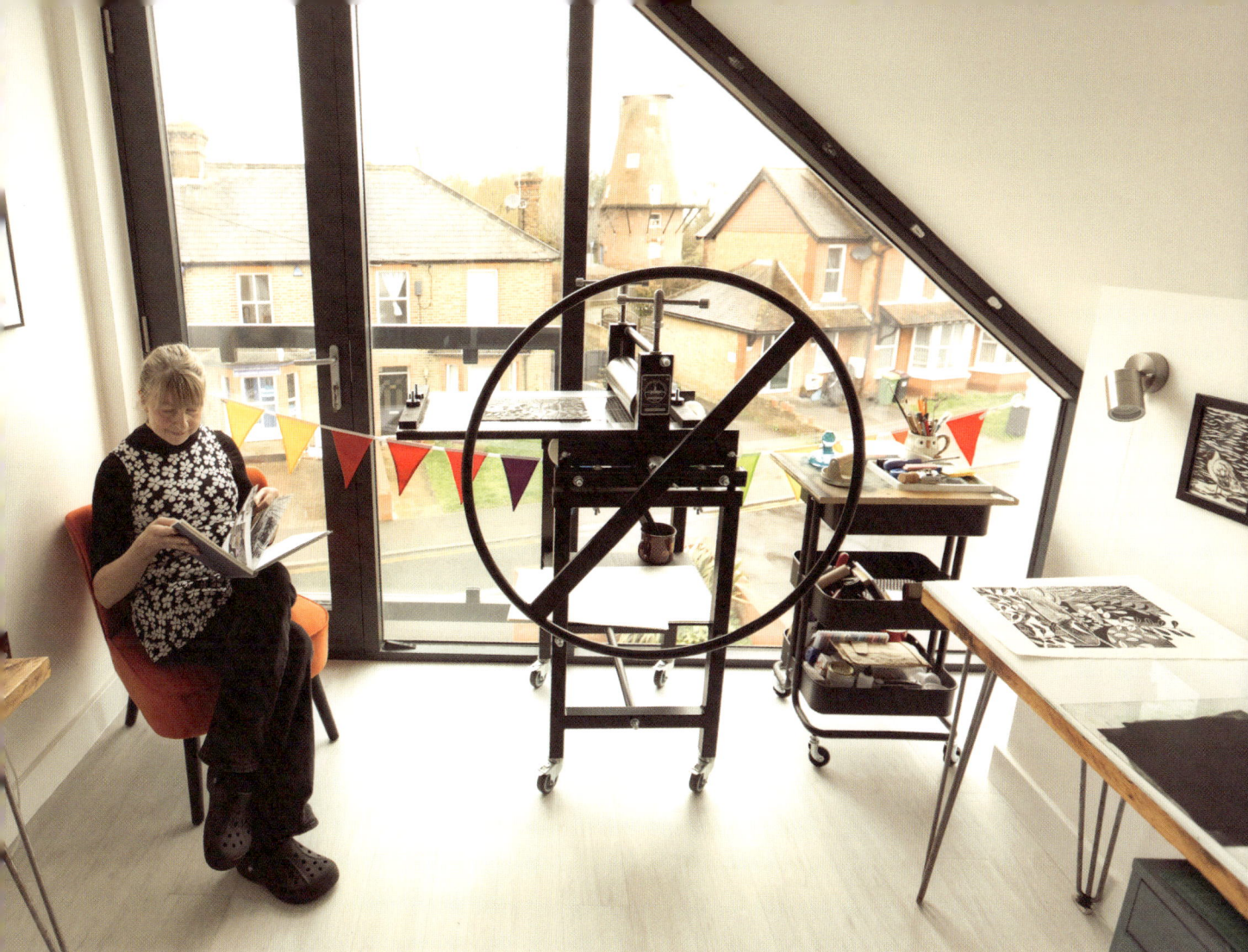

springboard for creating your own reference 'library' of carved marks and textures to use when carving your blocks. There is a simple, step-by-step demo project, which involves carving and printing a small stamp to get you warmed up before starting on the main projects.

In the 'Design & inspiration' chapter (see pages 64–71), I talk about my own inspiration, the starting points for my work and some of the outcomes of the pieces I've made.

I have also included a 'Troubleshooting' section after the 'Projects' section (see pages 140–147), which may help you to resolve some of the more common frustrations that can occur when creating a linocut print!

All that's left to be said now is let's design, let's carve, let's print – your journey starts here!

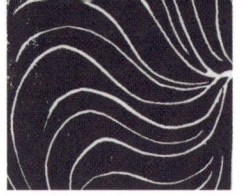

WHAT IS LINOCUTTING?

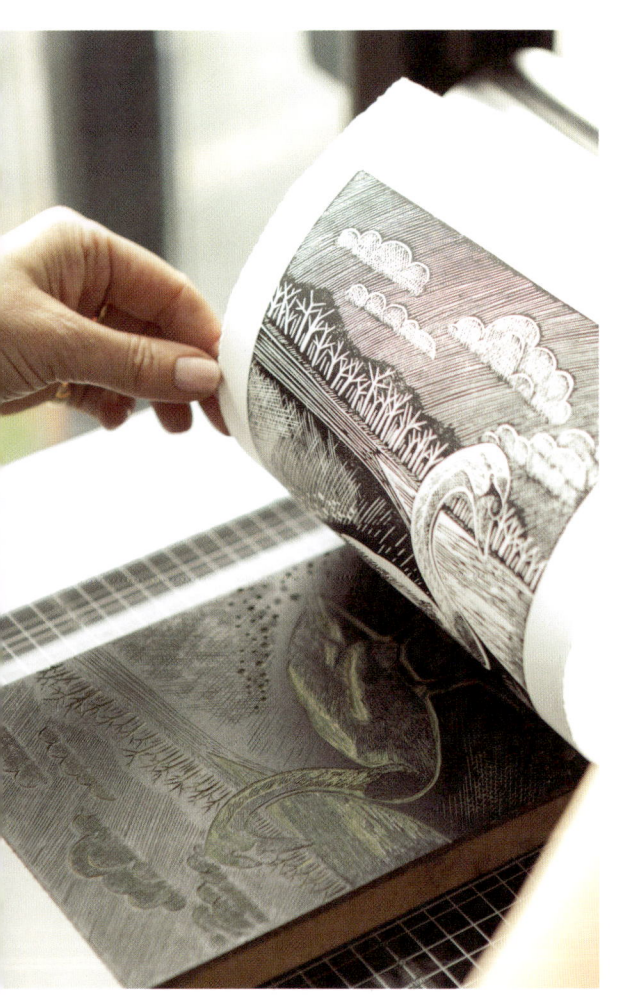

*Revealing 'My Walk Today' project
(see pages 109–115).*

A brief word on relief printmaking

Linocut printing is a form of 'relief' printmaking. The term refers to the fact that it is the 'raised' (uncarved) areas of the block or plate that form the print.

A 'printing plate' is made by carving into a linoleum block. The design is carved out from the block, in negative format, using a sharp metal tool. By 'negative format', we mean that the actual areas carved out are the parts of the block which *won't* be printed (they will appear as the 'white' areas of the print). Once the design on the block is carved out, a thin layer of ink is applied evenly with a brayer or roller. The ink will be applied only to the areas of lino that have not been carved out, therefore these are the areas which will print onto the surface (paper, fabric, and so on).

The opposite process to relief printing is the 'intaglio' process (see the tip box on page 28), where ink is rubbed into the plate and gathers in the areas that have been carved or scratched away. Unlike relief printing, intaglio prints are always made on damp paper and need a powerful press to make the print, such as an etching press. During this process, the rollers on the press push the dampened paper down into the inky scratched-out crevices of the plate, and in doing this, make a print.

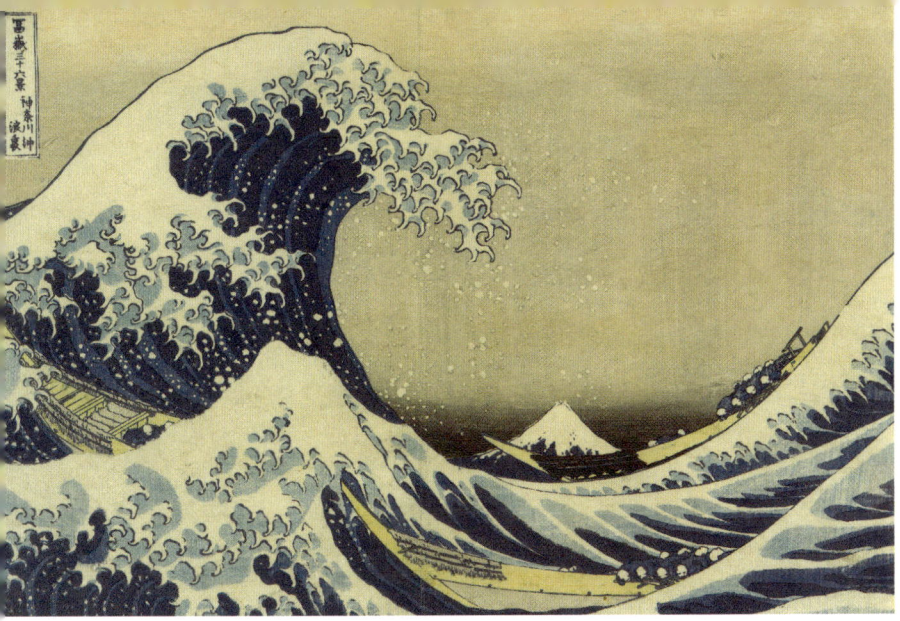

Hokusai, Katsushika, 'Under the Wave off Kanagawa' ('Kanagawa oki nami ura'), also known as 'The Great Wave'.

A short history of relief printing

Woodblock printing is thought to be the first type of relief printmaking, and first appeared in China around 2,000 years ago. The technique spread to Korea and then Japan, where it has been widely practised over the centuries. As the name suggests, this process involves carving into a wooden block, rather than a linoleum block.

Woodblock printing took off in Japan around the start of the seventeenth century. The mastery of the printmakers and the beauty of the prints they created have meant that Japanese woodblock prints have enjoyed an enduring popularity, which extends to this day. The work of master printmakers of the Edo period (1603–1867), like Katsushika Hokusai (1760–1849) and Utagawa Hiroshige (1797–1858), have been widely reproduced, and prints such as 'Under the Wave off Kanagawa' (see above) are instantly recognizable to many people.

The material 'linoleum' was invented in the UK by Frederick Walton (1834–1928) in the mid-1800s. A number of significant artists adopted this medium to make prints, including Henri Matisse (1869–1954) and Pablo Picasso (1881–1973). Twentieth-century British artist Edward Bawden (1903–1989) was also an accomplished printmaker, and produced a large number of works using the linocut printing process during the 1950s and 1960s. His prints included works depicting Kew Gardens and Liverpool Street Station, and he also created a series on the London Markets. Bawden's prints are clear, distinctive and often graphic in design. They are wonderful examples of the strong, bold style achievable through linocutting. This can be seen in his linocut print 'Autumn' (1950), in which he expresses his love of plants and gardening.

The bold, graphic characteristics of relief printmaking present many possibilities, and it is both interesting and inspiring to see how artists over time have used this technique to create powerful visual works. It's also worth looking at the work of German Expressionist artists, such as Ernst Ludwig Kirchner (1880–1938), Max Beckmann (1884–1950) and Otto Dix (1891–1969), whose bold style of woodcut prints can also be achieved by working with lino.

Finally, as an artist who takes my inspiration from nature, it would be impossible for me not to mention the work of wonderful English artist and illustrator Charles Tunnicliffe RA (1901–1979). Tunnicliffe produced a number of exquisite wood engravings to illustrate books, in the first half of the twentieth century. This includes 'Tufted Ducks' , which appears alongside many other mind-blowingly beautiful wood engravings in *A Book of Birds* by Mary Priestley, published in 1937.

TOOLS & EQUIPMENT

Linocut printing requires relatively little equipment to be able to begin designing and making your own prints, and relief printing is one of the few printmaking processes where it isn't essential to own a press in order to make prints. This makes linocutting one of the cheaper forms of printmaking to get started in.

In fact, there are 'starter kits' available at a reasonable price from a number of online and brick-and-mortar stores, which give you the key materials and equipment you need to begin your linocutting journey. Add to this a wooden spoon for hand-burnishing, and you have everything you need to get printing!

In addition to the essential materials and equipment you will need to begin your printmaking, I'll also share some future investment suggestions to help you develop and extend your practice as a relief printmaker in the future.

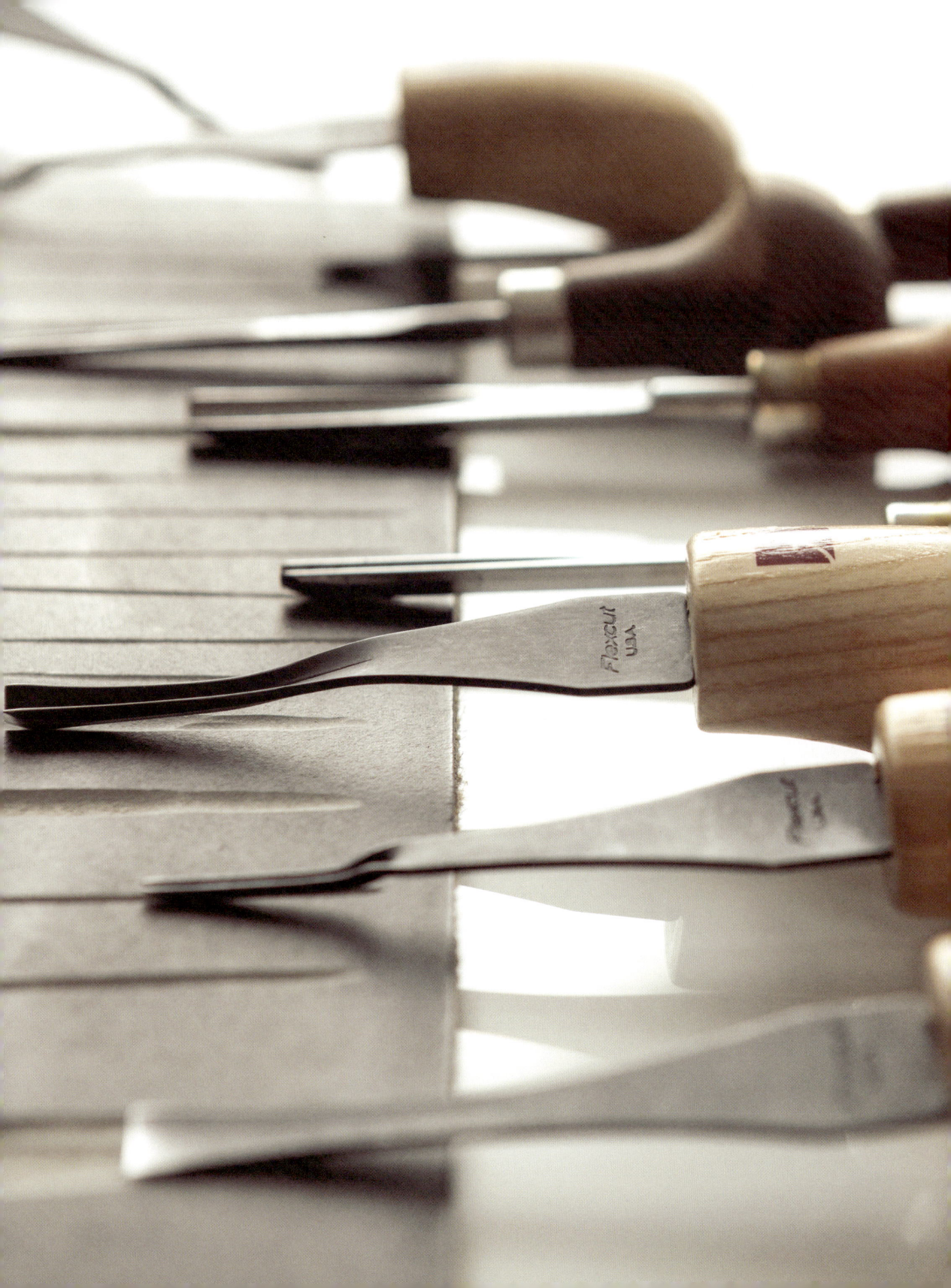

Cutting surfaces

Your cutting surface is the material you carve into, to make your printing block. There are three different options available:

— **Traditional linoleum** comes in colours 'battleship grey' or brown, and has a hessian backing (see the top-right photograph opposite).

— **Softer linoleum carving substitutes made from PVC**. There are many of these available and they vary in softness and thickness.

— **Japanese printmaking vinyl** is blue on one side and green on the other. This material is favoured by many printmakers, as it's seen as a 'halfway house' between traditional linoleum and PVC substitutes in terms of hardness, and how it feels to carve.

All of the above have advantages and disadvantages, which I will discuss over the next few pages. At the end of the day, it's down to personal choice and most printmakers will have their own particular favourite.

WARNING

It's not advisable to submerge hessian-backed linoleum in water, as the hessian backing gets soaked and causes the linoleum to curl as it dries. Also, if it's subjected to too many dunks in water, the surface of traditional linoleum will start to crack and crumble after a while.

TRADITIONAL LINOLEUM (LINO)

As the name suggests, this is the original standard lino and the go-to carving material for many relief printmakers. It is similar to the floor covering material we all know of as 'lino', but differs in that it is specially made for carving into. It comes in thicknesses of 3mm (⅛in) or 5mm (¼in), is widely available online and in brick-and-mortar art stores, and can be purchased in rolls or ready-cut in various convenient sizes.

Advantages:

— It's possible to achieve the finest of details in your designs. This is because the surface is rigid compared to softer PVC substitutes, and therefore the marks you carve in it will not change or 'close up' after cutting.

— Prints can be made either by hand-burnishing with a spoon or baren (see page 24), or by using a printing press (see pages 25–28). A block carved from traditional linoleum will print especially well with an etching press (see page 28), whereas a two-plate printing press (see page 25) may need a little help with some additional burnishing, before the paper is lifted. Performing this extra step will ensure that your prints turn out to be sharp, crisp and even!

Disadvantages:

— It can become hard and rigid if it has been stored in a cold place – warming it up on a radiator for a while before use can help with this.

— Traditional lino can curl up, particularly if it becomes wet or damp. For this reason, never wash your blocks in water (see the warning box, left, and the tip box on 'A note on cleaning up' on page 37). It may help to store linoleum blocks which have started to curl under a heavy weight, for instance a pile of books, to keep them nice and flat.

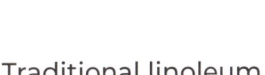

Mounted traditional linoleum:

You can purchase hessian-backed linoleum that comes ready-mounted on blocks of MDF or similar. These are available in a range of different sizes and have the advantage of being extremely sturdy and flat to work on – and, of course, they are totally curl-proof! They also feel nice and substantial to carve into, not dissimilar to a block of wood.

Please bear in mind that linoleum in this format will be more costly than purchasing it unmounted, in single sheets or by the roll. However, it is possible to make your own mounted blocks by glueing your sheet of linoleum onto a pre-cut MDF block of an identical size; this could possibly work out cheaper too. Personally, I prefer to buy my blocks ready-mounted, as the process of mounting them securely can be tricky; MDF blocks would also need to be cut neatly to the correct sizes, requiring access to a jigsaw or similar machinery.

If you like to use a press for printing, please be aware that, depending on the thickness of the block your linoleum is mounted on, it may not be possible to use certain types of two-plate press. When I use mounted linoleum blocks, either I hand-burnish my prints or use my etching press to print.

Traditional linoleum

Hessian-backed linoleum (see above) comes in 'battleship grey' and brown colours (see below).

Note: 'battleship grey' traditional lino is fully biodegradable unlike the other options, so this should be your choice if you wish to be more ecologically friendly.

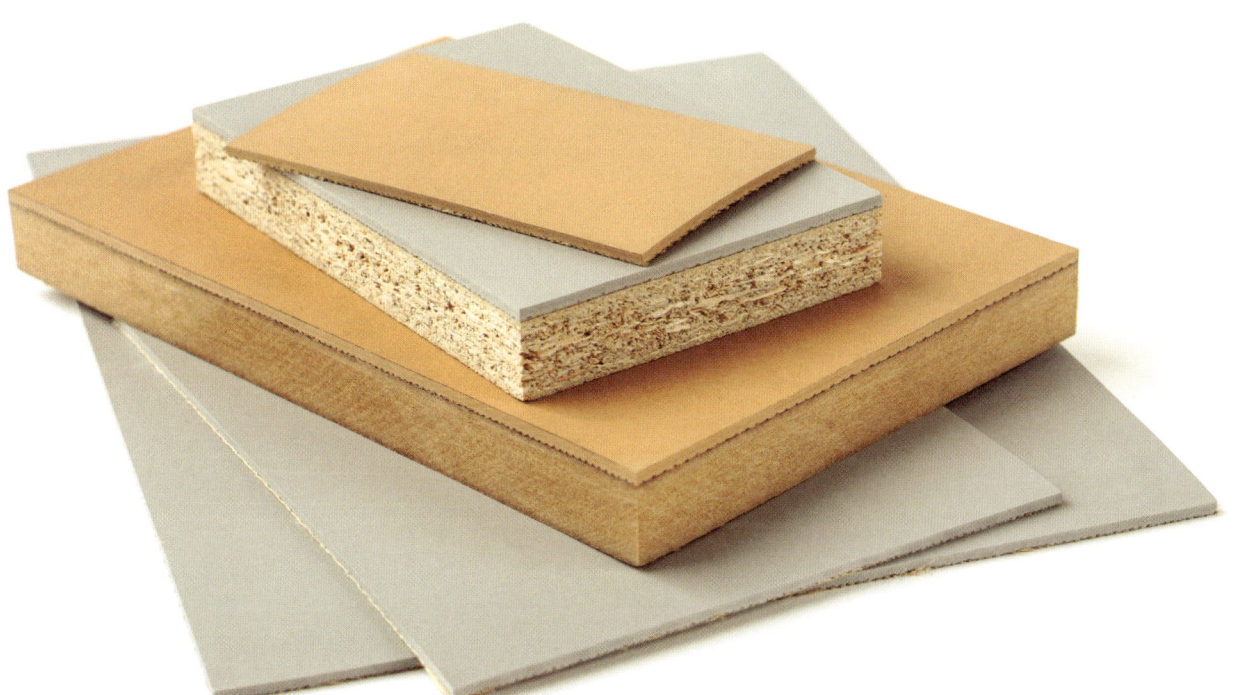

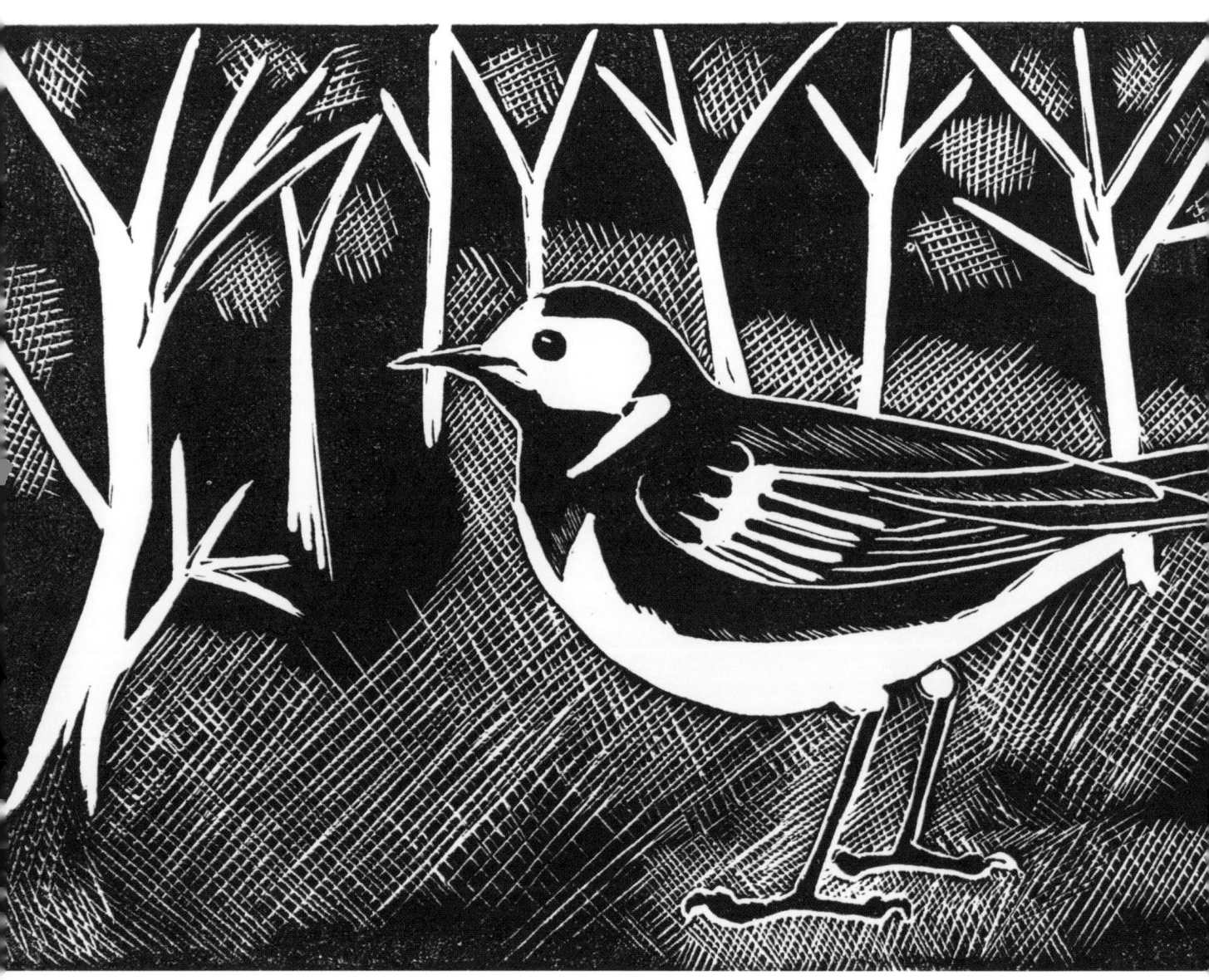

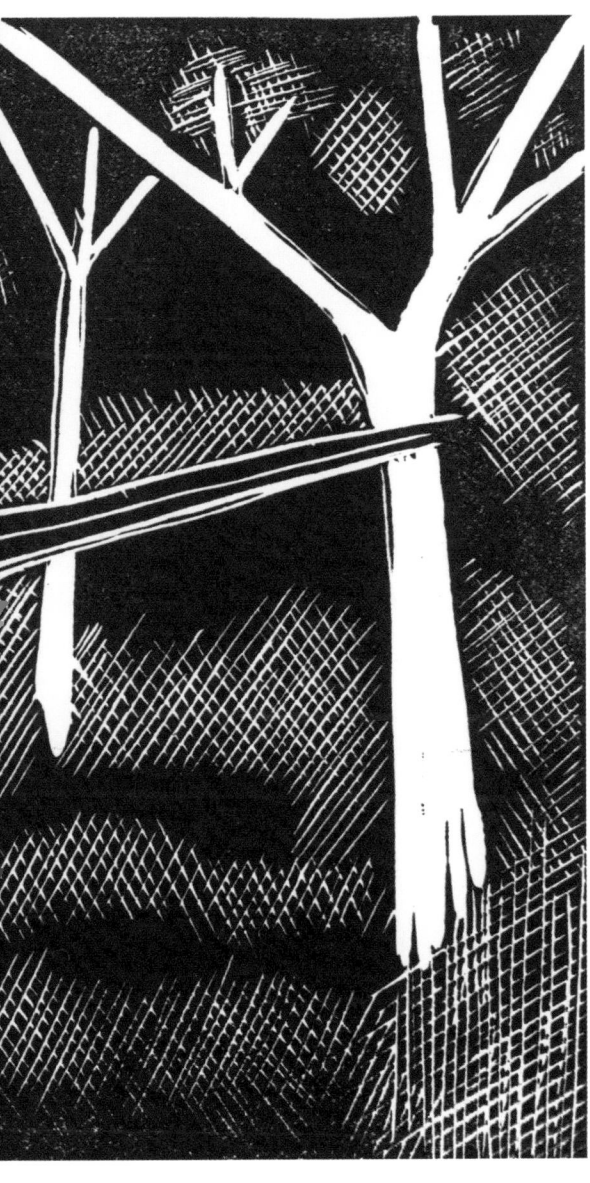

'A Study in Lino'
For the project, see pages 86–89.

PVC LINOLEUM

These lino substitutes are widely available online and in art stores. There are many different ones around and they come in a variety of different colours, with names such as Easy Cut by Zieler®, SoftCut™ by Esdee, Speedy-Cut™ and Speedy-Carve™. They come ready-cut in different sizes, but are also easy to cut to custom sizes and shapes with a craft blade, if required.

Although the most 'purist' printmaker might say that no other carving surface can touch traditional linoleum for the quality of detail that can be achieved, these PVC substitutes do have some advantages.

Advantages:

— PVC lino is easy to carve, as the softness and pliability of the material allows your carving tools to glide through the block with little effort. This makes them kinder to your tools too, and means you need to sharpen them less often.

— It's a good choice for anyone who might experience pain or discomfort when carving a less yielding surface, for example people who suffer from conditions such as rheumatoid arthritis or carpal tunnel syndrome. They are also good for beginners.

— Most PVC lino substitutes can be used with both water-based and oil-based inks, however there are certain brands that are only suitable for use with water-based inks. Do check the check your choice of lino brand, if you plan to use oil-based inks.

— Cleaning up is simple. The block can be washed in warm soapy water after use without fear of curling up, as hessian-backed traditional lino is prone to do.

— Contrary to popular belief, it is possible to achieve a high level of detail in your carving, using suitable tools. Speedy-Carve™ by Speedball®, a pink-coloured carving material, is used by printmakers the world over and is very good for carving fine marks and details.

Disadvantages:

— The softness of the PVC substitutes might be seen as a disadvantage by those who prefer to carve on a harder surface, with fine details being harder to achieve with some brands than with the traditional linoleum.

— If you wish to print with an etching press (see page 28), you will need to mount your block onto a sheet of plywood or a similar hard material before printing. This is because the softness of the PVC causes the block to 'squash' down under the high pressure of the press's rollers, and this in turn causes movement of the block when printing. Some brands will simply be too soft to print at all with an etching press, even if they are mounted.

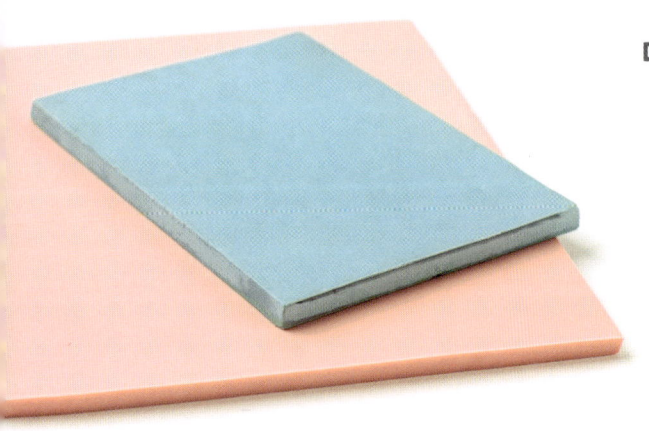

PVC Linoleum

Two PVC linoleum substitutes, Speedy-Cut™ (blue) and Speedy-Carve™ (pink), both from Speedball®.

JAPANESE VINYL

This alternative carving material is harder than the PVC linoleum substitutes, but its surface is more yielding than traditional linoleum, so could be seen as a good balance between the two. Interestingly, it is bi-coloured – one side is green and the other blue – giving it a distinctive appearance. Sheets of Japanese vinyl can be purchased in a variety of pre-cut sizes, and is easy to cut into custom shapes and sizes if required.

I haven't use Japanese vinyl to create the projects in this book, but I recommend experimenting with it if the advantages appeal to you.

Advantages:

— With its unique appearance and ease of carving, Japanese vinyl offers a good alternative to traditional lino to printmakers who use a lot of fine detail in their work.

— The vinyl is incredibly durable, lies beautifully flat and doesn't curl or bend, even after washing.

— It has a black core, which makes it very easy to see where you've carved.

— It's super easy to cut with a craft knife and is perfect for making multi-coloured 'jigsaw' prints, where different coloured areas of the design need to be seamlessly slotted together after inking, before they can be printed.

Disadvantages:

As always it comes down to personal preference, but from where I'm standing there are few disadvantages with this material.

— If you suffer from hand or wrist conditions that prevent you from carving into harder materials, you may still find Japanese vinyl too hard to carve. In which case, you can opt to use a PVC linoleum substitute.

Japanese vinyl

Sheets of Japanese vinyl, which can be purchased in a variety of sizes. The vinyl is green on one side and blue on the other.

Cutting tools

There is a wide range of cutting tools available to choose from, and they're essential for carving your designs onto lino.

The cutting tools you use dictate the size and shape of the marks you carve. If your tool has a small V-shaped tip, you will carve a thin line. If the tip of the tool is large, wide and U-shaped, you will carve a much wider, deeper line.

It stands to reason, then, that small V-shape tools are for carving fine details, while the larger U-shape tools are good for clearing larger areas of lino that are intended to appear 'white' when the block is printed onto paper.

The cost of carving tools varies considerably, depending on the brand, the quality and the materials the tools are made of.

1 *SlipStrop™ by Flexcut®, a kit which includes a gold polishing compound.*

2 *Speedball® No. 1 Lino Cutter Assortment (includes five interchangeable blades).*

3 *Swiss Cutting Tools by Pfeil, Set C. I have used sizes L 8/7 (large U-shape), L 9/2 (small U-shape) and L 12/1 (small V-shape).*

4 *Carving tools by Flexcut®. A selection from the Mini Palm Set, the Micro Palm Set and 'Beginners' Palm Set are shown here: the 1mm (fine) V-shape, the 1.5mm (medium) U-shape and the no. 8 10mm chisel tool.*

— It is possible to purchase a 'starter' set consisting of a **plastic handle and interchangeable cutting blades** for very little money, making this an affordable way to start out on your linocutting journey. The cutting blades don't need sharpening, as they are simply disposed of when blunt; replacement blades are then fitted onto the handle. **Do check with your local authority for the correct way to dispose of the blades!** Although it's possible to use these tools to carve on any of the three types of surface (see pages 14–19), I've found they work best on the softer PVC lino substitutes, where some good results can be achieved.

— Both from a personal perspective and if you are serious about developing your craft as a printmaker, I would strongly recommend investing in a small selection of high-quality **specialist carving tools**, or even just one, such as those made by Pfeil and Flexcut®. These tools have strong steel blades set in ergonomically shaped wooden handles and are wonderful to carve with. There is a large selection of tip sizes and shapes to choose from, for every imaginable carving task – from carving tiny details to sweeping away large areas of background lino. The tools can be purchased for a reasonable price, and are often available to buy in sets, which come in a nice storage boxes.

STORING TOOLS

It's important to store your tools safely, either by hanging them on a special rack or by keeping them in a storage box, to separate the tools, to prevent the blades from being damaged by hitting against each other, and to stop you from inadvertently cutting yourself too.

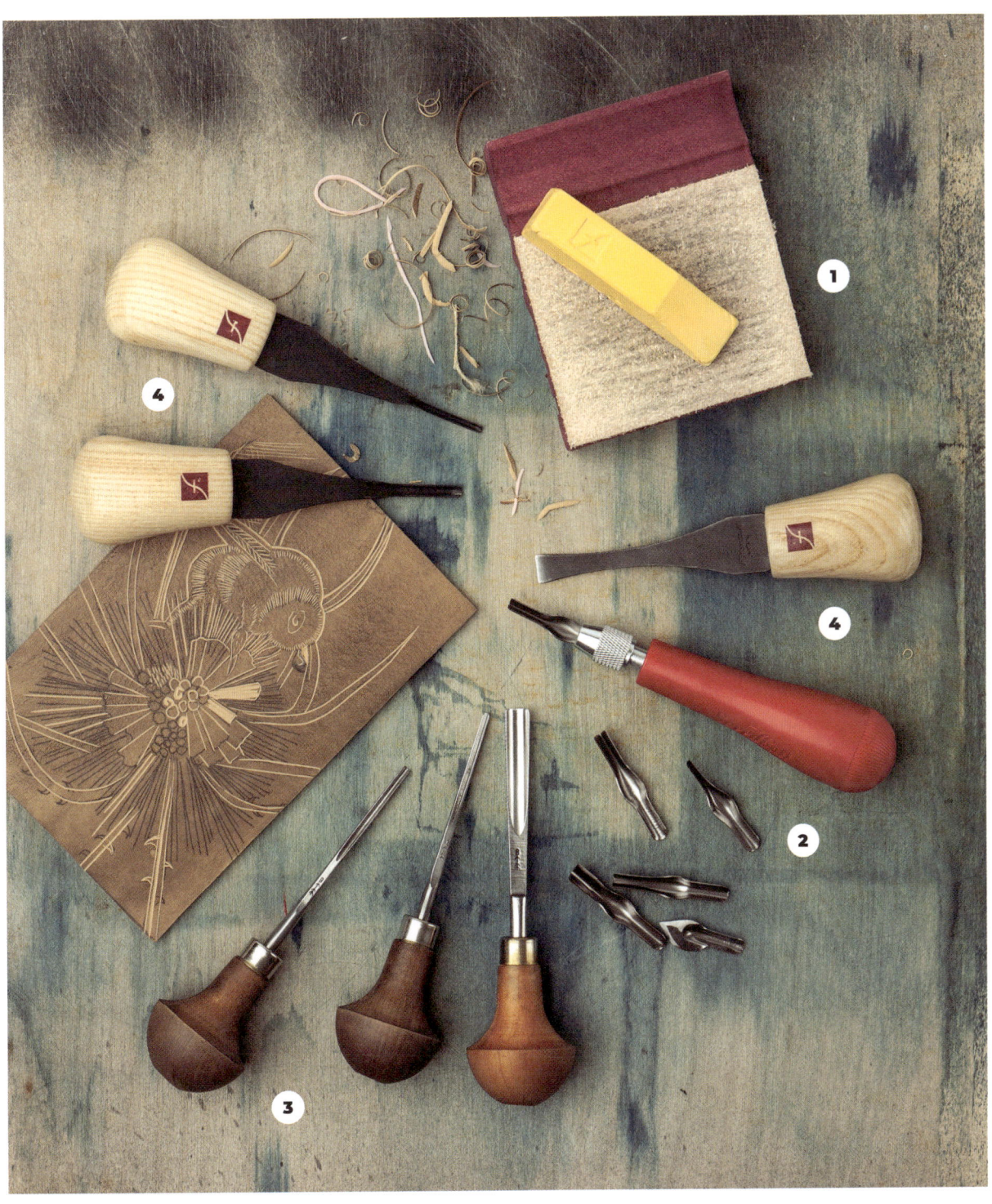

HONING & SHARPENING TOOLS

Unlike the disposable blades that come with the cheaper starter sets, your specialist carving tools will need sharpening from time to time.

Tools which are allowed to go blunt will cause your lino to crumble and tear as you carve, and are more liable to slip and cause injury. Honing and sharpening your own tools can be a little daunting, as it is possible to ruin them if it's not done correctly!

Sharpening can be done by purchasing a special 'waterstone' and rubbing the sides of the tools on the stone to sharpen the edges. If you'd rather not do this yourself, there are tool suppliers who offer a sharpening service where you send your tools to be sharpened. The tools will then be returned to you as sharp as the day you purchased them!

A less risky way you can keep your tools functioning well between professional sharpening is to use a leather 'strop', which hones the blades. It is possible to make a simple leather strop by attaching a piece of leather hide onto a small block of wood.

If you don't want to make your own strop, Flexcut® have made a 'SlipStrop™' that has leather hide attached on one side and a range of 'profiles' on the other. Also supplied with the SlipStrop™ is a special yellow 'polishing compound'. This is a kind of chalk, made of aluminium oxide and titanium oxide, that is rubbed over the strop and profiles prior to honing, making the whole procedure more efficient!

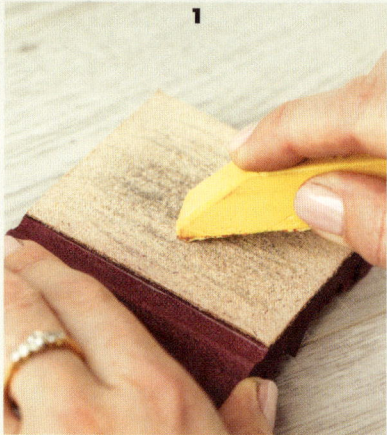

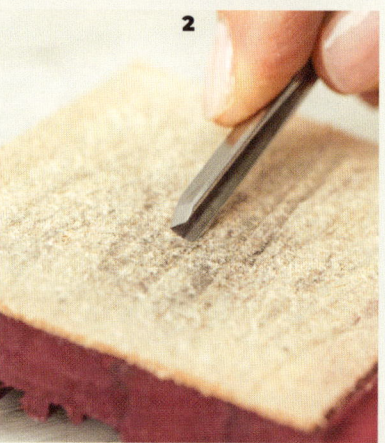

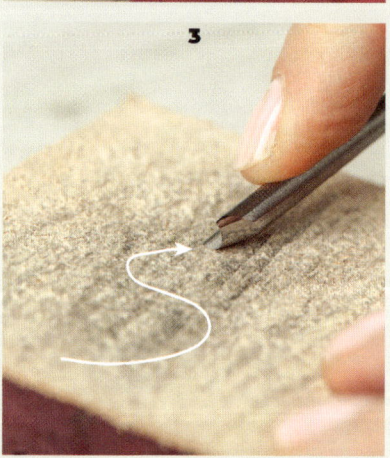

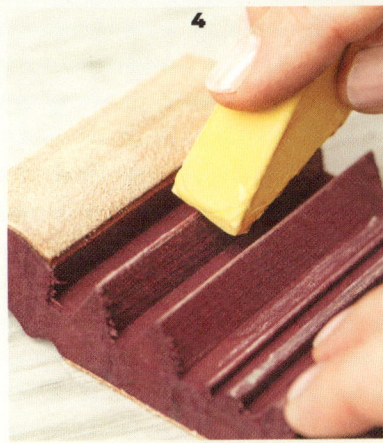

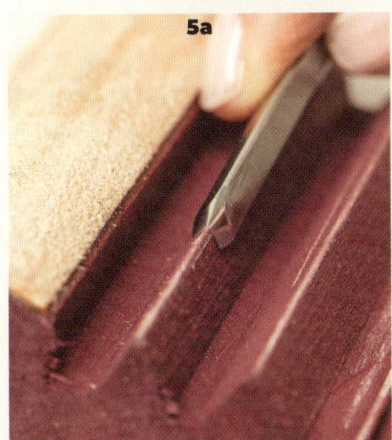

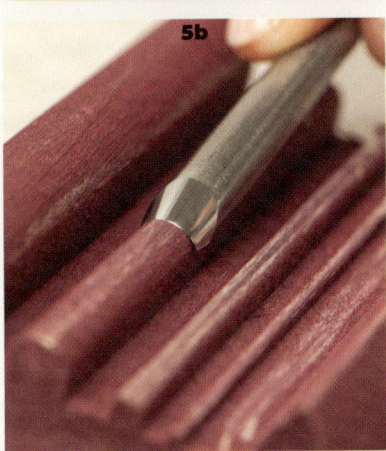

How to hone with a SlipStrop™

1 Rub the polishing compound on the flat leather side of the SlipStrop™ block. Liberally apply this, to prepare the surface effectively.

2 The blade is honed by holding the tool at a near 180-degree angle (almost flat), so the edge of the blade is in contact with the surface of the strop. Pull the blade towards you, applying enough pressure so that it 'scrapes' against the surface of the leather. If the blade is V-shaped, repeat these steps for each side of the 'V'. Never push the tool away from you, as you will damage the strop and possibly your blade too!

3 If your tool has a U-shaped blade, gently roll the tool from side to side as you pull it towards you (see the shape of the white arrow), so that the whole tip makes contact with the SlipStrop™ after one 'pull'.

4 After honing your tool on the leather side, flip the SlipStrop™ block so you can see the profile side, on which you'll remove any burrs that have collected on the inside of the blade. Prepare the profiles by rubbing the polishing compound over them.

5 Then gently pull your tools towards you, over the profile that matches the shape and size of the blade. There are pointed profiles for your V-shaped cutting tools (**5a**) and round profiles for your U-shaped tools (**5b**).

Pressing tools

It isn't essential to use a printing press for relief printing (which includes linocut printing), but it would be wrong of me not to include anything about presses in this section.

Printing presses come in a variety of different types, sizes and budget levels – so if you're already some way along on your printmaking journey, you may feel the time has come to invest in one of these wonderful pieces of equipment! If you're just starting out and your budget won't yet stretch to a larger investment, don't worry: you can make your prints by hand-burnishing and achieve the most beautiful results, as proven by master printmakers through the centuries who used this ancient pressing technique, creating works which now hang in museums and galleries across the world.

HAND-BURNISHING TOOLS

In its simplest form, a burnishing tool can be a humble spoon. Wooden spoons are often favoured by printmakers, but an everyday metal dessert or teaspoon can also be used! In the 'Techniques' chapter (see page 44), I demonstrate how to make a small print by burnishing with the back of a teaspoon. Other implements such as 'bone handles' can also be used to hand-burnish small prints.

If you can afford to invest in a piece of equipment called a 'baren' to burnish your prints, you may find this easier to use than a spoon or bone handle. A baren specially designed to have a proportionally large burnishing surface and an often chunky handle that is comfortable to grip and may give you greater control too. You can also buy barens made from glass, which glide smoothly over the back of your paper as you burnish.

If you're in a position to invest in a good baren, I would strongly recommend that you do so. Not only can you use it as a sole means of making your prints, it can also be used to burnish small areas of prints that have been printed on a printed press, but have slightly uneven areas of ink coverage. If you carefully lift one end of the paper before removing it from your block, it is possible to drop it back down again (in exactly the same position!) and burnish the uneven area, before lifting the print up from the block. In this way, you may be able to save a print which would otherwise be relegated to the reject pile!

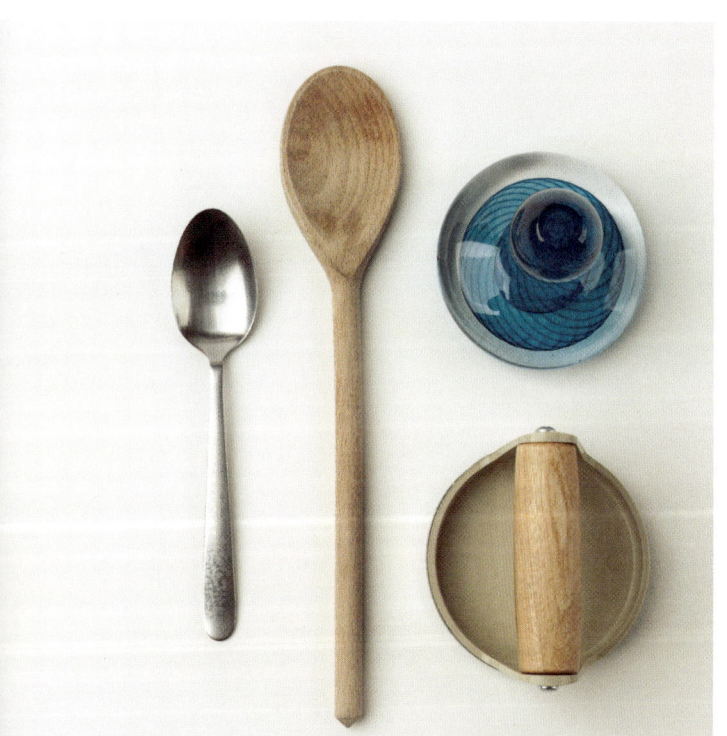

Barens
To start, a simple teaspoon or wooden spoon will suffice. If you continue in your printmaking journey, there are lots of specialist barens from which to choose, from those made of glass to wooden barens with a sturdy handle.

PRINTING PRESSES

A printing press is a mechanical device used to apply pressure to an inked block (with the chosen printing surface on top of it), thereby transferring the ink.

Printing presses come in a wide variety of shapes, sizes and prices. Depending on the type of press and the condition it's in (if it's been purchased secondhand), you can pay very little all the way up to hundreds of thousands of pounds or dollars.

Although, as we've discussed, a press isn't an essential item for linocut printing, most printmakers aspire to owning a printing press at some point in their career. Some save up their hard-earned money from selling their prints to buy a new press, others scout boot fairs or antiques fairs for that secondhand bargain. Some people even rescue non-working presses and lovingly restore them to their former glory! If you're in the market for making that investment to take you to your next level of printmaking, here's a brief roundup of presses you might consider – this is definitely not an exhaustive list though!

Lever-operated relief-printing press

These presses are designed for linocut and woodcut printing, and have a simple lever mechanism for applying the pressure to make a print. They consist of two thick wooden plates, the bottom of which is the 'bed' of the press. There are a number of brands currently available, all with similar operating mechanisms. Some are supplied with a 'printing blanket', which helps to achieve a more even pressure when printing. They make ideal entry-level presses as they are very simple to operate and are relatively inexpensive – for example the compact A5 (148 x 210mm/Junior Legal) size Woodzilla press, like the one I have. It's perfect for making small prints, printing your own greetings cards and even for small fabric printing projects. And when you're done with printing for the day, it fits beautifully on a shelf – ideal if you're pushed for space!

Lever-operated relief press

For very small prints up to A5 (148 x 210mm/Junior Legal) size, I like to use the A5 press by Woodzilla.

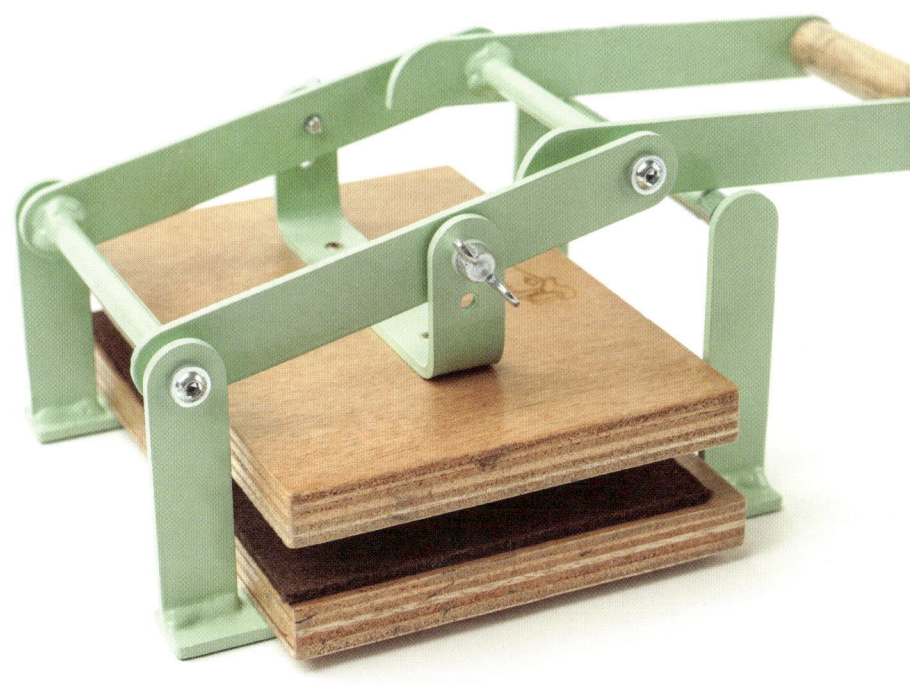

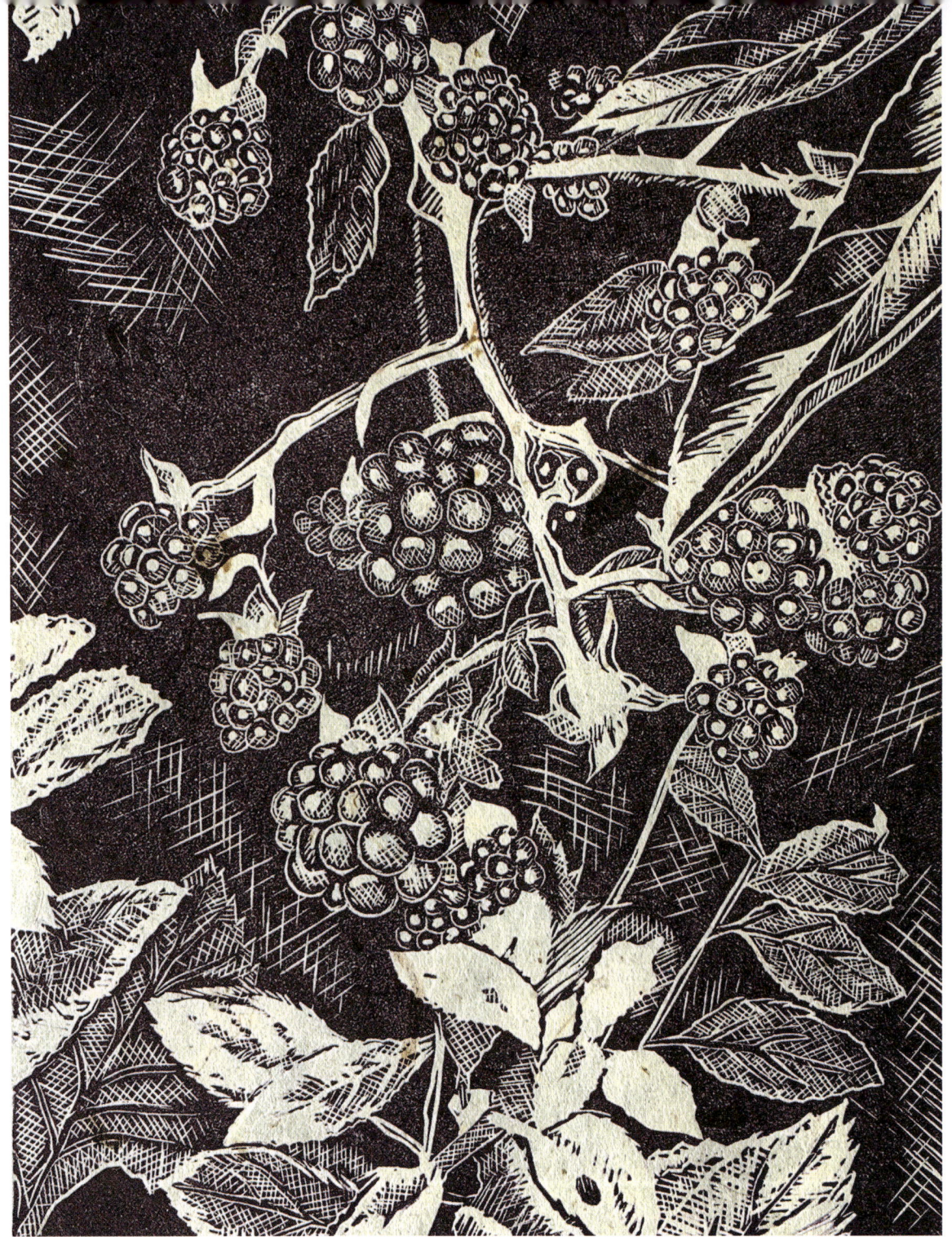

'Blackberries'

*This is a single-block print on hand-made Thai mulberry paper,
measuring approximately 12 x 15.5cm (4¾ x 6in).*

Book press

A book press is a two-plate press, in which the upper plate is lowered down onto the lower plate with a screw mechanism by turning a wheel or crank. Pressure is applied by tightening the crank as much as is needed to make a print.

Book presses, or 'nipping' presses, were traditionally made of cast iron and used for book binding. Today, original models are highly sought-after and can command high prices, particularly if they are in good working condition. It is possible to find a book press in an antiques market or online, but do bear in mind that the cast iron presses are extremely heavy and therefore only suitable for a ground-floor workshop or studio.

Book presses can also be made from wood. The lighter nature of the material means that it's not possible to get the same amount of pressure from a wooden press as from a cast-iron one, but they are cheaper to buy and much easier to transport. Also, there are some great secondhand bargains to be had if you look around – I managed to find mine on Facebook Marketplace for an extremely affordable price!

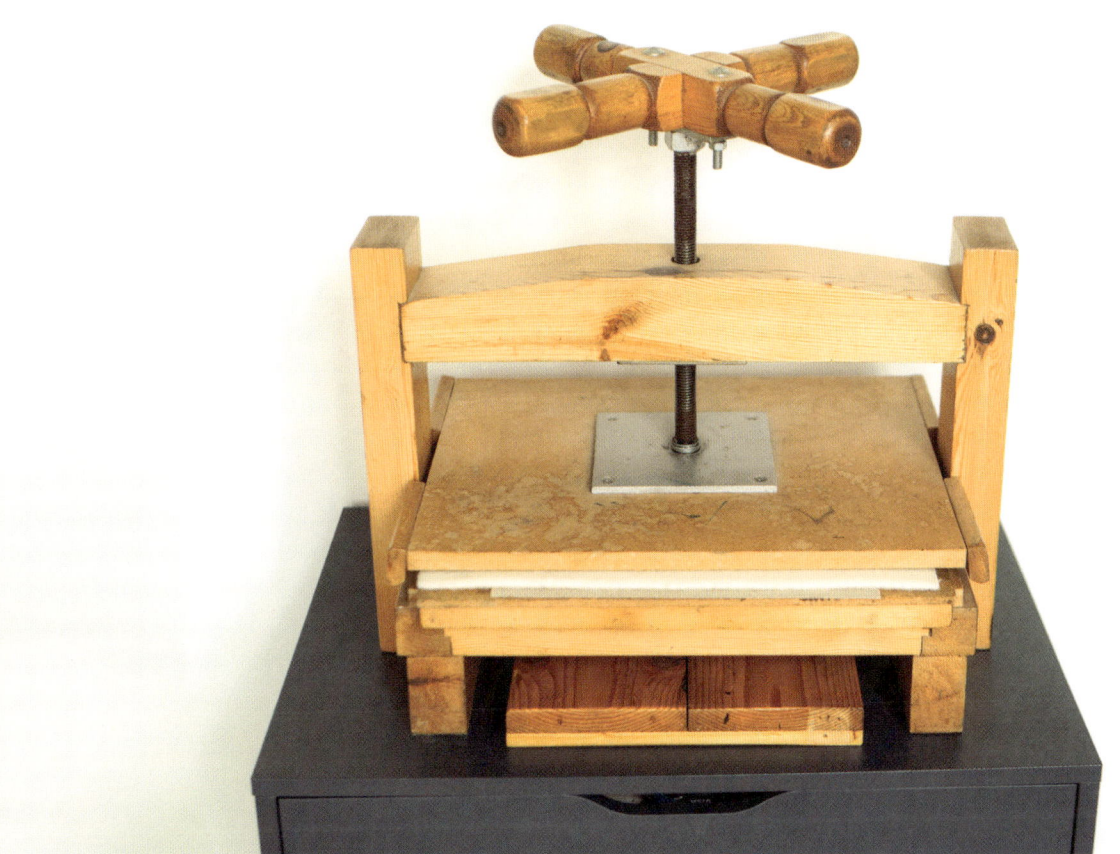

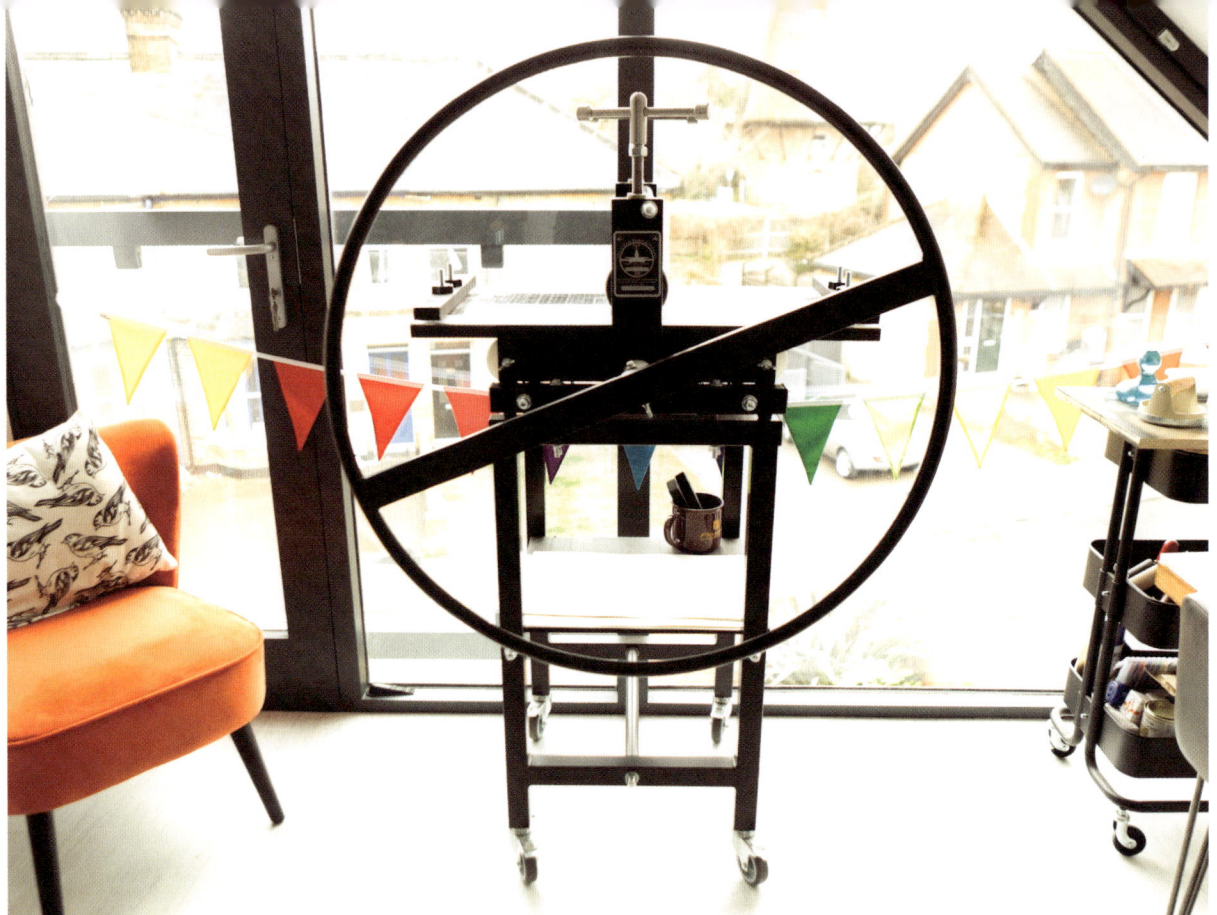

Etching press

With its roller-operated mechanism, an etching press is capable of exerting far more pressure than a press that is purely designed for relief printing. As its name suggests, you can make etchings (indeed, any intaglio process can be printed with one of these presses); however, it is also excellent for making wonderfully crisp, sharp, woodcut and linocut prints, due to the immense pressure that can be achieved between the rollers.

Etching presses come in a variety of sizes, ranging from small table-top models to giant floor-standing ones. They tend to be pricey, even for the smallest models, and go up to tens – or even hundreds – of thousands of pounds or dollars for the larger floor-standing presses.

If you're still fairly early on in your printmaking journey, an investment of that size possibly wouldn't make sense at this stage. However, if you eventually find yourself making large editions of prints, or want to explore other printmaking processes such as blind embossing or intaglio, purchasing an etching press could well be a future investment prospect.

INTAGLIO PRINTING

This is a form of printmaking that is, essentially, the opposite of relief printing: a debossed surface (a surface that has a design pressed or indented into it) is inked, with the ink sitting in the grooves, and then the paper or alternative print surface is pushed against the grooves (usually with a roller) to print.

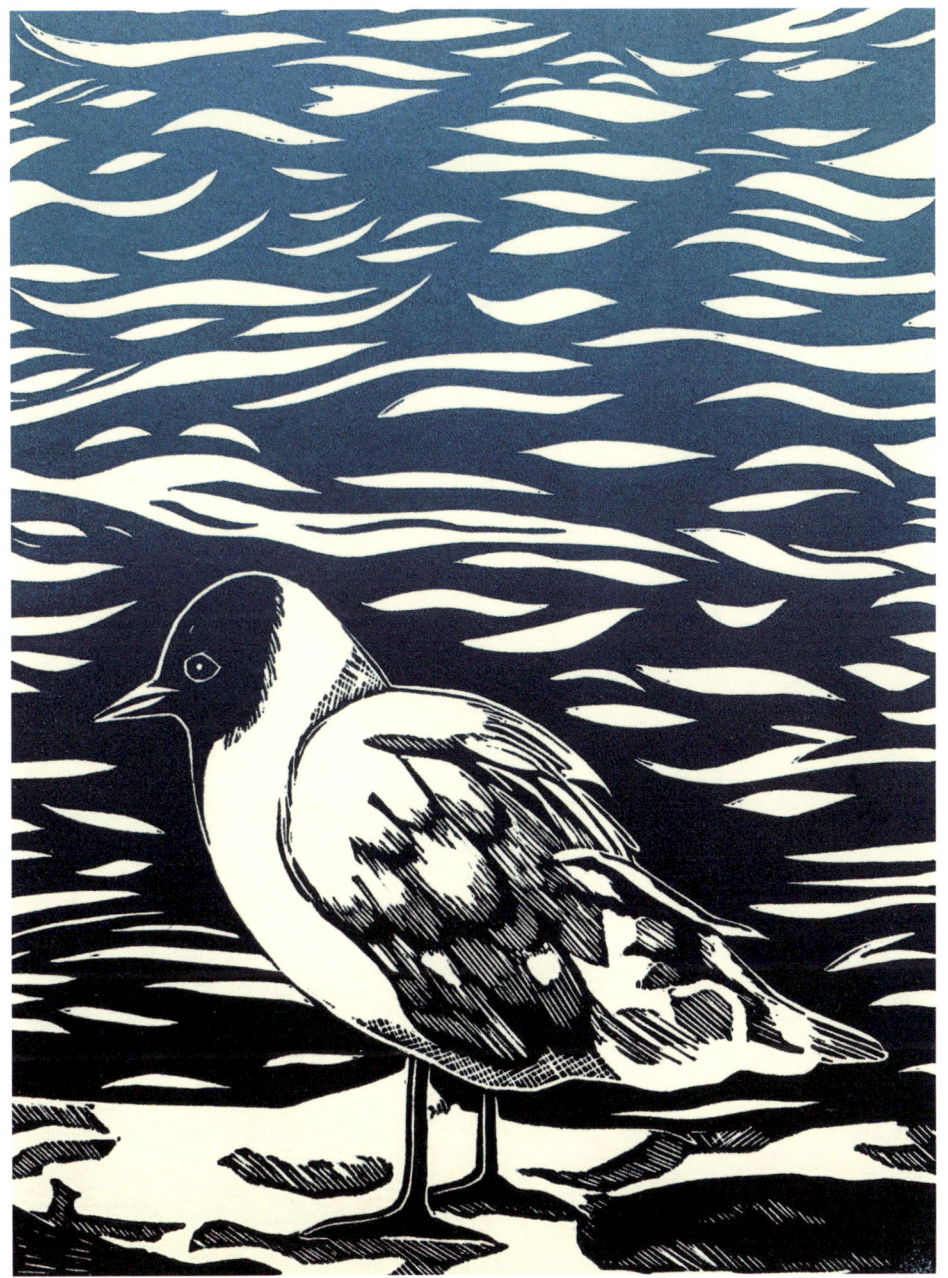

'Sea Gazing'

Carved in traditional grey linoleum, this small block printed beautifully on my etching press (see opposite), since the relatively hard surface of the linoleum tolerates the high pressure exerted by the rollers, resulting in a clean, crisp print.

Rolling tools

A printing brayer or roller is a small but vital component in the relief printmaking process. It's used for applying an even coat of ink onto the lino block, but before that it's used to roll out your ink onto a smooth surface (such as a sheet of plastic, glass or Perspex®), before transferring onto the block for printing.

Brayers come in a wide variety of sizes and widths. The biggest ones are called 'spindle rollers' and have a handle each side to hold onto, like a giant rolling pin. Printing brayers are made from rubber, and can either be hard or soft. Bear in mind that the softer the rubber, the more the ink will be pushed down onto the lino when it's rolled on. Therefore, a hard roller is better for inking up blocks that have been carved with lots of fine details. For evenness of inking-up, it's advisable to choose a roller that is at least the same width as your lino block.

You will also need at least one sheet of clear plastic, glass or Perspex® on which to roll out your inks before applying them onto your lino blocks. The glass or plastic from an old picture frame is ideal for this, although beware of using thin sheets of glass as these can break under pressure.

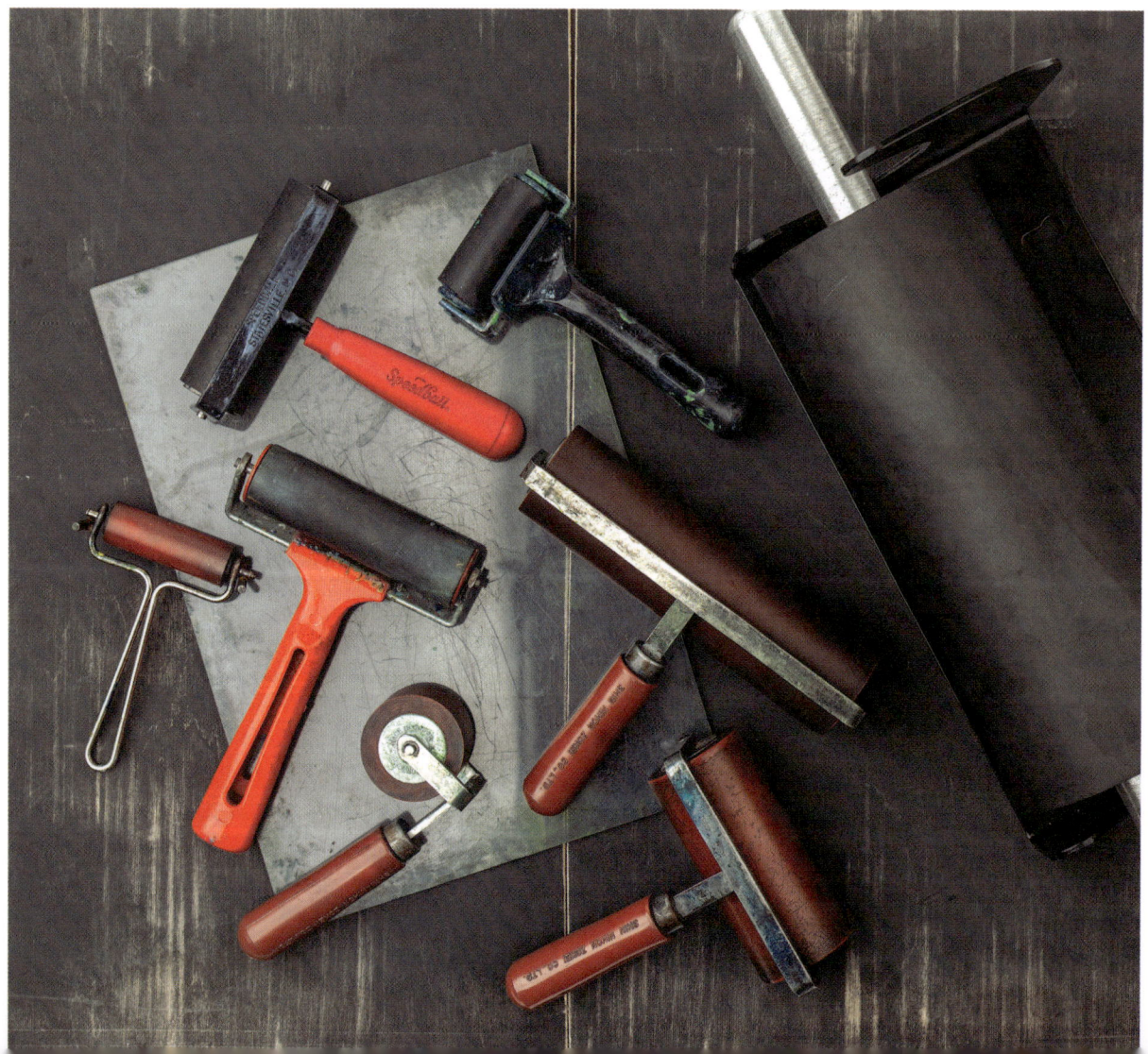

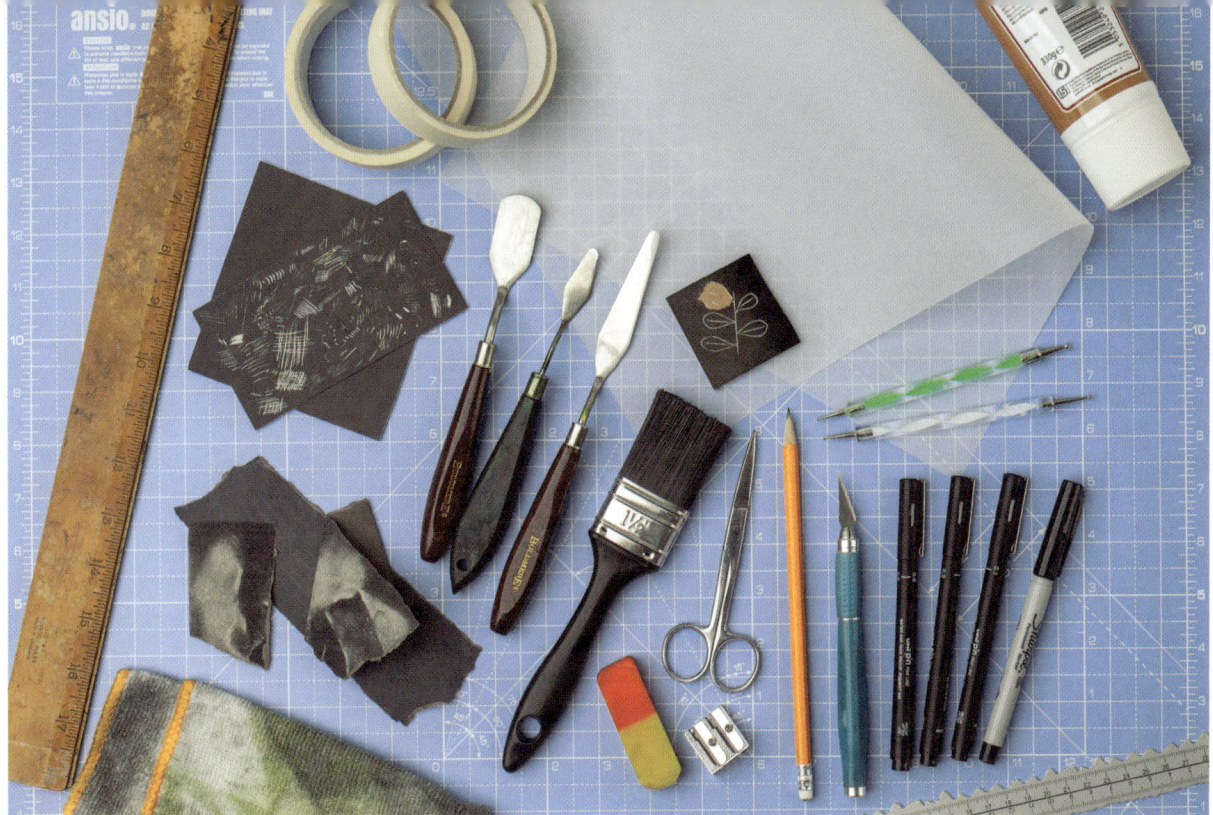

Additional printmaking essentials

In addition to the previous items described, there are some inexpensive 'extras' you will need to keep in your supplies drawer as part of your printmaking kit. These include:

- **tracing paper**, for transferring your designs onto lino

- rolls of **masking tape**, for securing and marking

- **pencils**, for tracing and drawing onto the lino

- **stylus** or the blunt end of a **ballpoint pen**, for rubbing over the lines on a tracing

- **fine-liner pens**, to go over any faint lines after you've transferred your design

- a sharp **scalpel or craft knife** for cutting paper and lino

- some **palette knives** for mixing your inks

- a household **paintbrush**, useful for brushing away those annoying particles of lino that can accumulate when you're carving

- a **scratchboard**, for experimenting with designs before committing to print

- a **ruler**, for measuring up

- an **old cloth** and **printmaker's cleaner**, for cleaning up messes and worktops

- a **deckle-edged ripper ruler**, for adding a deckled edge to paper when cutting it to size

- finally, if you can, I recommend investing in a **large cutting mat** with a grid to keep on your work table. Mine is A2 (420 x 594mm or approximately 18 x 24in) in size. It makes a nice surface on which to carve your lino blocks, and the grid is really useful for measuring and cutting or tearing your sheets of paper!

If you're using traditional linoleum, it's a good idea to keep some **sandpaper** to roughen the lino surface, and possibly some **wood filler** for trying those emergency carving repairs. If you are interested in making editions, I recommend purchasing **Ternes Burton registration pins** and **stripping tabs** for accurate printing.

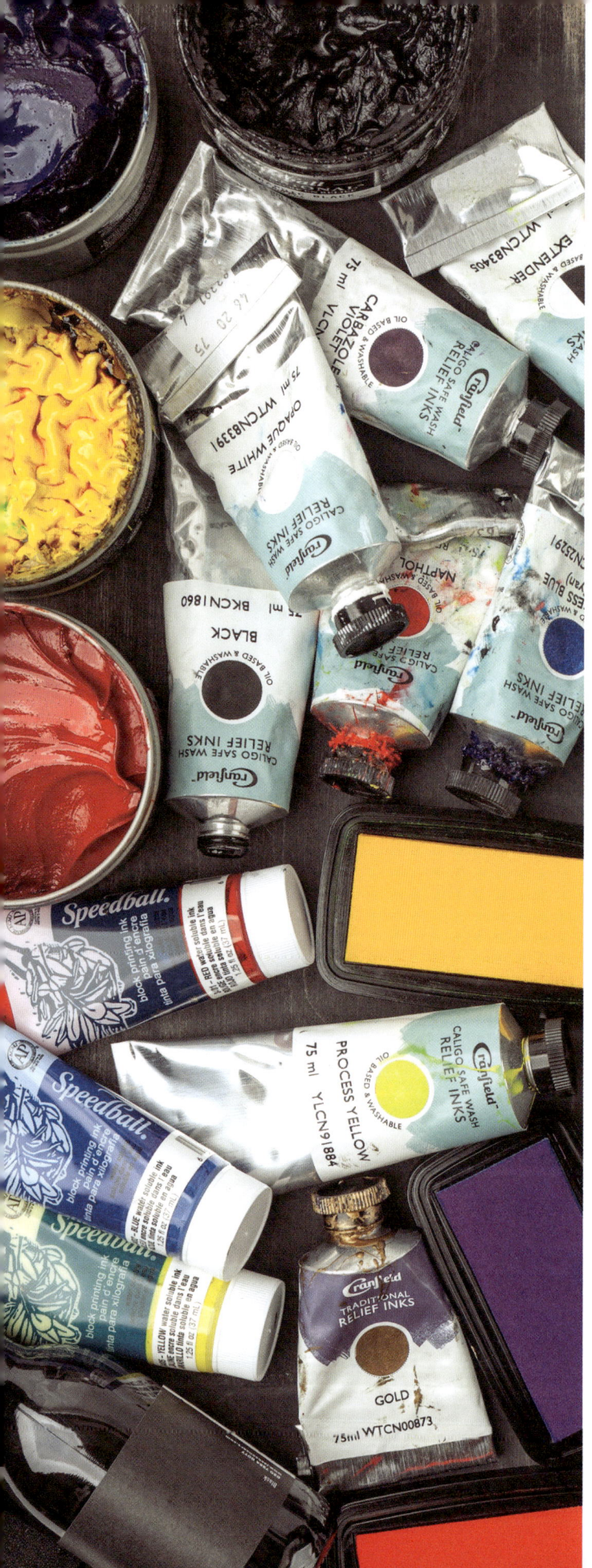

INKS

Ink is obviously an important component of printmaking (although it is possible to make an inkless print!). The ink you print with comes down to personal choice and most printmakers have their favourites, which they discover by trying out some of the many different types and brands available.

If you're just starting out on your printmaking journey, the fact that there are so many to choose from can be confusing. Setting aside the different brands, there are basically two types of printmaking ink available: water-based and oil-based.

Over the following pages, I will discuss these inks and attempt to point out the pros and cons associated with them.

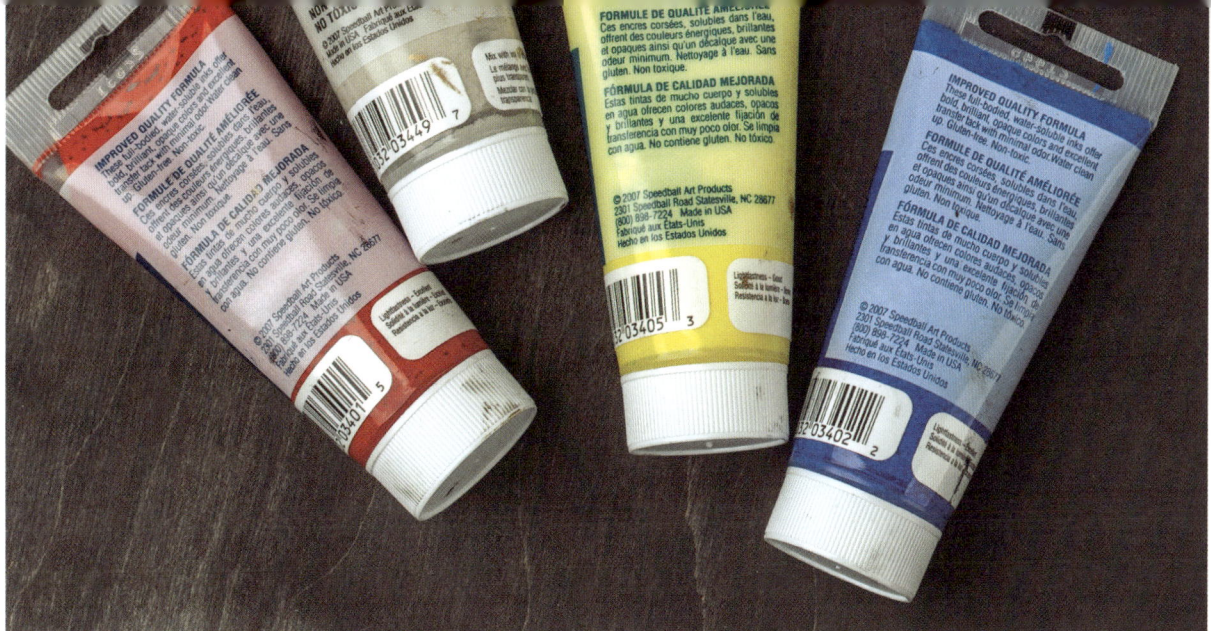

Water-based inks

As the name suggests, these inks are water-soluble and can be broken down by wetting them with a damp cloth or brush. This makes cleaning up after printing with them a very simple process and is a clear advantage of these inks over others.

Water-based printing inks mostly come in tubes and are available to purchase in many different ready-mixed shades, as well as the primary colours, if you prefer mixing your own. There are also extender mediums available, which you can mix in with the regular inks to achieve various subtle translucent shades of your colours.

Water-based inks can be used with all types of lino, both traditional hessian-backed and PVC substitutes. However, from the cleaning-up point of view, I find that the PVC substitutes are better to use with water-based inks, as the blocks can literally be washed up in a bowl of warm soapy water, rinsed and left to dry.

Advantages:

— Due to their ease of cleaning up, water-based inks are excellent if you're just starting out on your printmaking journey, or if you print in a small 'multi-purpose' space such as a kitchen or dining room which has to be kept clean and tidy.

— These inks are also great for teaching linocut printing to students, where print sessions are time-limited and clearing up has to be built in!

— It also has to be said that most brands of water-based ink tend to be cheaper to purchase than their oil-based counterparts!

— Water-based printing inks dry rapidly (even more so in a hot, dry environment), which can be an advantage, particularly in a student setting where there are large quantities of prints being made and taken home on the same day (therefore it's desirable for prints to dry quickly).

Disadvantages:

— The quick-drying nature of water-based inks can also be a disadvantage, particularly if you are printing in hot weather, when I have known the ink to dry on the block, even before I was able to print!

— Although it is possible to achieve a good, even coverage when printing with water-based ink, my personal opinion is that you don't get the same 'glossy' finish as you do with oil-based inks.

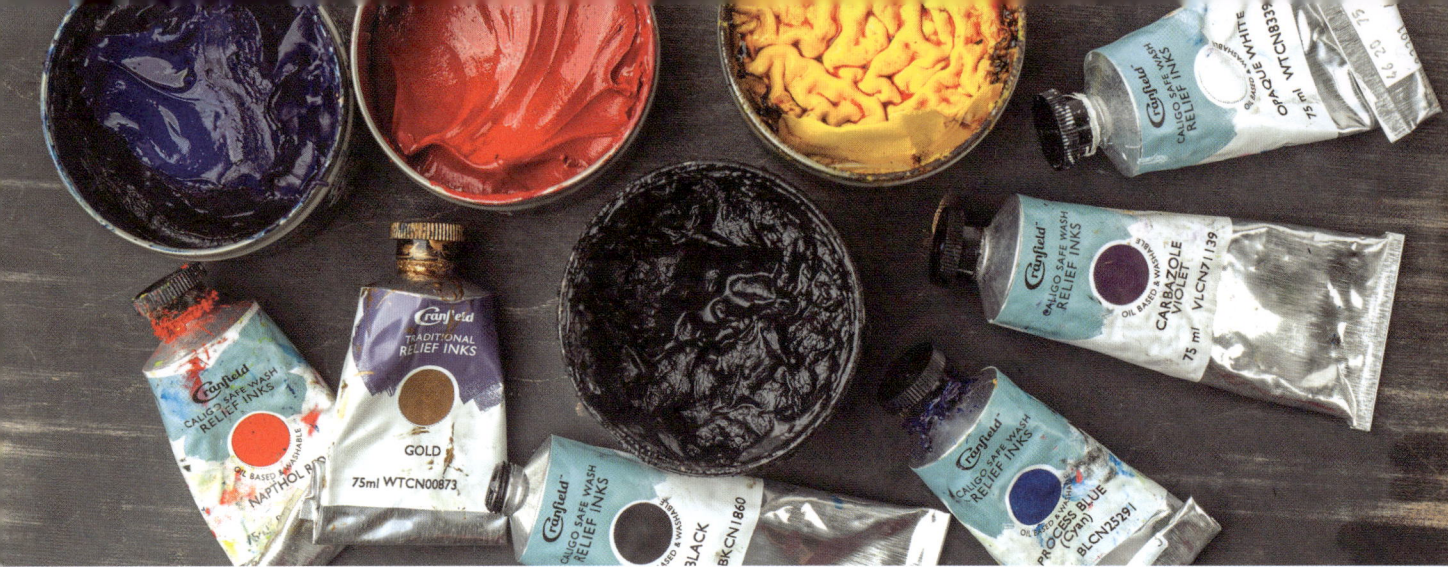

Oil-based inks

As a professional printmaker, I favour the wonderful, lustrous results you can get from printing in oil-based inks. For me, there's nothing quite like the smell of my oil-based inks that lingers in the studio after a successful printing session – it really does (almost) compensate for the extra effort required in cleaning them up!

The inks can be purchased in 75ml or 150ml tubes, or in larger pots. If you're purchasing the latter, be aware that, if the ink is not sealed properly, it will form a 'skin' over the top. Even when the lid is sealed thoroughly, if the ink is left unused for an extended period of time, it could dry out altogether and be unusable. For this reason, I prefer to buy my ink in tubes (making sure I always squeeze from the bottom, as per the 'toothpaste tube' rule!).

Important note: When purchasing oil-based inks for your linocut printing, please remember that it's *relief printing* inks you need, not etching inks. The latter have a stiffer consistency than relief inks, and are designed for – and more suited to – intaglio printmaking processes (see page 28).

Advantages:

— The vibrancy of the colours and evenness of coverage mean that oil-based inks are a very popular choice with professional printmakers.

— They come ready-mixed in every imaginable hue and tint, but you can easily mix your own colours – there is no limit. There are also some wonderful metallic inks available, which are perfect for those festive-season prints!

— Since the inks don't dry as quickly as water-based inks do, you can leave them out overnight and continue your printing session the following morning, as long as the space you're working in isn't too hot. Being able to do this can reduce wastage (if you squeezed too much ink out to start with!) and is not something you could do with the quick-drying water-based inks.

Disadvantages:

— Generally, oil-based inks are more difficult to clean up from your blocks, equipment and other surfaces than their water-based counterparts. Some brands – for example, the Caligo Safe Wash range of oil-based relief inks from Cranfield – are actually 'washable', meaning you can largely clean up with warm soapy water. This is a real game-changer for printmakers! Any stray traces of ink can then be wiped off with a little vegetable oil or a cloth dampened with a few drops of a non-toxic solvent such as 'Zest-it' (see 'A note on cleaning up' on page 37).

— Most brands of oil-based relief-printing inks are pricier to buy than their water-based equivalents. However, the superior printing quality that can be achieved by using them could make it worth the extra outlay.

Archival pigment ink pads

You may think that ink pads for stamping are not 'proper ink' – but this isn't necessarily true! High-quality archival pigment ink pads come in a dazzling array of colours and can be a very useful addition to your printmaking supplies cupboard. The lightfast pigment colours are oil-based and the pads can be dabbed directly onto the surface of your carved stamps to ink them up. These ink pads are perfect for using with small stamps, both on their own or to add extra colours to larger prints (see 'Let's Add Colour' on pages 102–108 and 'Inspired by My Garden' on pages 128–135).

There are a number of brands available, but my favourites are the 'Versafine' and 'Versafine Clair' ranges from Tsukineko. Because these inks are oil-based, cleaning up can be done using a little vegetable oil or a few drops of Zest-it or similar non-toxic thinning solvent. Certainly, though, printing with these ink pads is far less messy than with regular inks and for that reason are particularly useful for test-printing small areas of carved blocks-in-progress.

Block-printing inks for fabrics

I can't end this chapter without mentioning fabric printing inks. Printing onto fabric with linocut stamps is great fun, and it's possible to create some wonderful items to adorn both your home and your person! If the fabric you're intending to print on will be washed, you will need to use a waterproof ink that will not wash away. Fabric printing inks are oil based and specially designed for printing onto fabrics. In appearance, the inks are very similar to regular oil-based relief inks (and can be used on paper too!). Once dry, the inks are fixed by applying heat with an iron. After this, depending on the type of fabric (cotton, silk, linen, and so on), the item can be washed and cared for in the same way as any other item of clothing or soft furnishing. Fabric-printing inks come in an array of different colours and are widely available online or in art and craft stores. If you fancy printing some of your designs onto fabrics, it's definitely worth investing in some of these inks!

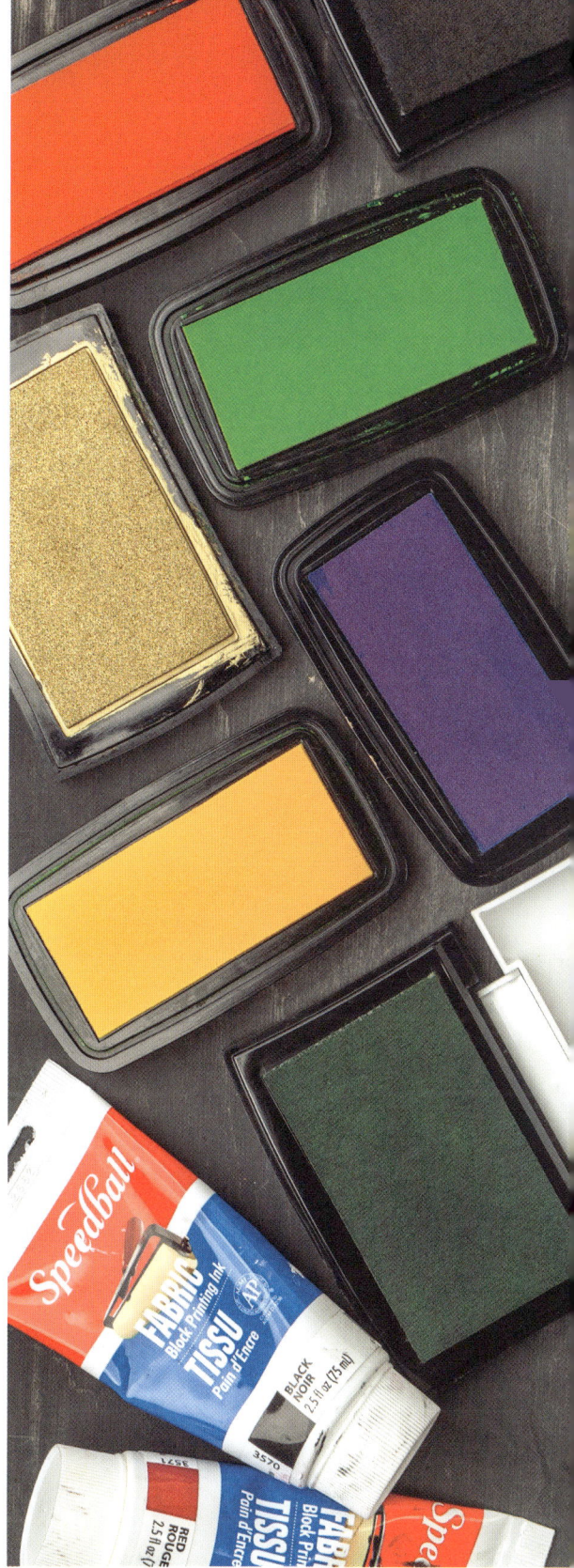

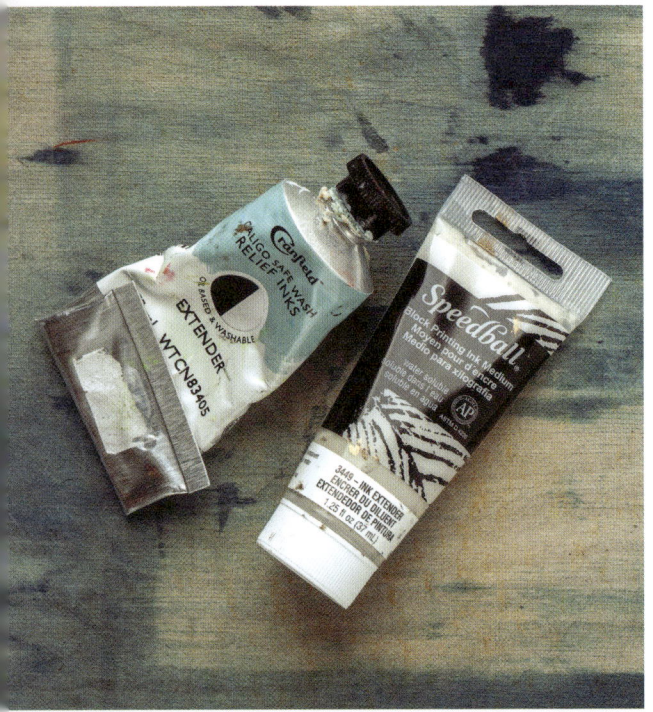

Extender medium

On a separate matter – I must mention extender medium. In my opinion, extender medium is a definite 'must-have' to feature in a printmaker's box of inks! It's a wonderful medium used for mixing with your coloured inks to make lovely subtle, translucent shades. As it makes inks more transparent, it's perfect for building up layers of colour in a print and creating blended effects too. It's also a little more forgiving with misregistered prints – any areas of misplaced translucent colour will not be so glaringly obvious! There are both water- and oil-based versions, so you can use either depending on which inks you choose for printing. Adding an extender medium to your colour will also make your ink go further too.

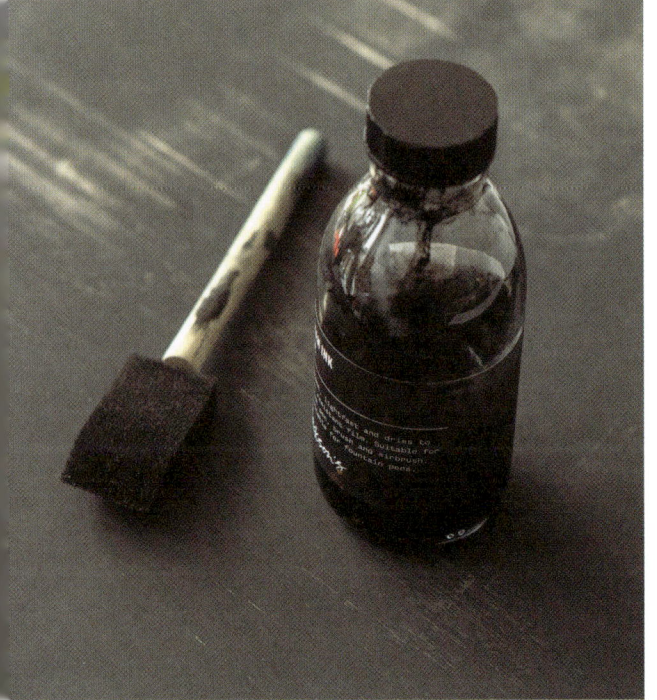

Indian ink

Sometimes I coat my lino with a black Indian ink solution to 'stain' the surface before carving. This isn't essential, and doing this won't affect how the lino prints, but it does make your carved marks show up well, which in turn gives you a good idea of the effects you're achieving as you carve.

Simply brush the ink over the lino using either a normal brush or a sponge brush, then leave it to dry completely before carving into it.

If you do want to stain your lino before carving, it is advisable always to dilute the Indian ink with water before using, as undiluted ink may change the surface of the lino slightly when it dries, affecting the way it carves and prints.

A NOTE ON CLEANING UP

It's inevitable that, after an intense, inky printing session, there follows the arduous but necessary task of cleaning up.

Cleaning your printing brayers, lino blocks and any other equipment is vital after printing. Brayers and carved lino blocks will spoil if ink is left on them and allowed to dry.

If you are using water-based inks, a damp cloth should be sufficient to wipe down work surfaces and clean your lino blocks. Wring out your cloth and wipe your lino block vigorously to remove as much ink as you can. With traditional linoleum, avoid getting the block too wet, otherwise it will curl up. I recommend using warm soapy water and a cloth to clean your brayers (make sure you dry them thoroughly afterwards before printing again!).

Oil-based inks are harder to clean up and require thinning down before they can be removed. Zest-it Printmakers Cleaner is a great product for cleaning oil-based inks. Large bottles can be somewhat expensive, but you need very little and a bottle this size lasts for ages! Pour a small amount onto a soft cloth, or shake a few drops onto the areas to be cleaned, before wiping.

Alternatively, you could squeeze a little vegetable oil on some kitchen paper then apply this to thin the inks, before wiping away with a wet, soapy cloth and patting dry.

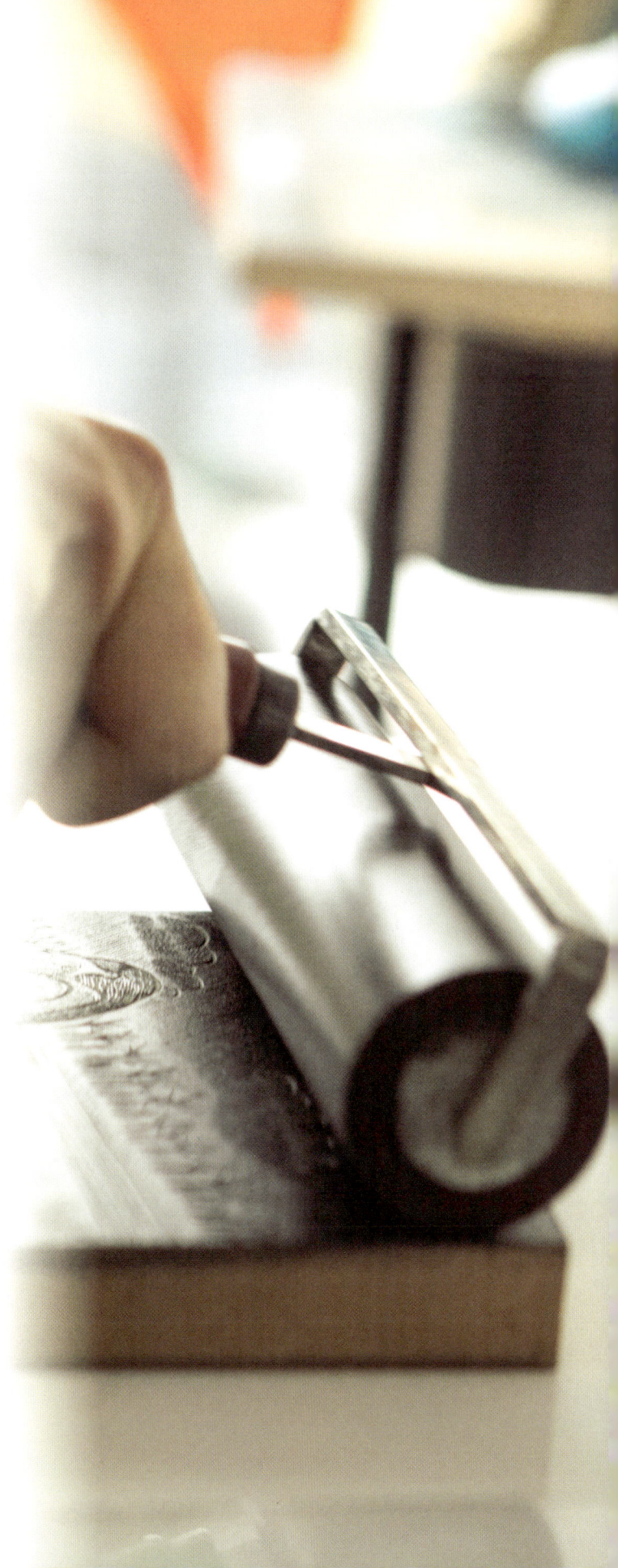

SURFACES

The surface on which you choose to print your image is arguably one of the most important decisions to make when creating a print. By 'surface' we mean paper, fabric or even hard materials such wood, glass or stone – or whatever the artist wishes to use!

As a printmaker, I find myself excited by paper. There is a unique beauty in a sheet of hand-made paper – there is a tactile as well as visual quality that is hard to capture in photographs. The type of paper a print is made on can dictate whether or not you, as the artist, considers the work to be visually successful – it can be that important! A hand-printed image is usually positioned on a sheet of paper in such a way that there is a margin or 'border' around it, making the paper an integral part of the print.

The strength of the paper is an important consideration, as it needs to withstand the processes necessary in order to achieve the finished print. Unlike intaglio methods of printmaking (see page 28), where paper has to be soaked first, relief prints are made on dry paper, which widens your choice of papers somewhat!

When deciding which paper to print on, also think about the type of image you've carved and how you want it to look when printed. Is it a bold, clean and minimalist design? Or intricately detailed, with lots of texture? Or possibly somewhere in between? Bold, simple designs often work well when printed onto a smooth, heavyweight paper, such as Somerset® Satin, while nature-inspired prints with textural details can work beautifully when printed onto 'flecked', hand-made paper embedded with plants (such as Thai mulberry) as the paper almost acts as an extension of the design itself.

All printmaking papers (whether smooth or textured) come in different 'weights', which simply refers to the thickness of the paper. The weight of a paper is stated in grams per square metre, or 'gsm' for short (or pounds/lbs). The higher the number is, the thicker the paper.

Some printmakers favour printing on thicker, heavier papers as they give a substantial, 'good-quality' feel to the prints, which some customers may like if the prints are being sold. However, in my opinion, the final choice of paper should depend upon how well it works with the print. Many suppliers will send out paper-sample packs, so you can try out the different weights and surfaces until you find your particular favourites.

If you're not sure which paper you'll eventually go for, you can have great fun trying your block out on different ones before committing to printing a full edition. You'll be amazed at the difference the various papers make to your design – it really is quite fascinating!

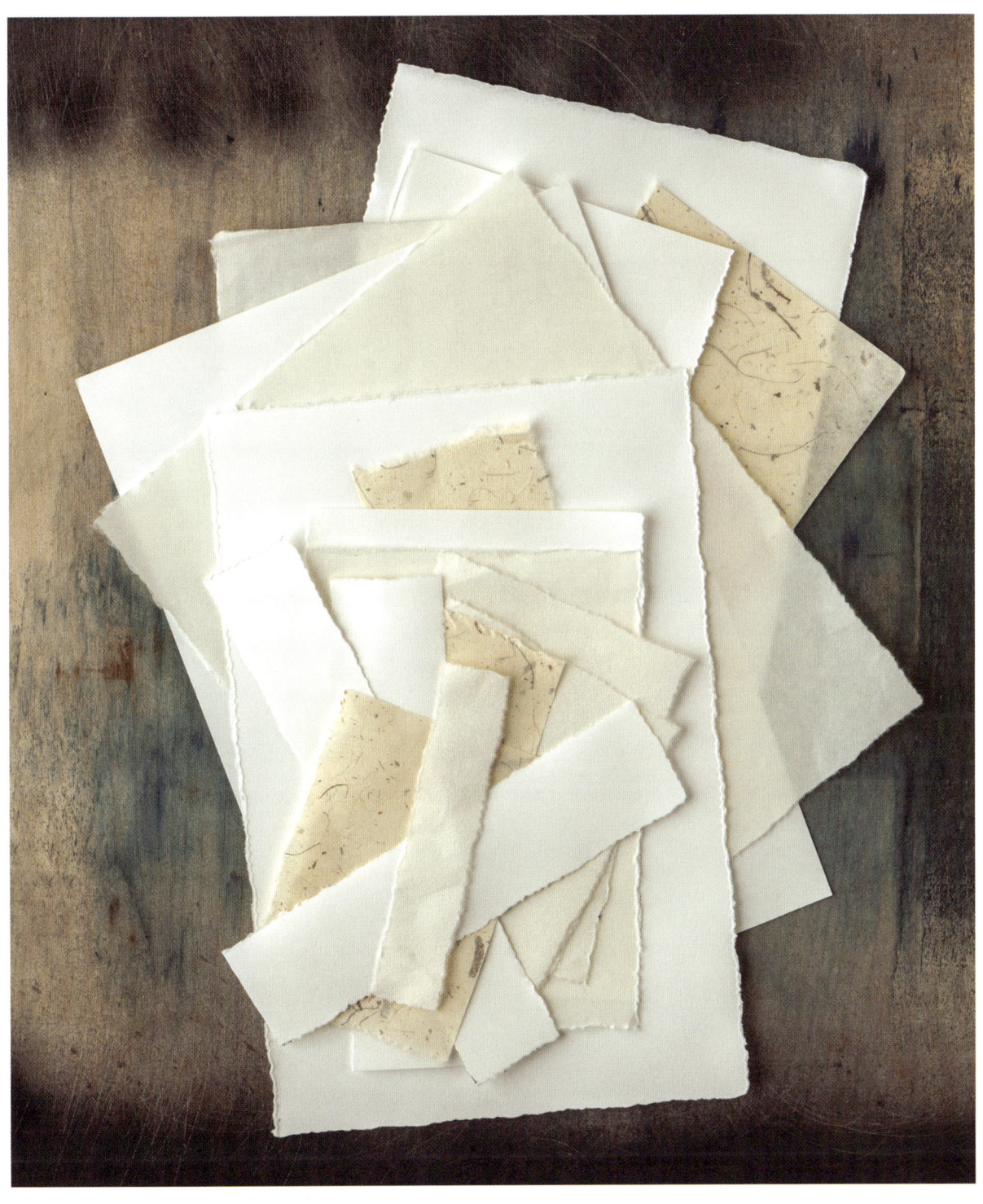

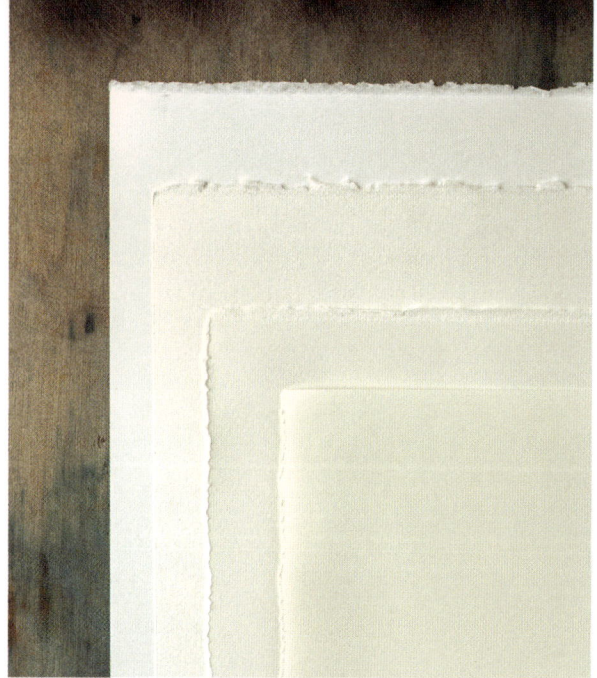

Smooth printmaking papers

High-quality, smooth papers are always a favourite with printmakers. These are acid-free, cotton-rag papers with a smooth surface that takes the ink well, enabling a crisp, sharp print and ensuring that all those small and painstakingly carved details are clearly visible.

The edges of these papers are often finished with a 'deckled' edge – an intentionally hand-torn finish that many people love, as they feel it gives extra charm and 'authenticity' to the print. Somerset® Satin, from the world-renowned St Cuthbert's Mill paper in the UK, is a thick, heavy paper that is around 300gsm (140lb) in weight, and a firm favourite of mine. Fabriano Botanical Ultra Smooth 300gsm (130lb) and BFK Rives 270gsm (100lb) are similarly good choices. If you are looking for a lighter weight paper, Zerkall Smooth 145gsm (54lb) is a good choice, with a beautifully smooth surface that picks up all the fine details of your blocks.

Japanese printmaking papers

Used for centuries in the ancient art of Japanese woodblock printing, these papers are always a wonderful choice for other forms of relief printmaking, such as linocut. The smooth surfaces, delicate colours and durability make these papers a firm favourite with many printmakers. My particular favourite is Okawara Select. At 51gsm (20lb), this seems like a pretty thin paper, but its durability belies its weight. The surface colour is a delicate creamy colour, and like all these papers, the edges have a lovely, 'feathery' deckle that adds to the beauty of the hand-made print. Bunkoshi Select 71gsm (26lb) is another favourite of mine and comes in a deeper, richer cream colour.

When printing on these papers, you will notice that one side is very smooth, while the other is slightly textured. I always print on the smooth side, as I find it gives a clean and crisp print – but do try both, to see which you prefer! There are a number of these wonderful papers to choose from, and to help you make up your mind, a sample pack is available to purchase.

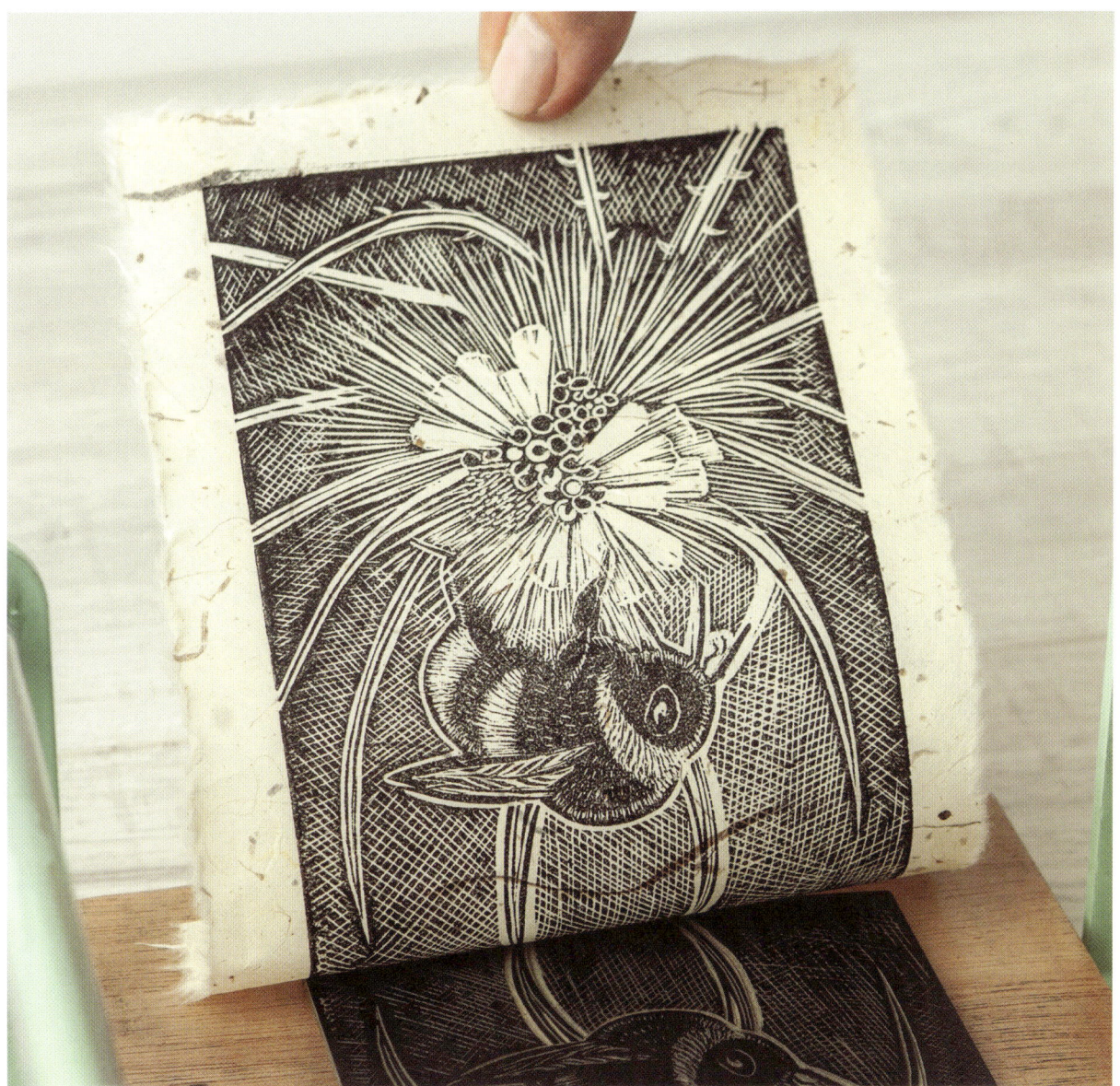

Printing 'It's All in the Details'

The project is on pages 96–101. I explored different papers for this design, and one was this hand-made Thai mulberry paper (see overleaf for more information). This paper ties in nicely with the design's natural subject matter, and adds texture too.

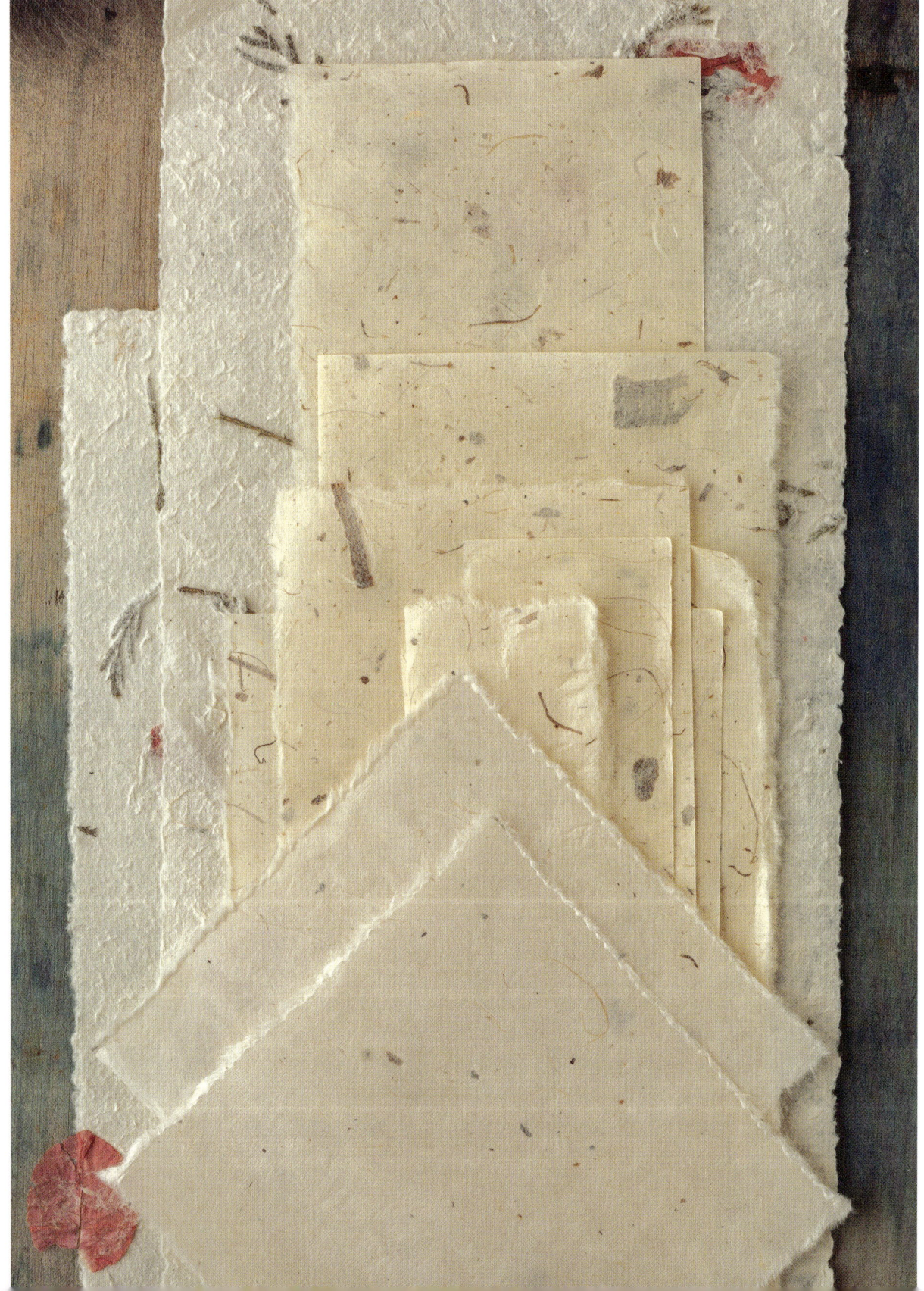

Specialist hand-made papers

If you are after a different type of paper from the fairly standard (but good!) branded smooth and textured papers, there is a vast selection of specialist hand-made papers available which may be worth exploring. These papers can come from all over the world, some commercially produced on a large scale and others lovingly made by individual craftspeople. They can be purchased in individual sheets, generally around 70 x 50cm (27½ x 19¾in) in size, so one sheet can be used to make several prints, depending on the size of your block.

A sheet of hand-made paper can often be a work of art in its own right, even with nothing printed on it. It may feature beautiful surface textures, or be embedded with natural plant fibres, or sometimes actual flower petals. Collecting these papers can be pretty addictive, even before you decide to try printing on them – and could well lead to you wanting to have a try at paper-making yourself! If you are wanting to explore the properties of different papers, it's best to purchase a selection of different sheets, which will help you to find your particular favourites.

One thing to note is some prints will look wonderful on a certain specialist paper, but not so good on another. It really is a case of try and see, but it's all part of the never-ending process of discovering what excites and delights you. For example, when I noticed some Nepalese flower-embedded Lokta paper on the website of one of my favourite UK online art suppliers, I was intrigued and had to try some. However, when it arrived, I was slightly disappointed. Although it was beautiful to look at, with its textured surface generously embedded with flower petals and small leaves, I was doubtful

of being able to make a sufficiently clean and sharp print. I decided to try printing onto the reverse side instead – and instantly fell in love with the result! The smoother side has a less pronounced texture, and although the flowers and leaves are still visible, they are more subtle and do not protrude, making the surface 'cleaner' for printing onto.

Thai mulberry has been a favourite of mine in recent years – I love how it complements my nature-inspired prints. It is a fairly thin, tissue-like paper, but even though it's so lightweight (around 40–50gsm/15–18lb), it's surprisingly strong and the edges look beautiful when the paper is hand-torn to size. It's produced on a large scale and therefore widely available from many online suppliers as well as art-supply stores. It comes in a huge range of colours and is often used in crafting. Rather like the Japanese editioning papers I discussed on page 40, Thai mulberry paper has a smooth side and a textured side. For sharpness and clarity, and as with the Lokta paper, I always use the smooth side for printing on.

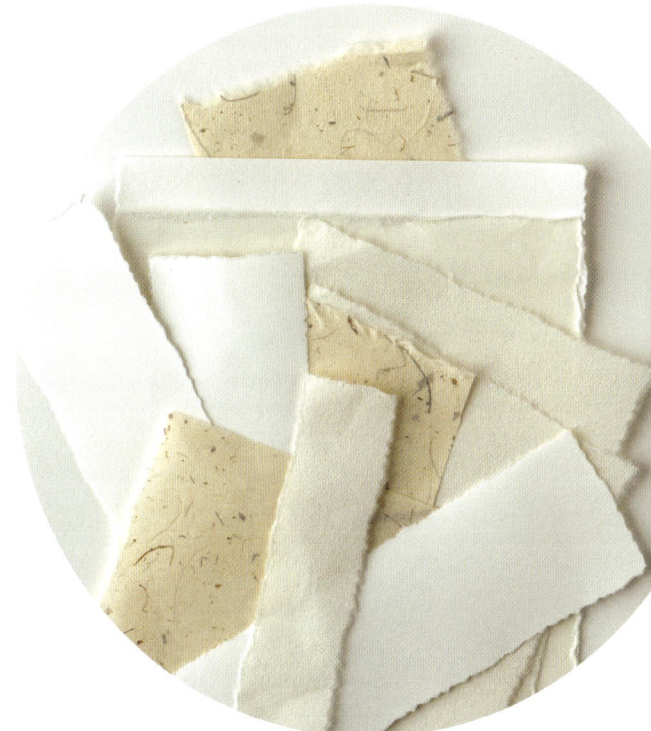

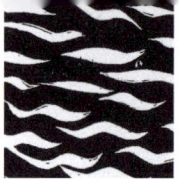

TECHNIQUES

Linocutting is a process that does demand a high level of precision and skill from the artist in order to achieve the desired images. Unlike other, looser and more forgiving processes such as drawing and painting, with linocutting it is harder to correct mistakes by 'working into' them. Once you have carved into your lino, your marks are pretty much there to stay and you can't rub them out or go over them!

That's not to say there aren't ways of remedying, or at least disguising, carving errors. Despair not! There are ways of rescuing your work, or at least minimizing the damage, which I will discuss in the 'Troubleshooting' section on pages 140–147.

I'm going to be walking you through some basic techniques for using tools and making marks on lino (which, after all, is what it's all about!). Then, using a simple demo project example, we will design and carve a small block before inking it up and trying out some test prints. I always think 'learning by doing' is the best way forward. Making a small and fairly quick project is a great way of starting to find out what works for you, and then what you need to improve on too.

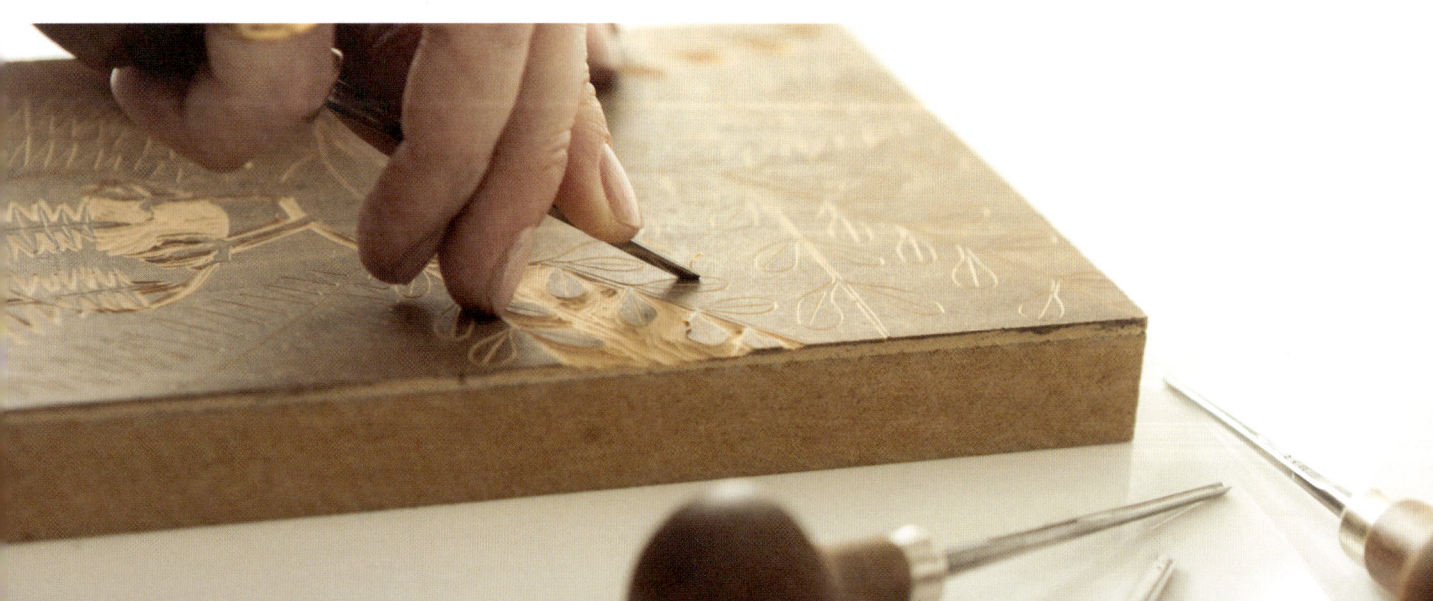

Get a grip

Firstly, let's talk about the tools you'll be using and how to find the best, most comfortable way of holding them.

Shown below is one of my favourite and most-used tools – a Pfeil L 12/1 with a tiny V-shaped cutting blade (**A**). As with all my Pfeil tools, the lovely solid walnut wood handle looks great and is ergonomically shaped – the round side nestles comfortably into the palm of my hand as I carve. Most linocutting tools have handles which are designed to nestle into the palm of the printmaker.

Begin by 'nestling' the round part of the handle in the palm of your hand, then grip the rest of the tool firmly (but not too tightly) with your fingers (**B**). Then place the forefinger on the metal part of the tool, about 1–2cm (⅜–¾in) above the tip (**C**). This enables maximum control when cutting.

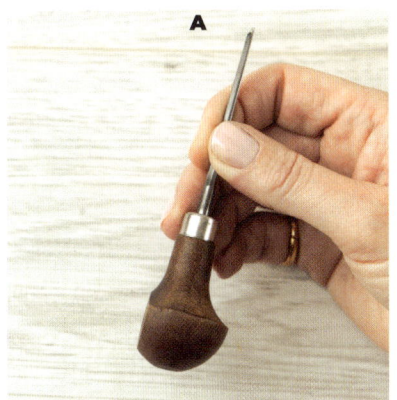
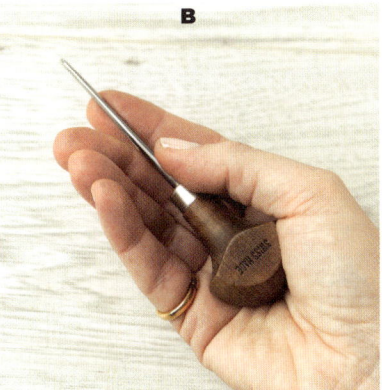
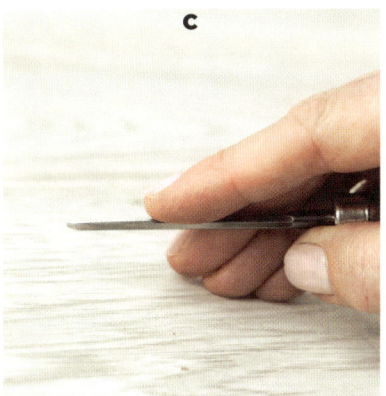

The most important thing with linocutting is to have control over your tool as you carve. You should always keep the above grip and retain the close distance from the end of your finger to the tip of the cutting blade. For extra stability, you can support your carving hand by gently placing your other hand onto it. This can be an effective way to minimize shaky hand syndrome!

Always carve away from you, and away from your other hand. If you need to turn a corner or change direction in your design, don't be tempted to twist your carving hand around so the tool is carving towards your other hand. Rather, turn the lino so that you are continuing to carve away from your other hand (**D**). Don't try to 'shortcut' this movement; it could result in the blade slipping off the lino and into your hand, resulting in a nasty cut.

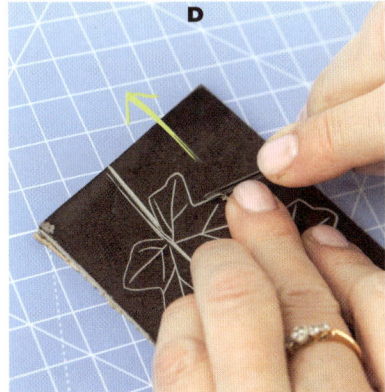

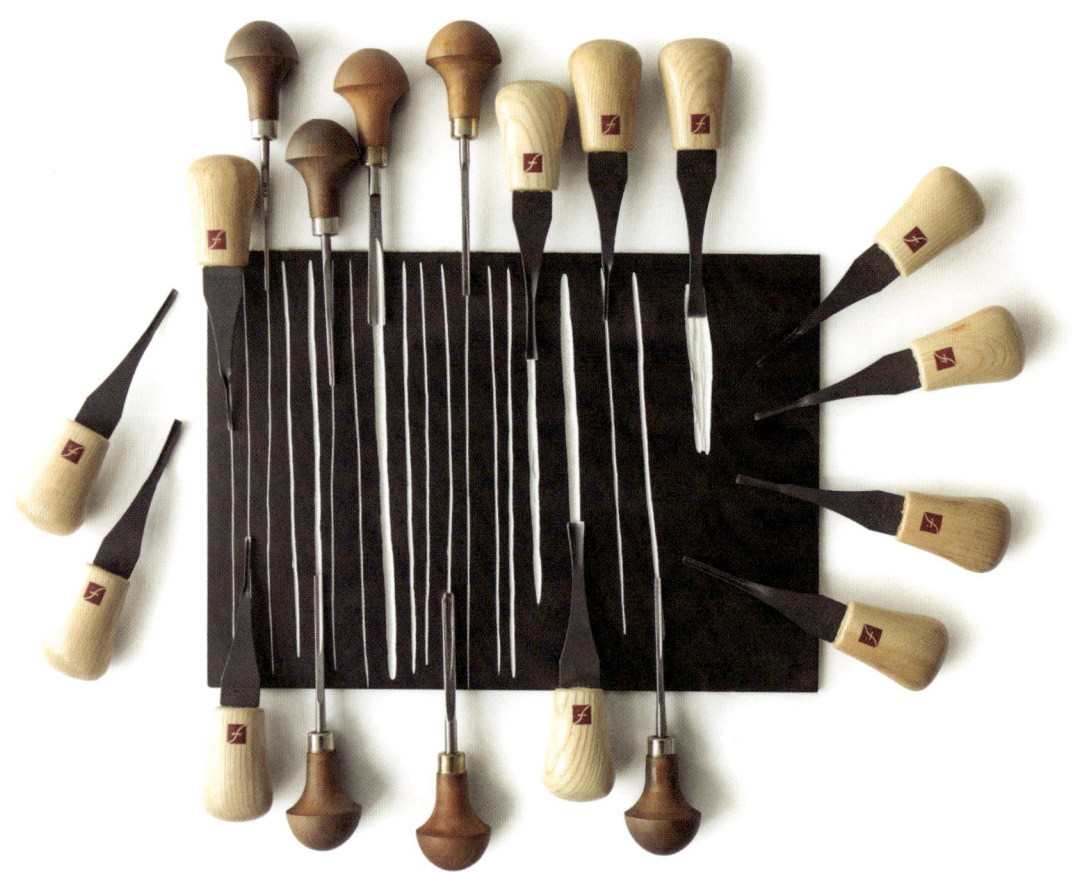

Your first lines

The tools with which you carve will dictate the size and appearance of the marks you make in your lino. Ideally, you want a selection of carving tools that will allow you to create the widest possible range of carved marks.

The best carving tools to go for are the micro (1mm or 2mm) V-shaped and U-shaped tools, as they're not only useful for carving those extra-small details but also for outlining shapes to make carving out larger areas of 'background' lino much easier.

At all times, remember the golden rule of linocutting (and any form of relief printmaking): **only carve out the areas of lino you don't want to print**. These will appear white in your print. The areas you leave in will be printed black (or whatever colour ink with which you choose to print).

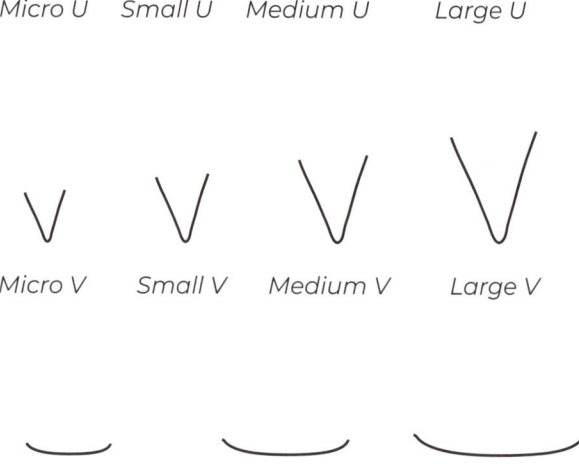

Micro U   *Small U*   *Medium U*   *Large U*

Micro V   *Small V*   *Medium V*   *Large V*

Small scoop   *Medium scoop*   *Large scoop*

Making your mark

As an artist who makes pieces inspired by nature, my mission is to try to interpret the many incredibly beautiful markings and textures I see on the plants and animals around me, into the simplified marks that make up my prints. This is no mean feat and can feel daunting!

If you are making a single block print in black ink onto white paper, it can help to focus on the tonal (light and dark) areas of your subject. Sometimes I will squint my eyes so the contrast between the areas in my reference photograph or sketch appears exaggerated, helping me work out which areas I'll keep white, black or grey.

Remember that you won't be able to create actual shades of grey with a single block, black-on-white paper print. What you can do is to create an illusion of tonal values with your mark-making, rather like the half-tone patterns used to create the old black-and-white photographs in newspapers. To do this, in my own work, I tend to use a lot of hatching and cross-hatching. These sorts of marks are excellent for suggesting tonal values and textures. For darker areas I carve fewer lines, which are more spaced out. For lighter areas I carve more lines, and densely pack them together. For even lighter areas, I use cross-hatching, and multi-directional cross hatching for very pale areas that I don't want to be completely white.

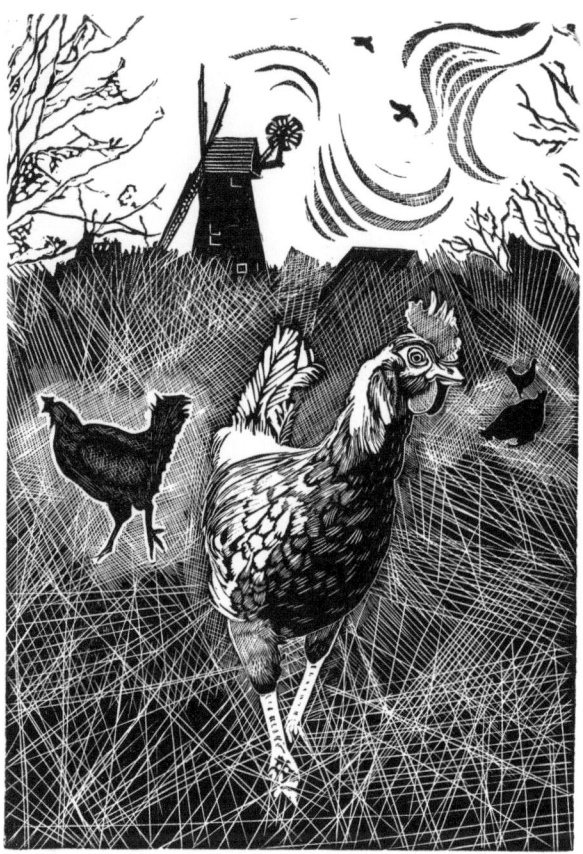

1/50   FOUR RESCUE HENS AND A WINDMILL   JFB '22

'Four Rescue Hens and a Windmill'

In my print above, I've used a variety of hatched, cross-hatched and multi-directional hatched marks (that cross over each other multiple times) to create a wider range of tones and textures. The white outline around the second-largest hen, on the left of the image, demonstrates how effectively the multi-directional hatched marks contrast with both the white and black areas of the print.

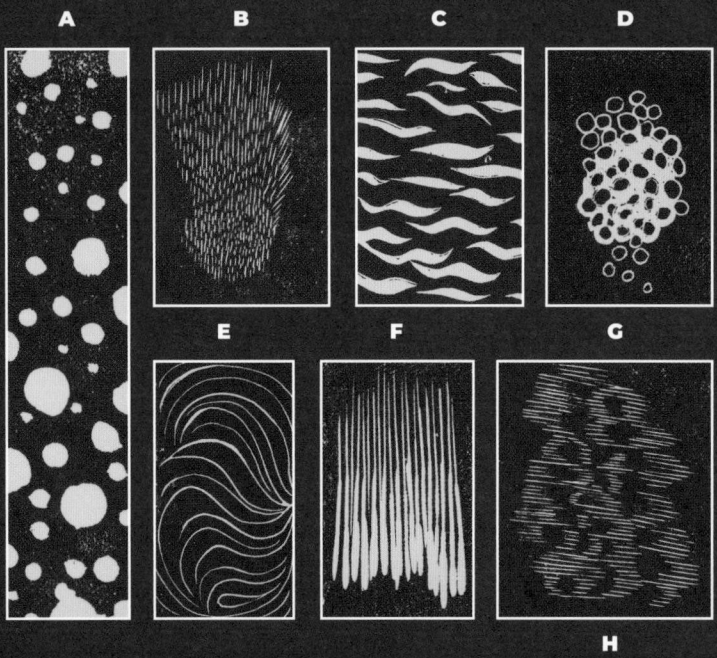

Lino doodling

Trying out a variety of mark-making ideas on tiny scraps of lino is a great way to build skill and confidence with your carving before embarking on a finished project, and will also help you to become used to working with your tools.

It's always useful to build up a 'reference library' of different marks and textures, as these can help you when planning and executing your future projects. If you need to remind yourself of anything, I encourage you to look back through the previous pages.

'Doodling' on a small piece of lino with a carving tool is really no different to doodling on a piece of paper with a pencil. Both are relaxing, no-pressure ways of trying out marks, textures and ideas for a potential print, without fear of 'ruining' a precious block of lino in which you have already invested many hours of work.

Artists are never happier than when they have some kind of mark-making implement in their hand. It may be a brush, pencil, pen, stick of pastel or graphite or – in the case of a relief printmaker – a carving tool!

Note: these are just suggestions for how the markings could be used.

A Ground textures (soil, stones, etc.).

B Fur.

C Water.

D Centre of a flower, ground texture, frog-spawn.

E Water variation.

F Wood.

G Feathers and fur.

H Ground texture.

I Background texture tree bark.

J Cross-hatch background texture.

K Large pebbles.

L Multi-hatching background texture.

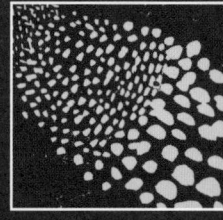

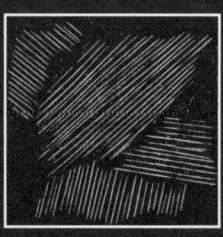

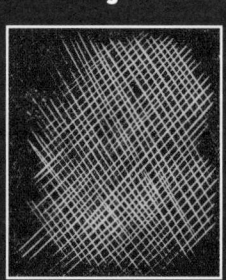

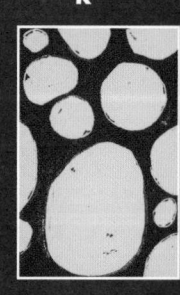

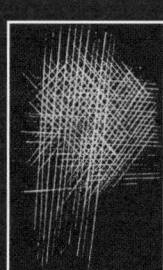

HATCHING & CROSS-HATCHING

Hatching is simply a collection of parallel lines drawn (or carved) closely together, and is a technique used by many artists to indicate the shaded areas in a drawing. Since we are unable to create actual shades of grey when carving a lino block, using hatched areas is an effective way of showing tonal values.

Hatching tends to be a 'bread and butter' mark for me, as it is so useful in representing the many different tones and textures in my pieces.

Cross-hatching, as the name suggests, is simply hatched lines that cross over each other in a 'criss-cross' pattern, rather than lines which go only in one direction. Cross-hatching is useful for creating lighter tones that can't be achieved as easily with single-direction hatching.

Using a combination of hatching and cross hatching, it is possible to create a whole range of rich and complex-looking textures in a print.

Carving such straight lines does take a little practice, and it's important to hold your tool close to the cutting tip for maximum control. It also helps to support your carving hand lightly with your other hand, which helps to prevent any 'wavering'.

Finding your style

When carving a new lino block, there is the challenge of working out how we are going to create the kind of printed image we are aiming for. How are we going to achieve that fur or feather texture? How shall we interpret those reflections on the water, or those pebbles on a beach?

It's impossible to replicate an image or object(s) completely using linocut techniques – but this isn't what we should be aiming for. To start, let's look closely at our subject: analyze the areas of contrasting light and dark, shapes and textures. A linocut print is essentially a collection of shapes and textures (or marks) printed onto a surface, if figurative giving an illusion of the subject, or if abstract simply a pleasing composition.

When studying the work of other artists, you will see prints where the marks have been made with such skilful detail that they look almost photographic, but you will also see prints of a more 'naive' or abstract style, which have enormous charm. There are just so many different styles of work out there – each one unique to the artist who made it – and you will eventually find yours!

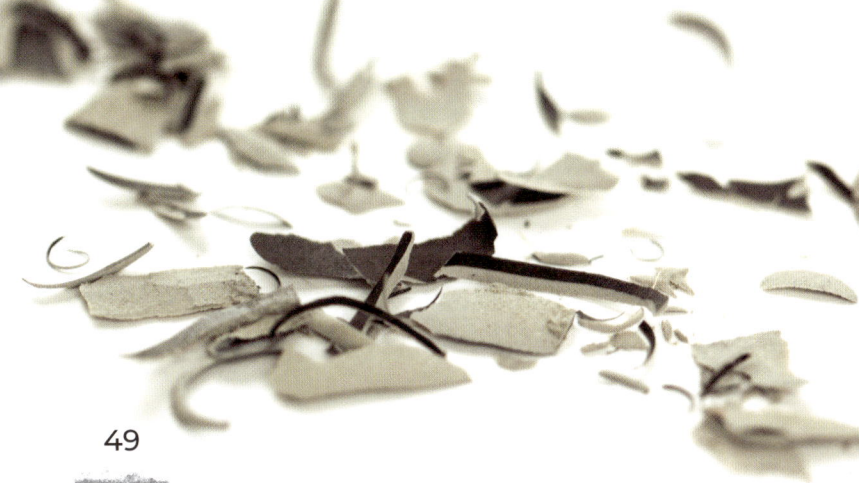

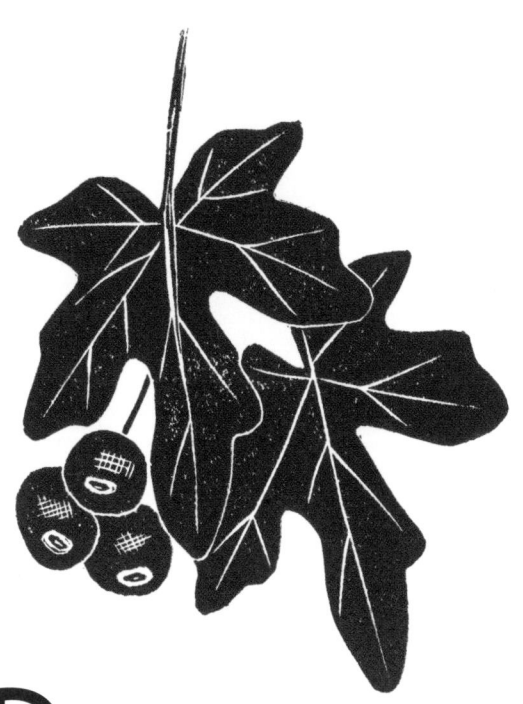

DEMO PROJECT:

STYLIZED LEAVES & BERRIES

On the following pages, I will take you through the basic process and techniques I follow for making my linocut prints, using a sample project. This project is a perfect opportunity to experiment with different markings (see page 48) and print onto different surfaces. A variety of paper scraps and off-cuts, different types of card and even fabrics can all be tried out with your block, in a fun, no-pressure environment! Any mistakes or issues at this stage will only result in a minimum amount of wastage – a tiny piece of lino, very small amount of ink and your cheapest paper.

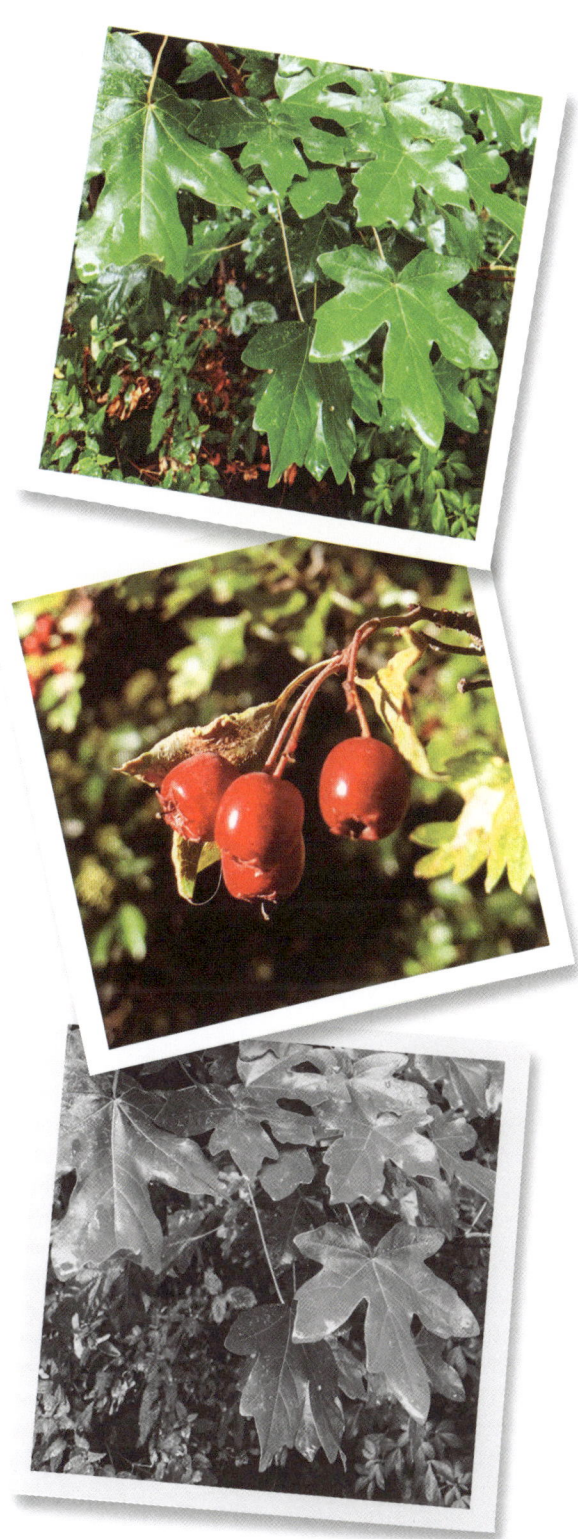

Designing & transferring

When designing my prints, I always like to use sketches I've made or photographs I've taken as references for shapes, colours and details. Even if my planned design is going to be made more abstract, I still like to aim for recognizable plants, birds, insects or animals in my prints. For this example, I am using some close-up photographs I took of leaves and berries as a starting point. Using artistic licence, I will incorporate both of these elements into the same design.

Often, I will I convert any photographs I use for inspiration to black and white on my mobile/cell phone or on my computer, and sometimes adjust the levels of contrast or exposure (depending on the photograph) to create images which have strongly contrasting areas of light and dark. Making the images greyscale gives me a better idea of how they could work as linocut prints. If you don't have photo-editing software on your computer, most camera phones have the facility to convert photographs to black and white, and also to adjust the contrast. You then upload the photograph to your computer to print out, or send it directly to your printer via WiFi or Bluetooth.

If you don't have a printer, don't worry – just sketch a simple outline onto paper, using the image on your phone or computer, then refer to the photograph to add a few key details. If you are making sketches instead, to use for your main design, be sure to make boldly contrasting lines and areas of shading. This will make it easier to decide which areas to carve out (the white areas) and which to leave in (the black areas).

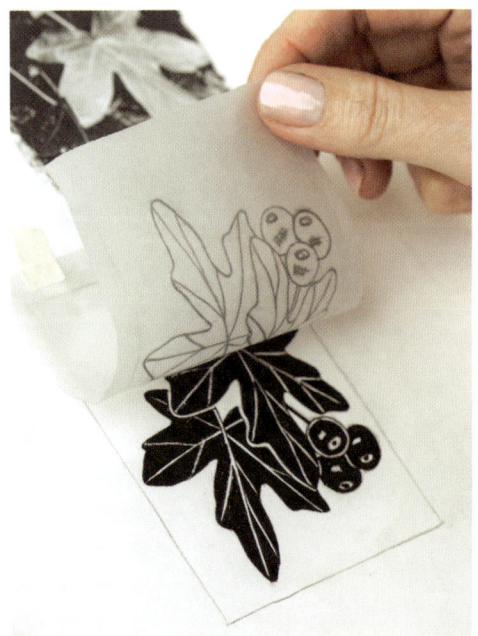

TRANSFERRING METHOD

1 I start by creating a small design in my sketchbook, using simplified and adjusted images of the leaves and berries. For this design, I am focusing on making strong shapes and looking at how they interact with each other on the page. If you wish to use the same design, use the template on page 152.

2 Once I've drawn out the design, I need to transfer it onto a piece of lino for carving. There are several different ways of transferring designs onto lino, but my tried-and-trusted method is to use tracing paper.

Place a small piece of tracing paper over your photograph or sketched image and secure at the top with two tiny pieces of masking tape. This will prevent your tracing paper moving while you're tracing, and also allow you to lift the paper up to make sure you've traced all of the lines you need.

You do not need to include much detail in your tracing, just the outline plus any strong dark areas. When you start carving, you will have your image and the actual object to hand to help guide you.

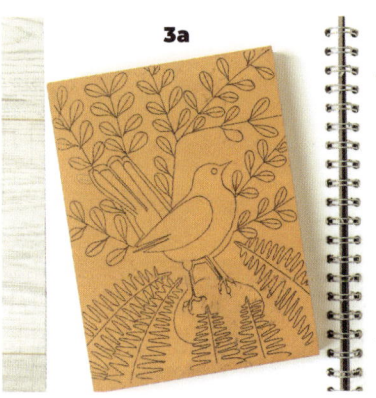

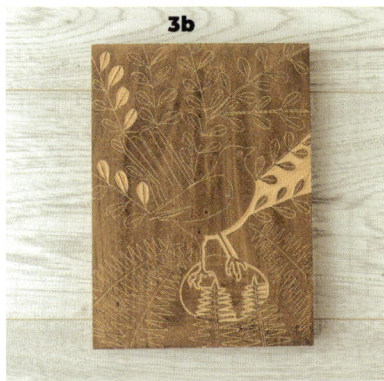

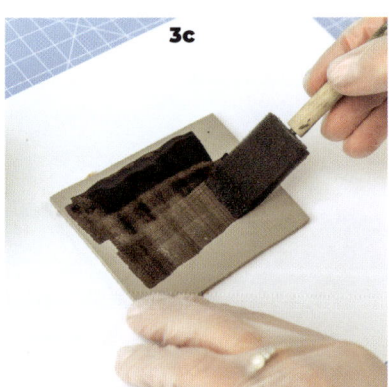

3 Depending on your design, you can choose to stain your lino with ink – **3a** is of a design simply traced onto the lino, and **3b** is when the block has been stained and carved into. Staining the lino helps me to see my carving progress more clearly, and also gives an idea of what the design will look like once it's printed onto paper or fabric (although remember, the carved block is always a 'mirror image' of what the finished print will be!).

For the leaf and berries design, I'm using a small piece of traditional, hessian-backed lino to make this stamp. Before I transferred this design onto the lino ready for carving, I 'stained' it with quite a strong black Indian ink solution (see **3c**). You can use a much weaker solution if you wish, as long as it darkens the lino sufficiently to help you see your carved lines more clearly. Either way, you need to allow the lino to dry thoroughly before carving.

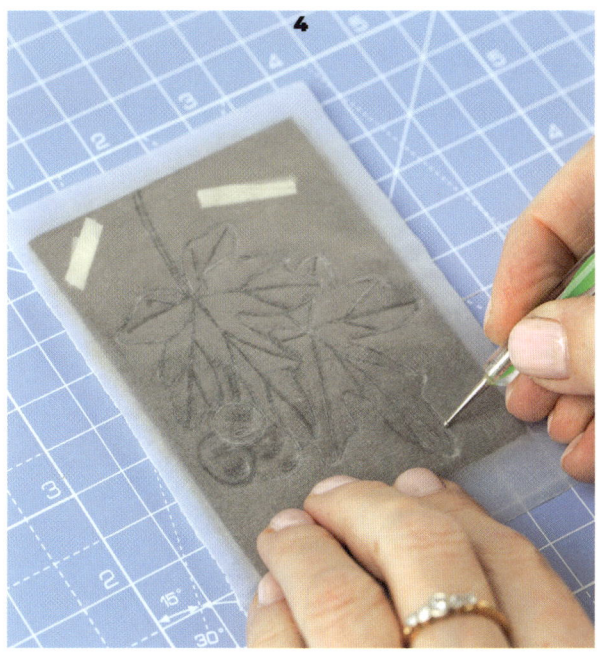

4 I flip over my tracing and place it onto the stained linoleum block, making sure that I place the image in the correct position. The image is now the reverse of the original design, but don't worry about this: when the carved-out design is printed, it will be 'flipped' back to the original image!

Before I begin transferring, I like to fix the tracing in position along the top of the lino with some small pieces of masking tape. This helps prevent the tracing from moving out of position during the transfer process, and also allows me to carefully lift the tracing paper from the bottom to check that the transfer I'm making is a clear enough guide for carving. My preferred method is to 'draw' firmly over the lines using the end of a ballpoint pen or a stylus. This way, I can easily see if I've missed a bit!

5 The stylus pushes the graphite from the tracing into the lino. Once the image is transferred, carving can begin!

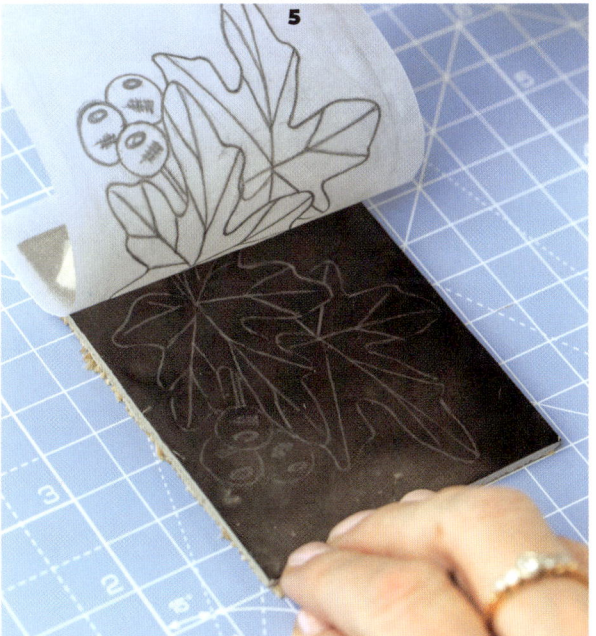

TRANSFERRING TIPS

— If you have missed out any lines, you can put the tracing back down in position and rub over them once again.

— If you feel the pencil lines are too faint, or parts of it are in danger of smudging or rubbing off, you can go over it gently using a black fine-liner pen.

Carving

How you approach your carving, and the order in which you cut out elements of your block, is very much a matter of personal preference. Some people like to carve all of the fine details first, while others prefer to 'skip' around the block until it's complete. If there are any tricky and extra important bits, I usually begin with these as I feel these are essential parts of the image to get right. Once these are done, I can relax more into carving and enjoy the rest of the process! Try out different ways of working until you find what works best for you.

Depending on the complexity of the design, the carving process can be lengthy and parts of it may require great concentration – particularly when cutting out small details.

For this design, I have decided to remove the background area of lino around the motif, so that the leaves and berries will be the only things printed in the final print.

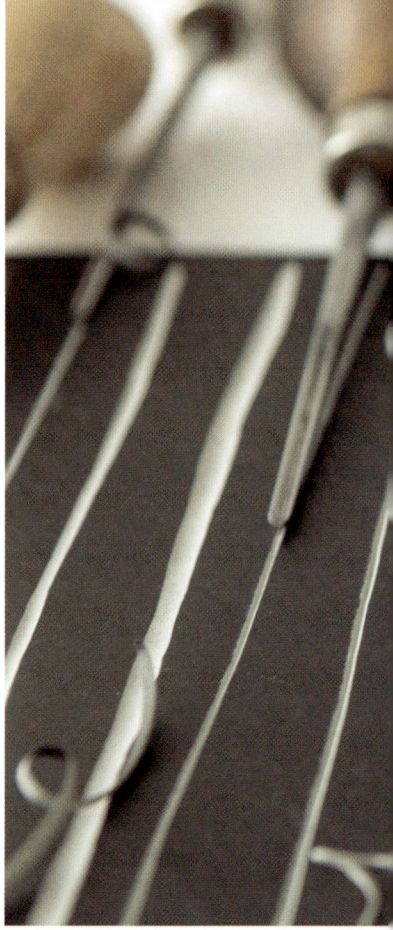

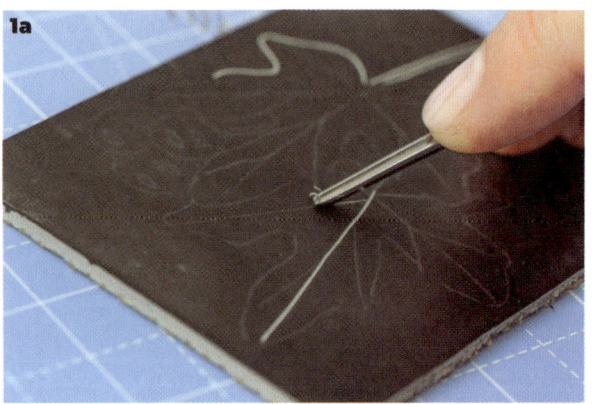

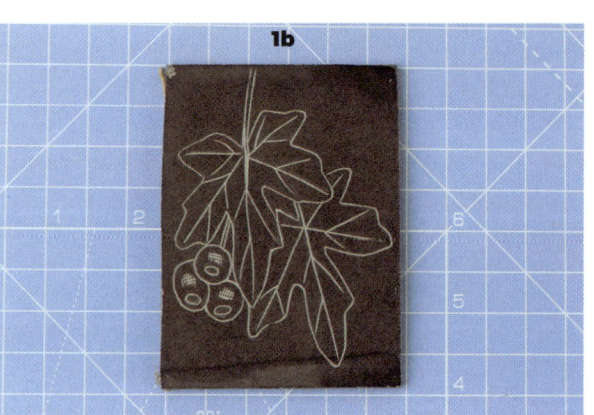

1 I start by carefully carving an outline around the motif (**1a**), using my smallest tool, which is a 1mm V-shaped cutter – perfect for outlines and small details! I then carve out the main outlines/details inside the main design (**1b**). For this little block, I'm adding the details such as the veins of the leaves and highlights on the berries. Sometimes I carve these details at the same time as carving the background; I find working in this way makes the carving process more varied, and seeing the block slowly 'come to life' always heightens my enjoyment and excitement of a project as I work on it!

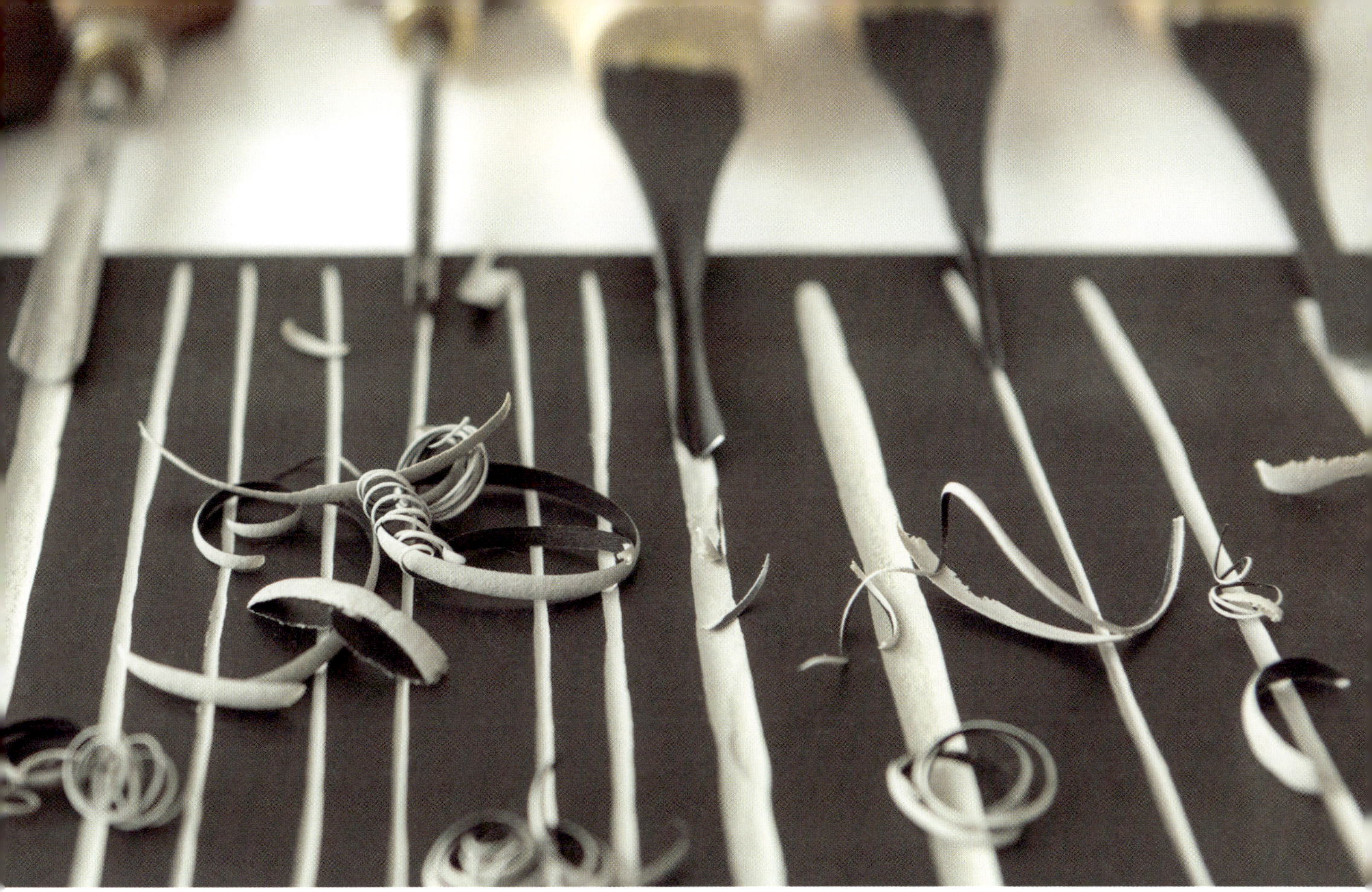

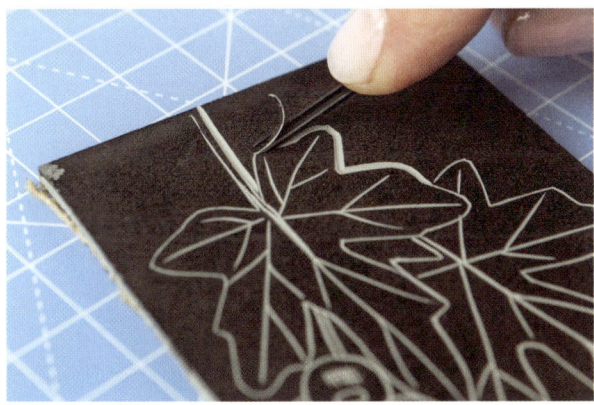

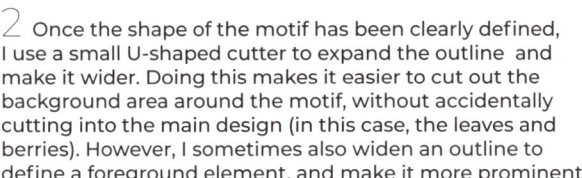

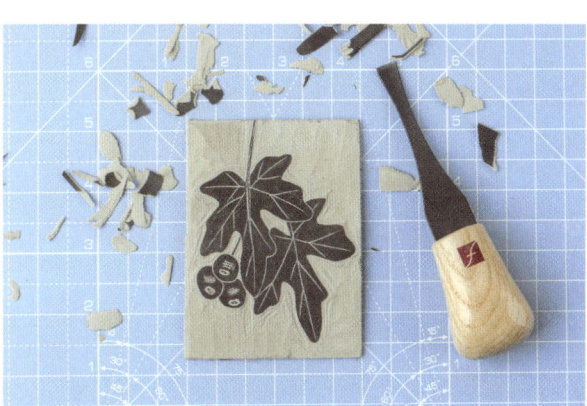

2 Once the shape of the motif has been clearly defined, I use a small U-shaped cutter to expand the outline and make it wider. Doing this makes it easier to cut out the background area around the motif, without accidentally cutting into the main design (in this case, the leaves and berries). However, I sometimes also widen an outline to define a foreground element, and make it more prominent.

3 For carving out larger areas, I like to use a larger, U-shaped cutter or a wide 'chisel' or 'scoop' tool, as shown. A chisel is ideal for removing larger sections of background where there's no danger of cutting into the design; it also flattens the cut-away sections, preventing 'noise' (see page 146). Cutting out larger areas tends to be quicker and easier than the smaller, fiddly bits – and it's pretty satisfying! When the carving is complete, we are ready to print.

Rolling

We start by laying out the equipment we need to print. I'm using some of my favourite black oil-based relief ink, but a water-based ink is fine to use instead – with the added bonus of being easier to clean up! A small roller or brayer is needed to roll out the ink and apply it to your block. I am using a hard rubber brayer for this print – please revisit page 30 for more information on printing brayers. You will also need an even, wipe-clean surface to roll out the ink on, before applying it to your block. I'm using a small sheet of Perspex®.

When rolling, what you are aiming for is a thin covering of ink on your brayer and on the wipe-clean surface. If there is too much ink on your brayer, continue to roll it out onto the wipe-clean surface and, if necessary, roll any surplus ink onto a second wipe-clean surface or a sheet of scrap paper. This is really important, as too much ink on your brayer will translate into too much ink on your lino block! (See also page 144.)

A well-inked brayer will have a nice 'glisten' to it when held up to the light (see middle right). An under-inked roller will be patchy (though, arguably, it is better to under-ink so you can gradually add more); an over-inked roller will have thick blobs of ink on it – either on parts of it or all over.

Getting it right (most of the time) will come with practice, although I can tell you that even experienced printmakers have the occasional struggle with over-inking!

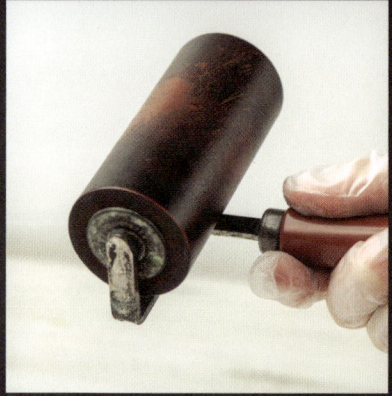

Under-inked brayer

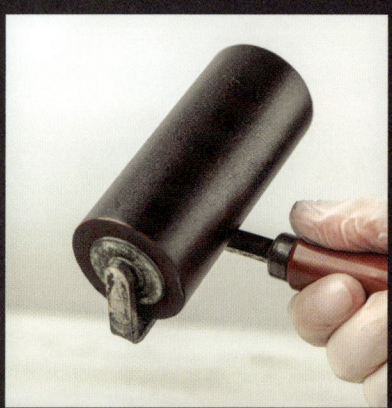

Well-inked brayer

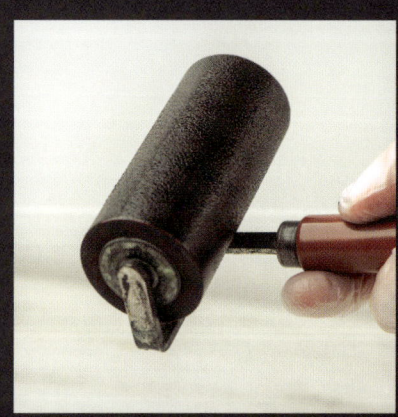

Over-inked brayer

OVER-INKING LINO

If you apply too much ink at the start, your lino block will become clogged up and the resulting prints will look 'gungy' and over-inked, causing your small details to disappear. It's more difficult to remove surplus ink from your block than it is to apply it, so for this reason it's definitely preferable to build up with thin layers of ink, gradually applying more as needed.

ROLLING TIPS

— Remember, use a roller that's at least the width of your lino block, as this will make it easier to achieve an even coating of ink. Don't worry if your roller is smaller though; this just means you will take a little longer to apply your ink evenly.

— If you do end up getting ink onto parts of your background, it's not the end of the world – it just means that these tiny areas may be printed in the background of your print, along with your design. This is called **noise** in printmaking (see page 146), and opinion is divided as to whether it's a good or bad thing. Some artists like it and feel it gives a certain dynamism to their prints; others aim for a completely clear and pristine background.

— As you are applying ink to your lino block, you need to look closely at it from different angles, to ensure you have covered all of the areas you want to print (particularly if the block was stained in black ink before carving). This can involve bending over it and adopting some rather strange poses!

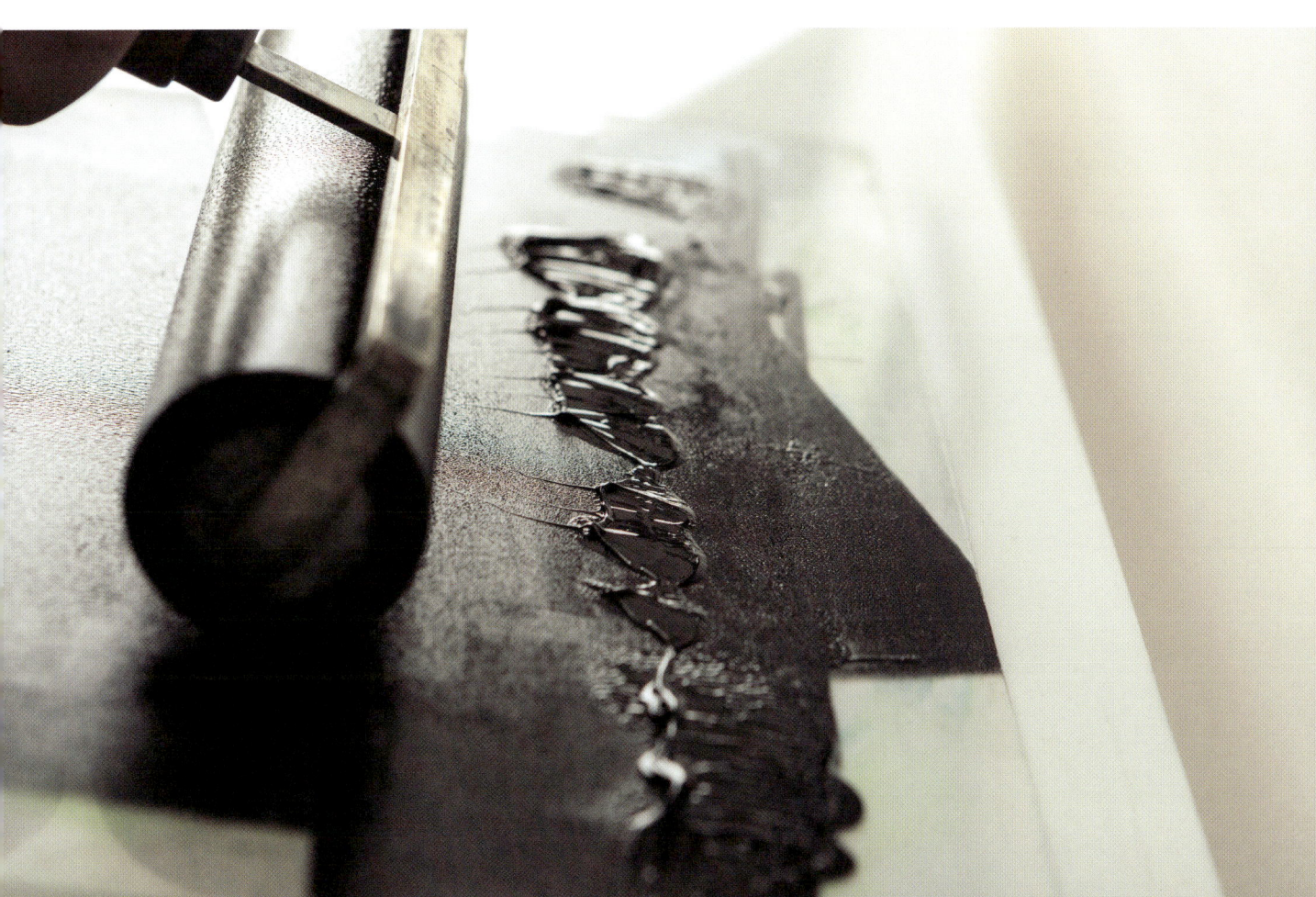

ROLLING METHOD

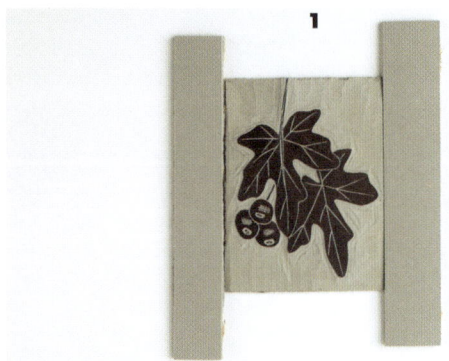

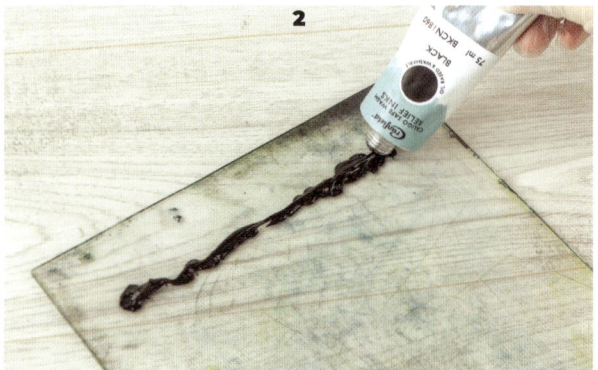

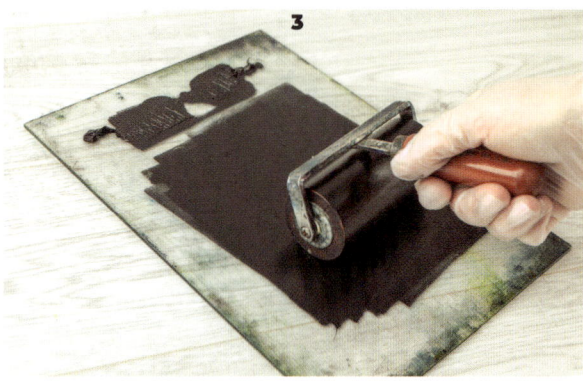

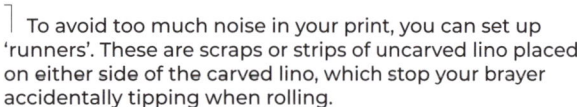

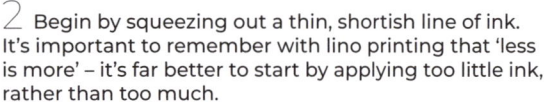

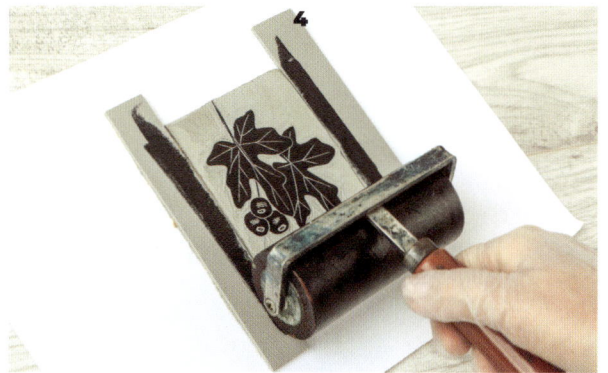

1 To avoid too much noise in your print, you can set up 'runners'. These are scraps or strips of uncarved lino placed on either side of the carved lino, which stop your brayer accidentally tipping when rolling.

2 Begin by squeezing out a thin, shortish line of ink. It's important to remember with lino printing that 'less is more' – it's far better to start by applying too little ink, rather than too much.

3 Now to roll out your ink! Firstly, dip your brayer gently but firmly into your line of ink then start to roll it out onto the wipe-clean surface, rolling back and forth. This is pretty satisfying, and your brayer will make some wonderful 'sticky' noises as you roll the ink out! Remember, you are aiming for a thin covering of ink on the brayer.

4 To apply ink to your lino block, simply glide your brayer over the lino block, and the raised (uncarved) surface will be coated with ink. There's no need to press down hard, just glide the brayer lightly over the lino; as the brayer passes over, you will hear a slight sticky noise.

When rolling your ink, try to keep the roller level, so that it just makes contact with the uncarved (relief) surfaces and not the carved-out background. When you feel that the block has an even and sufficient coating of ink, lift it up and turn it to the light: the inked areas should glisten and not look too 'blobby', which would indicate over-inking. (If you have applied too much ink, see page 144.)

Printing

Once you are happy with your inked block, you are ready to make your first print. For this demo I will show you two straightforward methods of printing: one with a spoon/baren, known as 'hand-burnishing' (see page 60), and the other with a two-plate press (see pages 61 and 62).

Under normal circumstances, I would make several test prints from my block on cheap paper (usually newsprint), before printing onto the final, usually more expensive paper. However, this little demo project is intended to be a way for you to test things out and gain confidence before you embark on the 'real' projects, which start in the next chapter.

Relief printing (the family of which linocutting is a part) is simply the act of transferring ink from the raised (uncarved) surfaces on your block onto a different surface (your paper), by using some form of pressure.

A NOTE ON 'PERFECT' PRINTING

I always find the act of lifting a print from the block for the first time exciting, with a little frisson of anxiety attached!

When I am working on a carved block, I usually have a specific idea of how I want the print to turn out. If the result isn't quite as I'd planned or hoped for, it can be disappointing. If this turns out to be the case, I will clean up the block and look at ways I can improve it – maybe I can work into some of the carved areas (see page 142) or, in extreme cases, I will re-carve the whole block!

When you check your print after pressing, ask yourself the following questions: have I carved everything, or did I leave something out? Is my print over- or under-inked? Have I positioned the paper on the block squarely, as best I can? If you do need to adjust anything at this stage now is the time, before you go on to make any more prints. Do also refer to the 'Troubleshooting' chapter on pages 140–147 if you're not happy with certain elements, which I hope will help you overcome some teething troubles you may encounter.

We all have an inner critic, but it's important to be positive and constructive when reflecting on your work. For every 'fault' you spot in your print, also note a good quality. Reflection and troubleshooting are vital for your development as an artist. Also remember that these are *hand-made* prints that we have created. In my opinion, small inconsistencies and 'quirks' between individual prints only serve to add to their charm and appeal – so we do need to avoid letting that inner critic take over and spoil our enjoyment of our work!

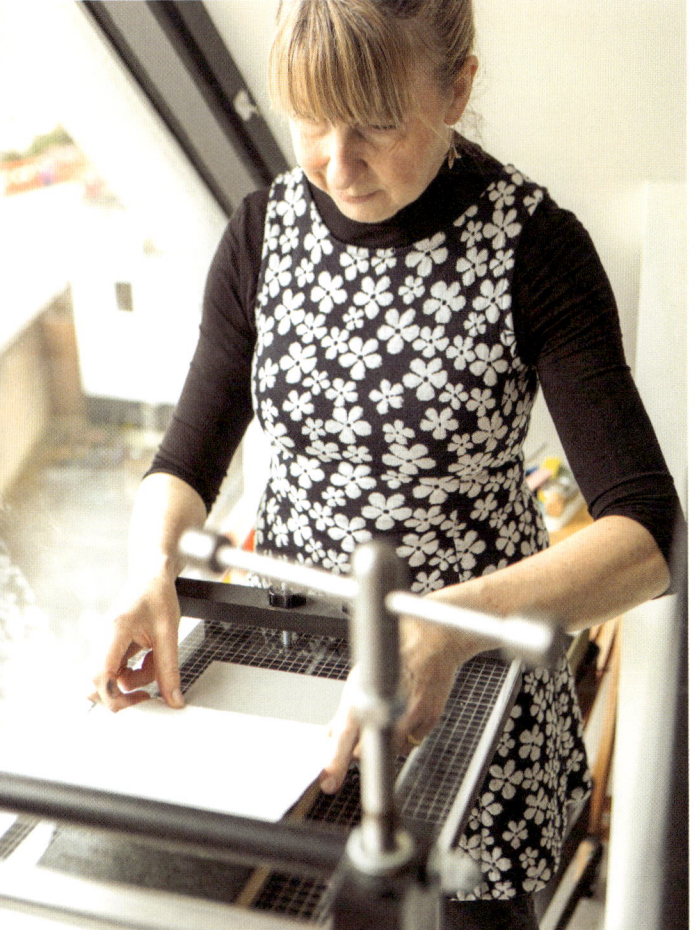

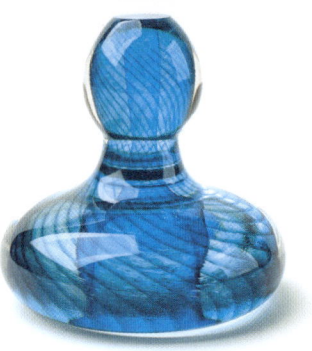

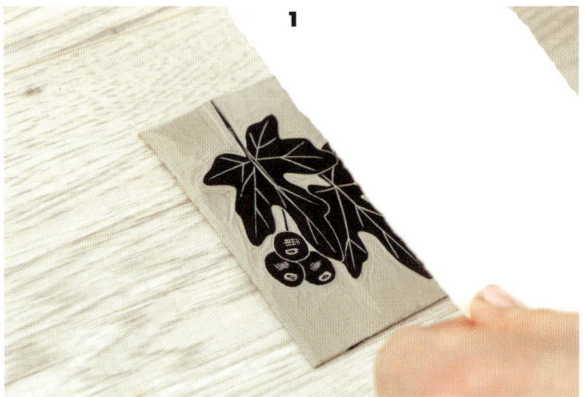

HAND-BURNISHING

Some printmakers prefer to use a wooden spoon to hand-burnish their prints, others prefer to use a baren (see page 24). Whichever you choose, it is vital that the paper does not move on the block when hand-burnishing, as this will result in the print being offset and having unwanted 'movement'. Hand-burnishing with the back of a spoon proves that you really don't need much investment to start out in linocut printing!

1 Carefully place a small piece of paper on top of the block, ensuring that it doesn't move (not even slightly!).

2 Holding the paper in place with one hand, use the back of a spoon or baren to rub firmly all over the raised areas of the lino.

3 Still holding down the paper firmly from one end, and being careful not to move it from its original position, lift the other end to inspect the print. If there are any areas that missed while burnishing, that haven't printed properly, carefully drop the paper and rub those areas again with the spoon.

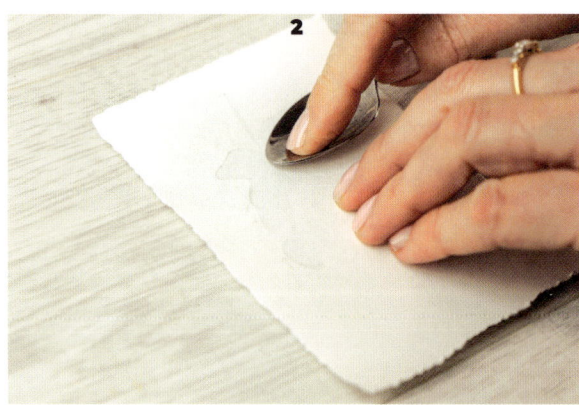

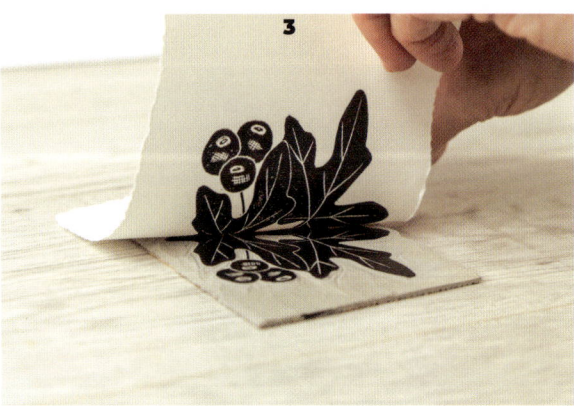

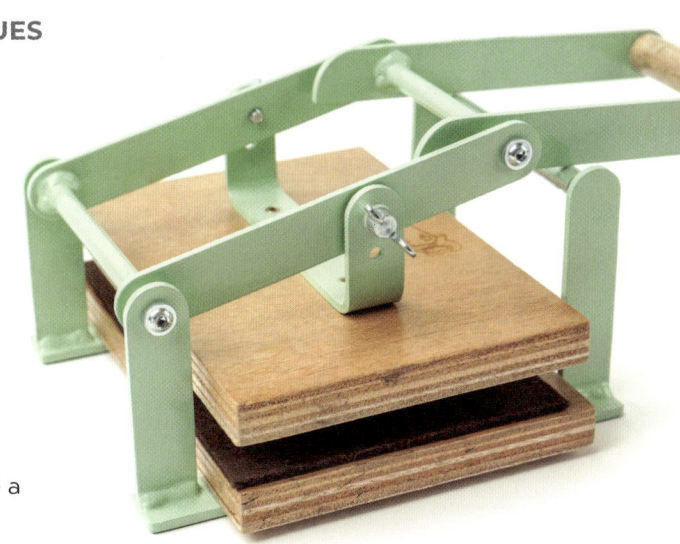

TWO-PLATE PRINTING

If you're ready to take that next step in your printmaking practice, a printing press is a great investment, and can be a game-changer when it comes to printing your lino blocks.

I'm going to be using my compact A5 (148 x 210mm/Junior Legal) Woodzilla press. It's small size and lightweight, which means it can be easily stored on a shelf and carried over to a table. It's particularly useful if your workspace doubles up as your kitchen or dining table!

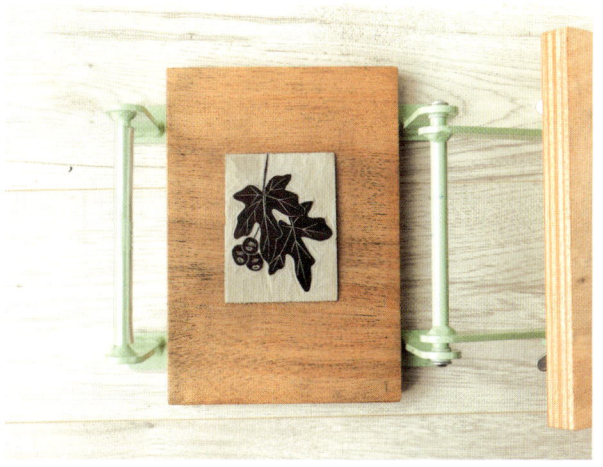

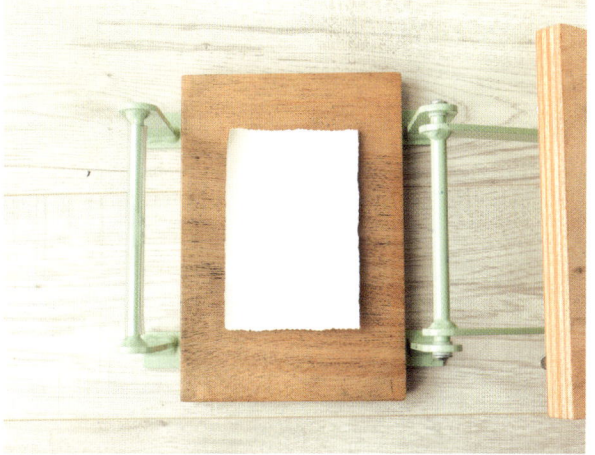

1 Pull the handle to lift away the top plate, revealing the bottom plate. Place your block nice and centrally on the lower plate of the press, the design facing up.

2 Carefully place the paper on top of the block, ensuring that it doesn't move. For this demo I'm not worrying about being too precise with positioning the paper. This is a practice exercise, and the main objective is to end up with a good-quality printed image, with no pressure for it to be perfectly placed on the paper.

Continued...

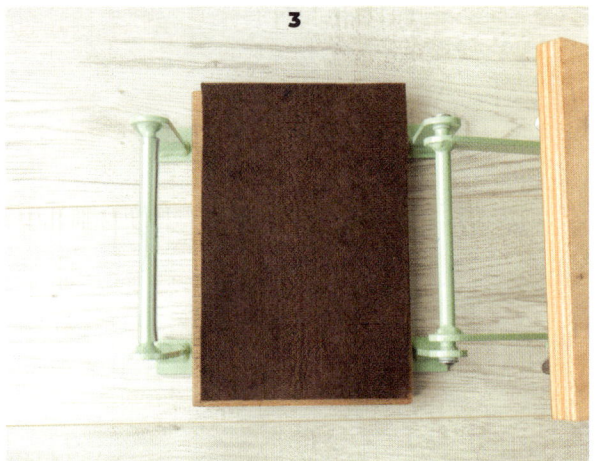

3 A felt printing 'blanket' is placed over the top of the paper. Using a printing blanket ensures even pressure when the top plate is lowered, resulting in better ink coverage. I haven't done it here, but if you're worried about ink getting through to the blanket, or onto the press itself, you can place a sheet of cheap paper between your printing surface and the blanket.

4 Lower the top plate of the press then apply pressure by squeezing the handles together, which have a spring mechanism. For help on how much pressure to apply, refer to the tip box opposite.

5 Lift the top plate of the press and remove the blanket. Your print is now ready to be revealed! As before, you can check the quality of the print by holding one end of the paper down while peeping at the other end, before fully committing to lifting it up. If you're not fully happy with the result, refer to the tip box opposite or the 'Troubleshooting' chapter on pages 140–147.

6 If you are happy with the print you've made, you can go ahead and print some more on your chosen printmaking paper. Lay the prints out to dry on a clean, flat surface, or place on a drying rack if you have one. Depending on room temperature, and whether you have used water-based or oil-based inks, your prints will take anything from a couple of hours to two to three days to dry properly.

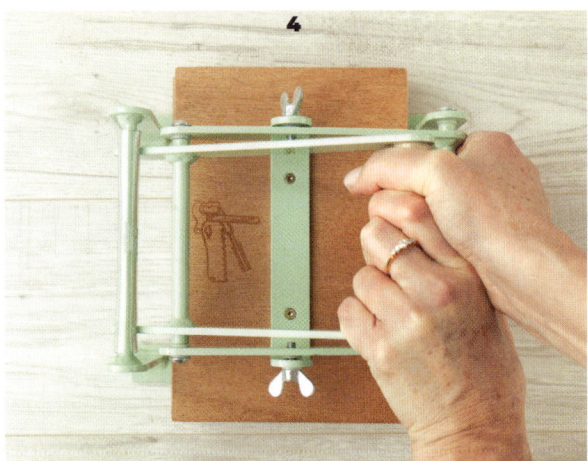

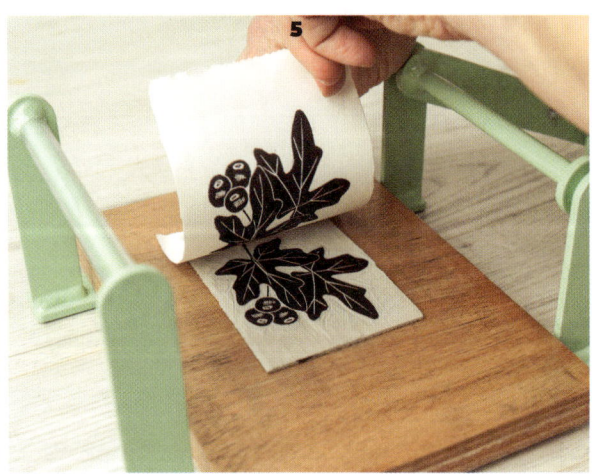

PRINTING BLANKETS

Using a printing blanket with a press is beneficial, as it enables a more even pressure to be applied to your block, and therefore improves the result of your print. If your press hasn't come with a blanket, you can purchase a blanket separately from most specialist printmaking suppliers.

Trying out different papers

The type of paper you print onto can make an enormous difference to the look and feel of the print. Paper choice can be influenced by a number of factors, including personal preference, subject matter, composition and size of the finished print.

Below is my design printed on three different types of paper. The Japanese paper (bottom left) gives a soft, delicate feel to the print, while the textures of grass and bark fibres embedded in the Thai mulberry paper (bottom right) beautifully complement the nature-inspired subject matter. The Zerkall (top right) gives a clean, crisp finish that many people like in a linocut print.

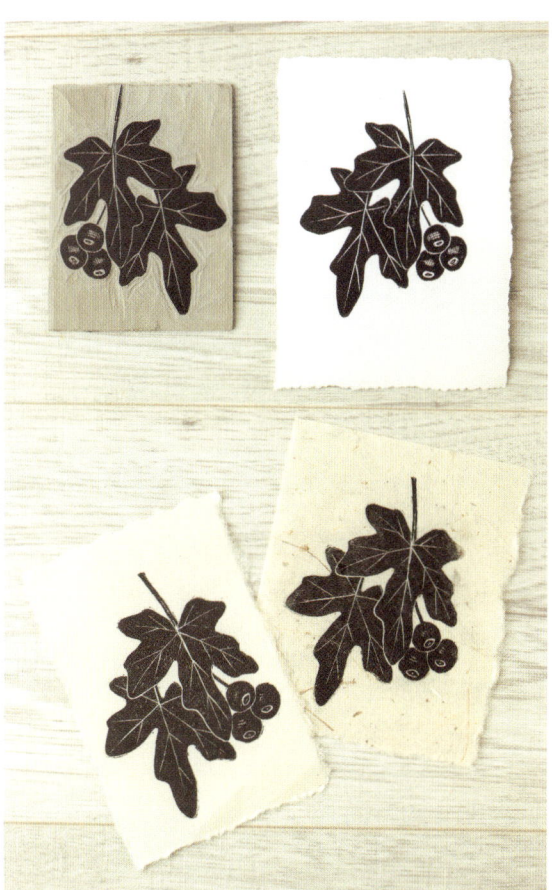

Left

Clockwise, from top right): smooth, off-white hand-made Zerkall (medium-weight, 145gsm / 54lbs); hand-made Thai mulberry (light-weight, 40gsm / 15lbs); Japanese Okawara Select (lightweight, 51gsm / 20lbs).

DESIGN & INSPIRATION

My linocut designs always start with an image that delights and excites me. It may be a photograph I've taken while on a walk, or of a bird I've seen in my garden, or maybe even a sketch I did years ago and never got around to developing...

I would love this book to act as a springboard for my readers' own unique ideas. During my years of teaching art to adults, I never stopped being thrilled and amazed at the creativity I saw in my students. They inspired me constantly and I felt privileged to be able to help and encourage them along their creative journeys!

Photography

I work a lot with photographs and tend to carry my smartphone with me everywhere I go. Consequently, I have literally thousands of photographs. A camera phone is such an instant, spontaneous way to capture an image, and the quality is pretty good! Most camera phones also have some simple editing tools, which allow you to zoom in and crop the photograph if there's just one part of the image which you find interesting.

Many camera phones and point-and-shoot cameras have a 'portrait' setting, which I find works really well when you want to focus on a particular object/subject when taking a photograph: if you tap your screen where the subject is, it'll make it sharp and clear in the foreground then give the background a pleasing blurriness/soft focus.

I often convert photographs to greyscale (black and white) and adjust the contrast to give images strongly contrasting areas of light and dark. This makes it easier to decide which areas to carve out (the white areas) or to leave uncarved (the dark printed areas).

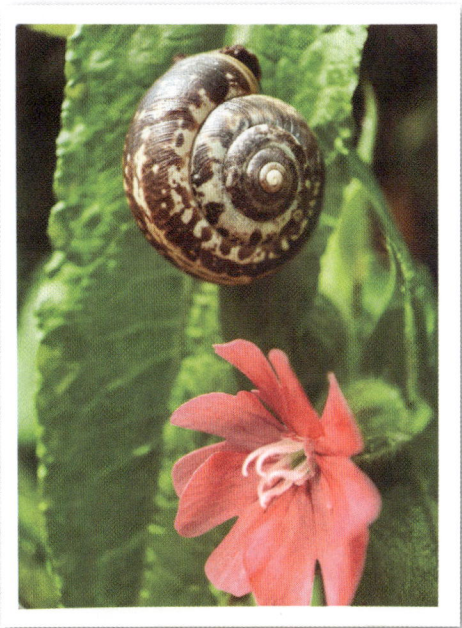

MACRO PHOTOGRAPHY

I have a fascination with close-up details, so I've invested in a special separate macro lens for my phone that can be easily attached with a clip-on case. It's allowed me to capture some wonderful close-up images of plants, flowers, textures and tiny creatures. I find it a useful piece of kit for taking images that I can't photograph with the in-built camera on my phone alone – details in tiny subjects that I may later decide to develop into print ideas.

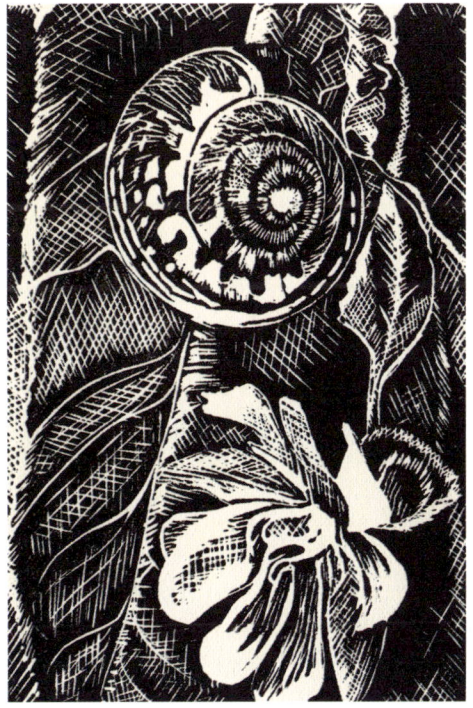

From photo to print

Many of my designs are inspired by my macro photographs. Sometimes I like the composition of the photograph so much that I recreate the image completely. The photograph of a little snail sharing a leaf with a tiny pink flower (top right) was made into a single-block print (bottom right). This ready-made design also has potential for adding colour to the flower later on! (See pages 68, 101 and 102–108.)

Process of creating 'Amongst the Brambles'
The coloured version can be seen on page 7.

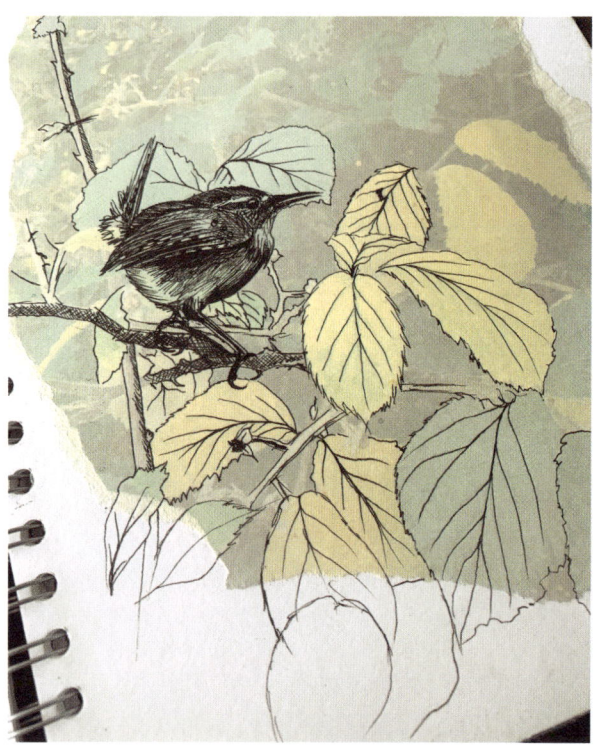

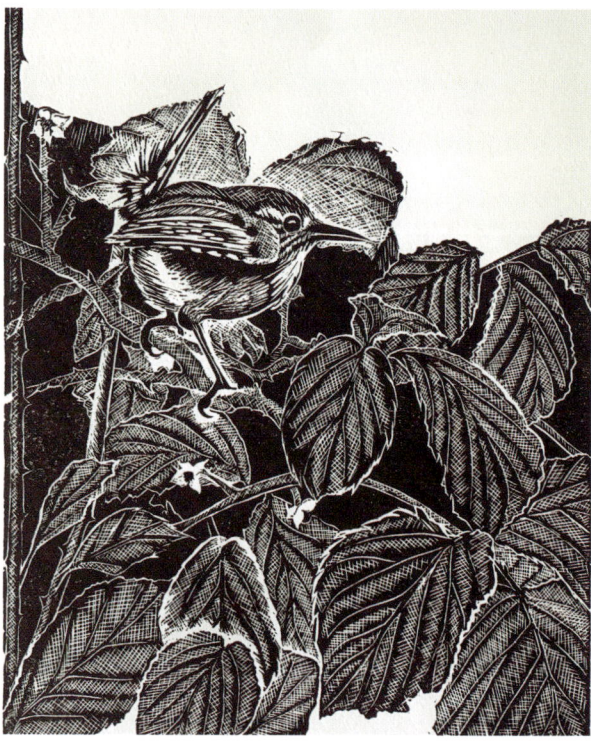

Sketchbooks

I like to use sketchbooks, although mine tend to be more like art journals or scrapbooks – containing collage, torn-up photocopies and mixed-media experiments – rather than just pencil and pen sketches and colour notes.

I enjoy using a mixture of traditional and digital media to develop my ideas. I often manipulate the photographs I've taken using photo-editing software, typically reducing the opacity to make the image more transparent and pale. I will then print out the photograph, tear roughly around it and stick it into my sketchbook, before starting to draw onto and around it. I like extending and adding to elements in the photographs, while simultaneously playing with mark-making to develop an image into an idea for a print.

For example, if a photograph features leaves, I may begin drawing onto existing leaves – emboldening them with my pen – then extend and add leaves beyond the torn edges of the photograph. I may then add a focus subject, such as a bird skulking among the leaves! When I feel I have a sufficient idea of the composition drawn out in my sketchbook, I transfer the design onto lino and begin carving. This is how I created my 'Amongst the Brambles' print (above).

I prefer this approach when working in my sketchbook, as starting a new, blank page can feel rather daunting! It also makes me feel bolder about drawing: if I've already torn into the image, I feel less precious about working into it. I always purposely draw with pen – it forces me to work into any 'mistakes' as I can't rub them out!

Using video stills

When you have in mind a subject that moves around a lot that you want to feature in a print, it can be hard to make sketches or take photographs that are suitable to create the composition you want to achieve. Recording a video and isolating still images from the video can sometimes be a helpful solution.

I used this approach to start off the design process for my 'Four Pigeons and a Primrose' linocut print (see below right). In my opinion, the common feral pigeon is one of our most under-appreciated species of wildlife. I love to see them congregate in their comical little groups as I walk along our local main street, and find the gentle sounds they make soothing amid the noise and bustle of the town centre through which they wander.

To begin my design process, I sat on a bench with my camera phone, videoing the birds as they moved and pecked industriously around the roots of one of the large trees that flank the street. I was then able to pause the video in playback mode and move slowly through the frames. Whenever I saw a frame with a pleasing composition, showing close-ups of the birds and clear details of their plumage, facial expressions, and so on, I saved a screenshot to my phone (see the top-right photograph). I repeated this process until I had a sufficient number of images of the birds to put together a composition for my print.

In the initial linocut design I had included some stylized tree roots in the top-right corner, which featured in the original scene. However, I ended up removing them from the final carve simply by carving them out. Even once I've started carving a block, I like to remain open to change, and will often refine and adapt my ideas almost up to the last moment. I like the cleanness of the composition I achieved in the final print (see bottom right), and feel that the single primrose being the solitary background element with the arrangement of birds does a satisfactory job.

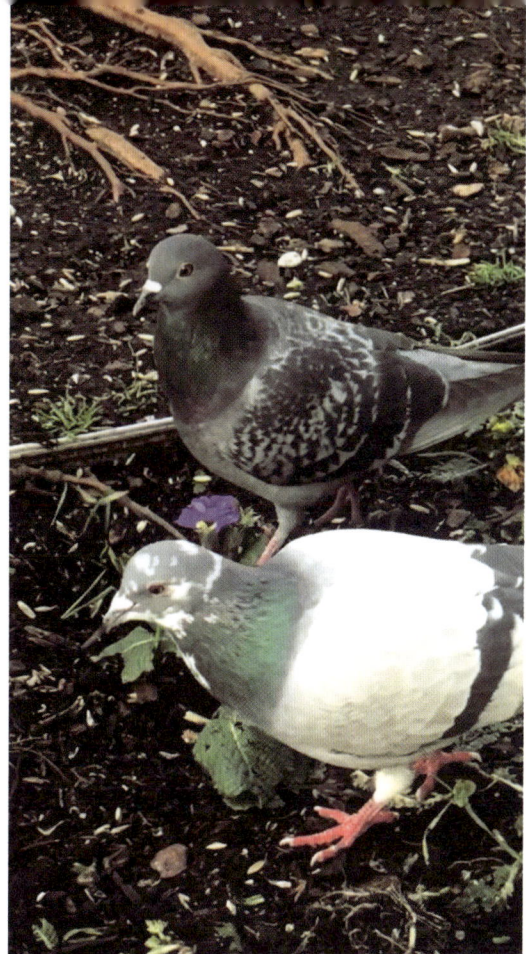

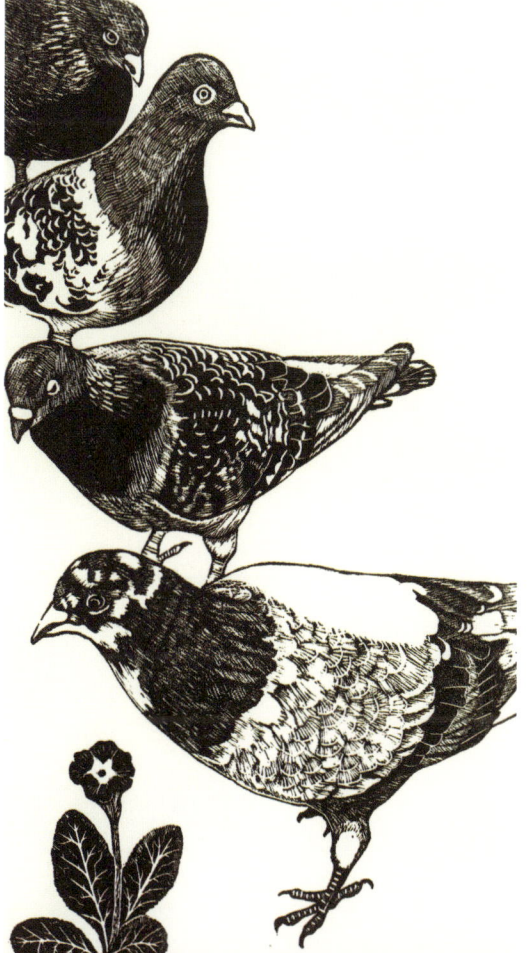

Bringing in colour

Many people think linocut prints are mainly bold, graphic images printed in black ink onto white paper – and I love to make single-block prints in this way. But I also love designs with colour and surface patterns (I can never quite leave my roots as a textile designer!).

Sometimes I will make a print, intending for it to be a single-block, single-colour image, but then I feel it needs an extra 'pop' of colour – maybe to give a little more focus on the main subject of the print.

My 'Waterlily' print, right, was such a print. I was thrilled when my waterlilies began growing and blooming in my reclaimed farm-trough pond, and I enjoyed photographing (and even filming!) the process. I was fascinated by the shapes of leaves and flowers, and the way they interacted together. They were the perfect combination for a print! Starting with a photograph, I added and rearranged leaf shapes until I was happy with the composition. I then transferred it to lino and began carving. After making the first test prints, I decided to see how a pop of colour on the flower would change the dynamics of the print. I applied the colour by carving a small waterlily-shaped stamp and applying a mixture of extender and inks with a small roller. I added the yellow to the centre of the flower by dabbing it on with my finger! These techniques for adding colour to your prints will be covered in more detail in the project 'Let's Add Colour' (see pages 102–108).

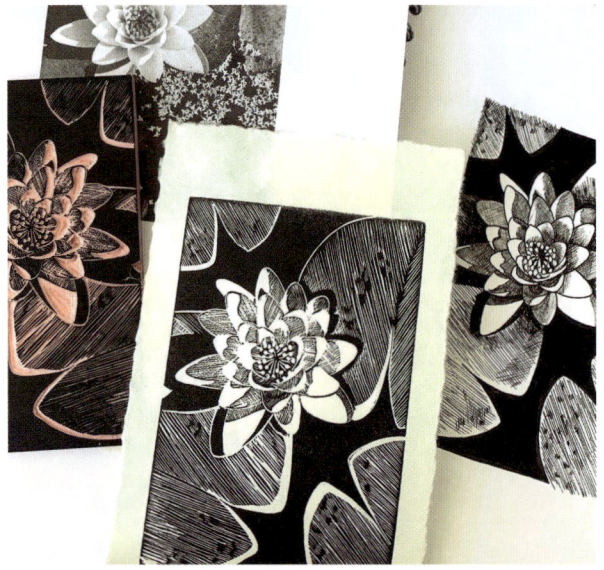

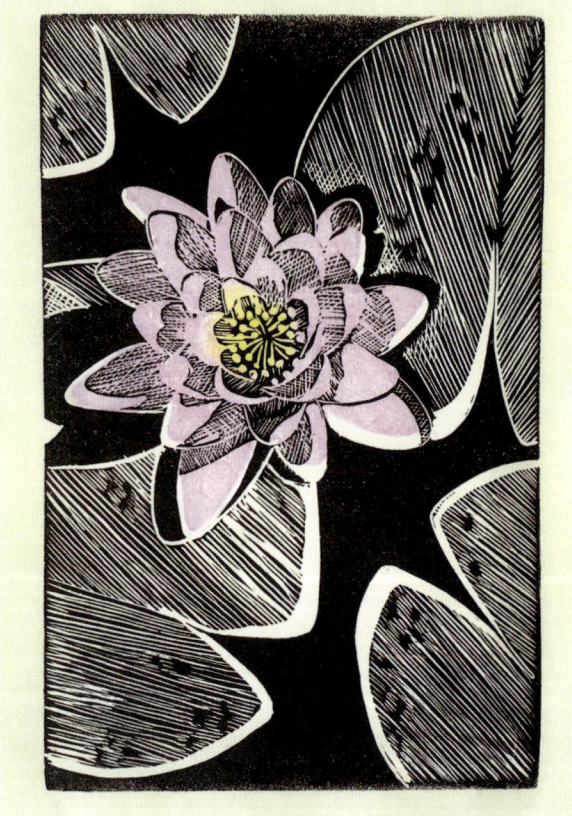

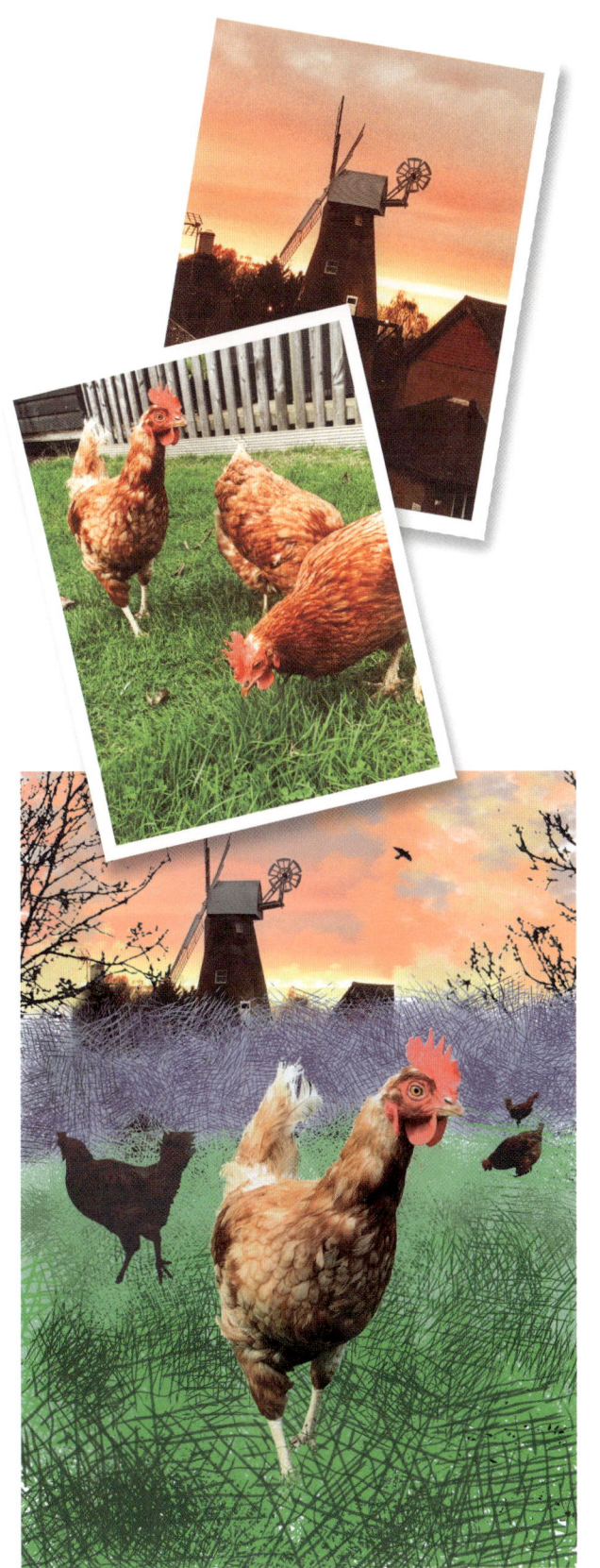

Designing digitally

In recent years, I have been dipping into a digital-art-studio app that I have on my phone. The app I use, called Procreate Pocket, allows you to create often quite complex digital artworks. You can either start an artwork from scratch, using the many drawing/painting tools, or you can work into existing photographs from your phone's camera roll to develop them into digital artworks. There are also digital-art studio apps for tablets too, which are easier to use as you have a larger screen. Whether you prefer using a phone or tablet, it is best to use a stylus to create digital artworks for greater control and accuracy. These can be purchased online for very little.

'Four Rescue Hens and a Windmill' (see page 47) was the first print for which I used Procreate Pocket as a development tool. The print is a fantasy combination of elements: it stars four lovely rescue hens, owned by a friend, and the windmill I see every day from my studio window!

I combined photographs I had of both subjects in the app; I then enjoyed playing with some of the texture brushes. The result was a very colourful combination of hens, green grasses, a windmill and a sunset! I liked how the composition and colours worked together, and decided to transfer an outline image onto lino and start carving.

The final print had a completely different look and feel to the Procreate artwork, although some of the cross-hatched marks on the grasses were retained in the prints. My linocut prints are very often black on white paper, but for this design I did print a small edition with some colour in the background (for more on editions, see 'More Blocks, Please' on pages 116–127). The main edition, shown on page 47, of only single-colour black ink, is my favourite as the fine details and cross-hatched marks printed well.

Copyright considerations

There is such joy in making a piece of art that is entirely yours – the outcome of a personal journey of creation, which started off as a mere idea in your mind's eye; an idea which you took through the various stages of development, before creating a real-life, tangible piece of art, in every way personal to you. There is far less joy in simply copying, or trying to reproduce an image of an artwork which you may have come across, either online or in print.

As an artist, my preferred way of developing an idea for a print is always to use my own references and source images where possible – be it from photographs I've taken or sketches I've made. However, there are times when, as artists, we need extra reference images to help us put together an idea, and we may not have immediate access to these. It may be a close-up of an animal in a certain pose, reflections in water, or perhaps a particular type of leaf or flower.

In these instances, we might search online. Image-sharing sites, like Pinterest, are probably the best-known ways of sourcing images on the internet. Try to use these images only when absolutely necessary, as a reference for just a part of your own original design, and do change and adapt the image to make it fit in with your own ideas. Please be aware that all photographs on Pinterest are the property of the original photographers and may be subject to copyright.

There are many commercial image libraries available online, such as Shutterstock®, where you can legitimately purchase a single license to download an image for a small fee. This way you are supporting the photographer and, in return, have legal access to a top-quality, unwatermarked photograph for your own, personal use.

There are also many wonderful wildlife photographers on social media who are often happy for artists to use their photographs as references, provided they are credited in any posts where the artist has made use of them. Always message the owner of the account before using their photograph, to check whether they agree to you using it!

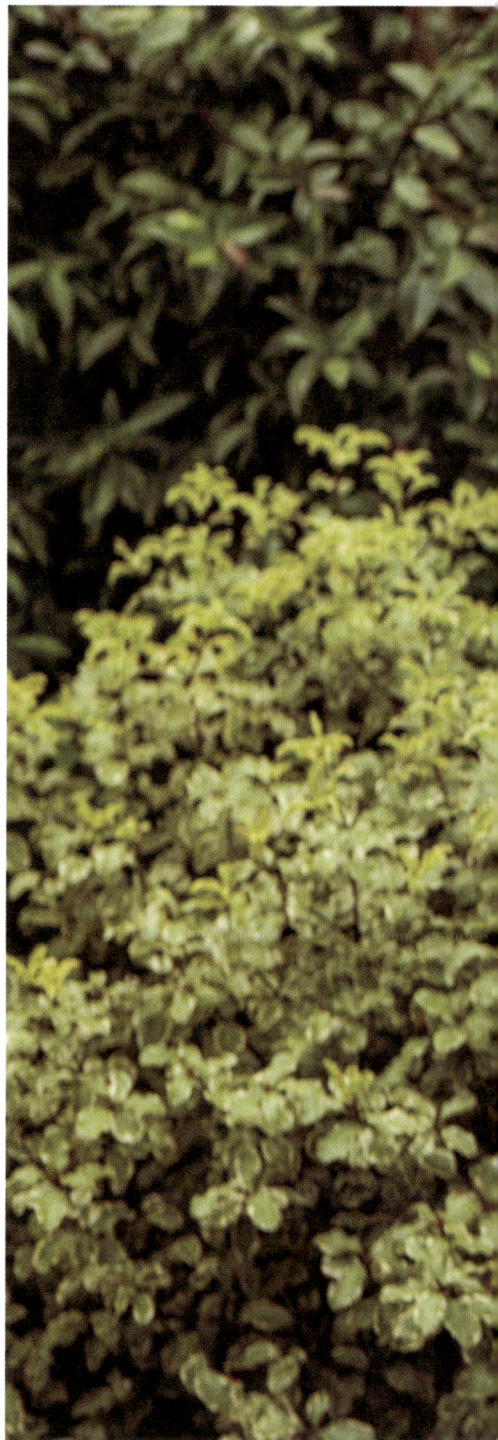

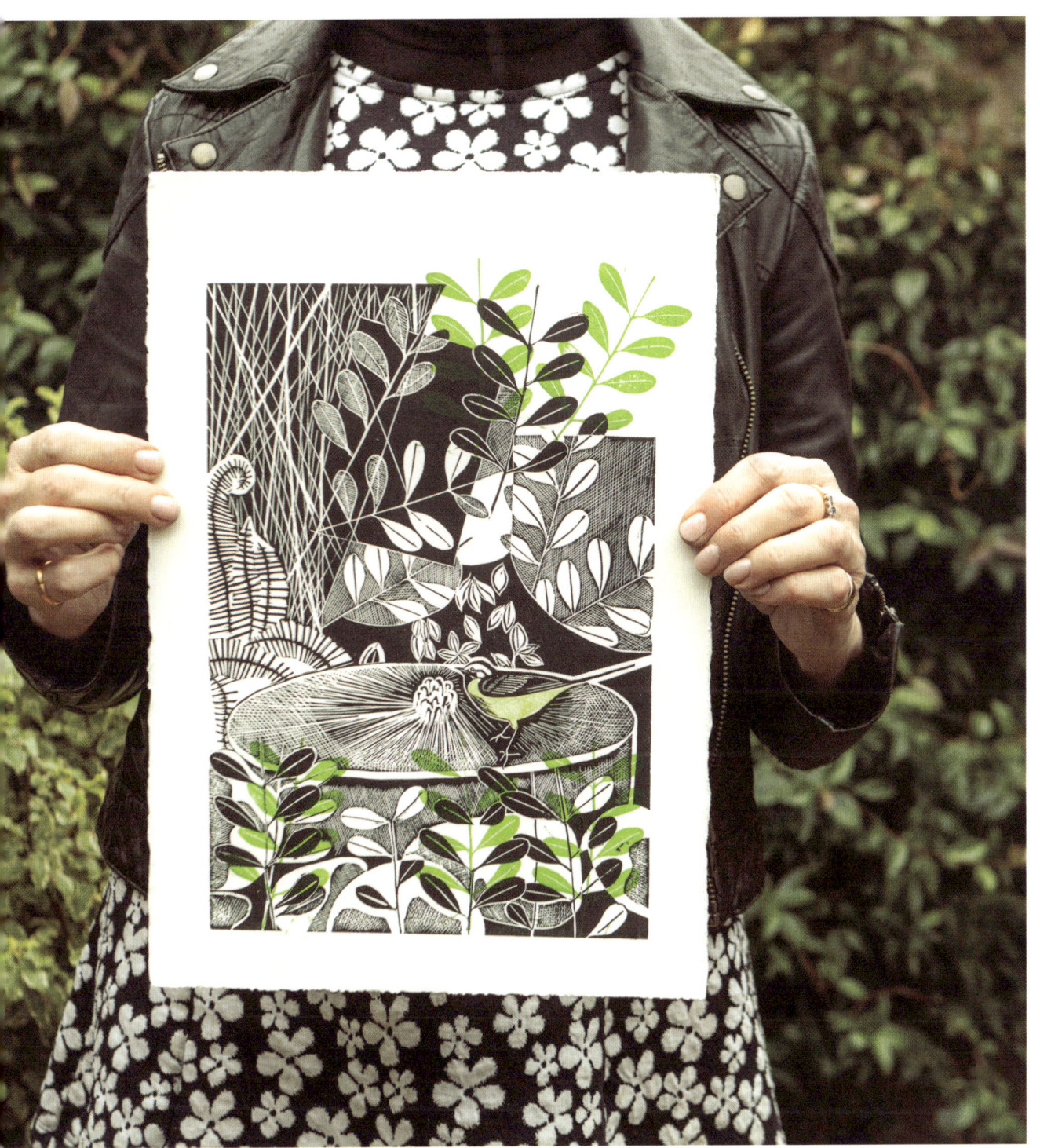

PROJECTS

On the following pages, you will find 10 different linocut projects to make, all inspired by nature in some form or another. Plants, flowers, animals, birds, insects and natural forms (such as shells, feathers and pine cones) provide an endless source of inspiration. As David Hockney once said: 'You can't be bored of nature, can you?'

Each project begins with a 'brief', consisting of some loose guidance on subject matter and design, and fairly open-ended suggestions for your starting points. My intention behind this is to encourage you to take ownership of your own subject matter and develop your ideas, so that each piece you create will be totally unique to you – so satisfying! However, you are perfectly free to interpret the projects exactly as you wish. Having this approach will help you grow and develop your own linocut printing practice.

There is a templates section at the end of this book, which you can use to help you with drawing the shapes of the various elements that appear in the projects. If you do choose to follow this path with any of the projects, I would ask that you use them just for personal and not commercial purposes.

All that's left to say is, please read on – and become lost in the wonderfully absorbing world of creating and making your own linocut prints!

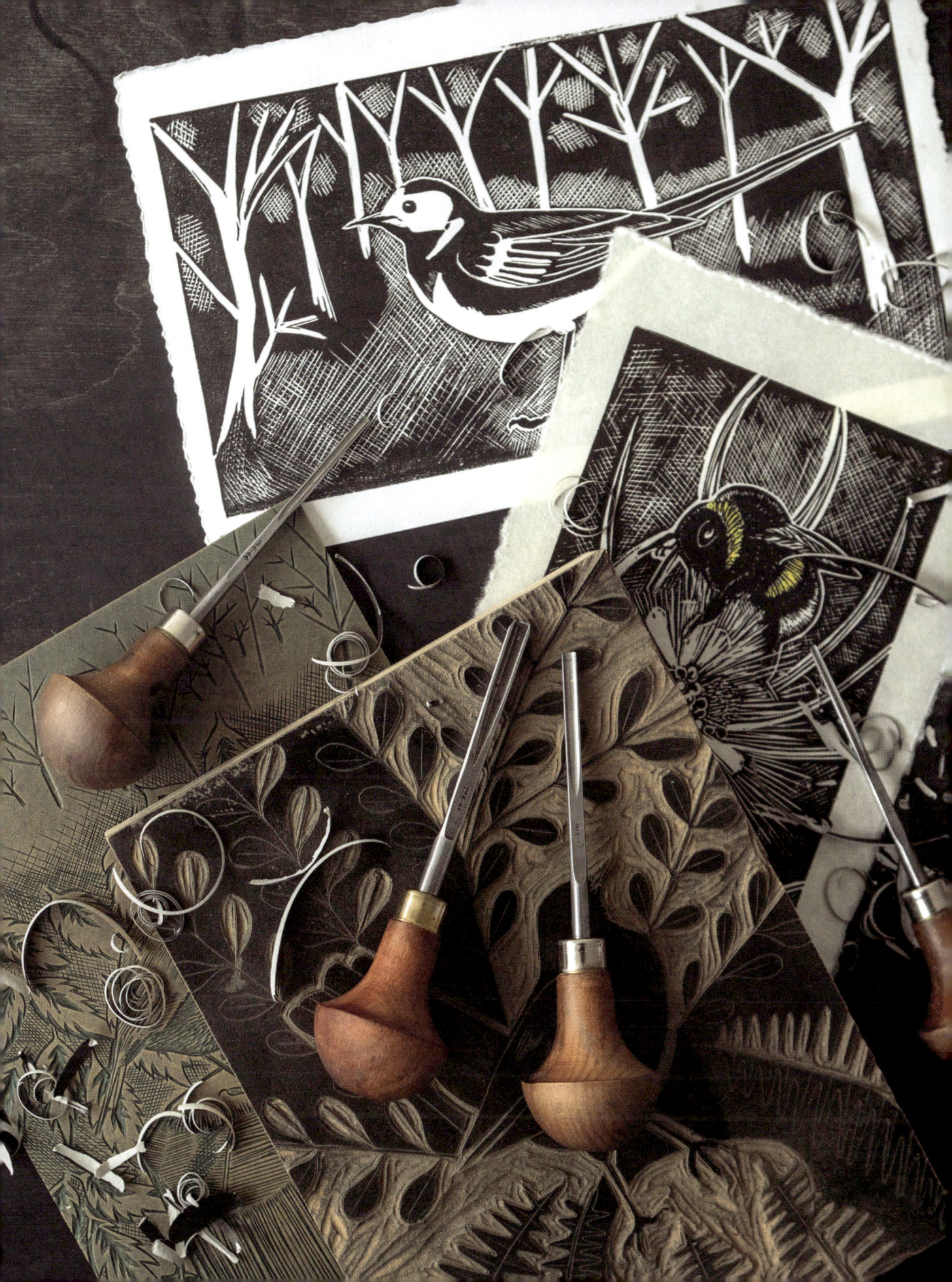

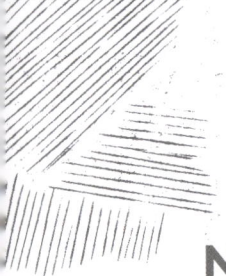

NO. 1

FIRST CARVES

Project brief

For this first project, you'll be working from small, found objects. Make some sketches of them in pen or pencil, or take some high-contrast black-and-white photographs of the objects. Working from these, carve a stamp then make a mini print on paper, card and/or fabric.

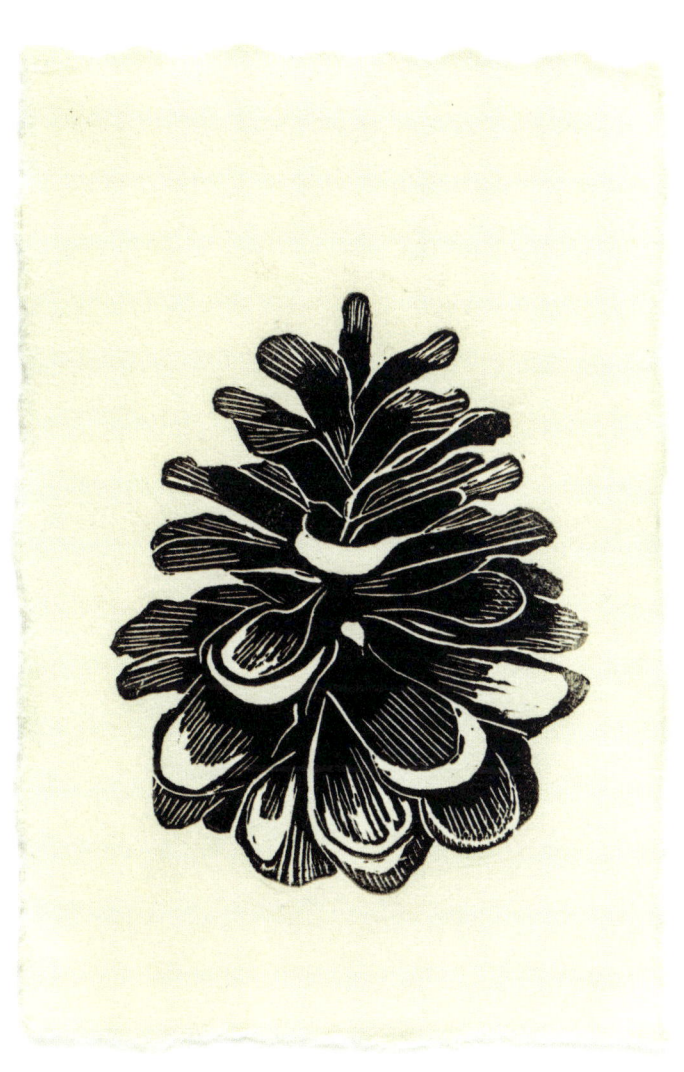

My starting point

I have never been able to resist picking up things when out on walks – be it feathers (maybe from a pigeon, crow, or something more exotic like a jay, mallard or even a tawny owl!); pine cones; horse chestnuts; sweet chestnut cases (beware of the spikes!); and seashells (I have an ever-growing collection, spilling out from pots all around my studio, from walks along the nearby estuary). It is small natural forms such as these which will be the subjects for the first stamps you will carve and print.

I have chosen a pine cone, which was lying around in my studio. The beautiful shapes, textures and the way the contrasting areas of light fall onto the pine cone makes it a perfect subject for carving into lino stamps. For your own stamp, please choose any object that inspires you. Three-dimensional objects, with surfaces and textures that capture areas of light and dark, are the most suitable subjects for a nice, strong printed image.

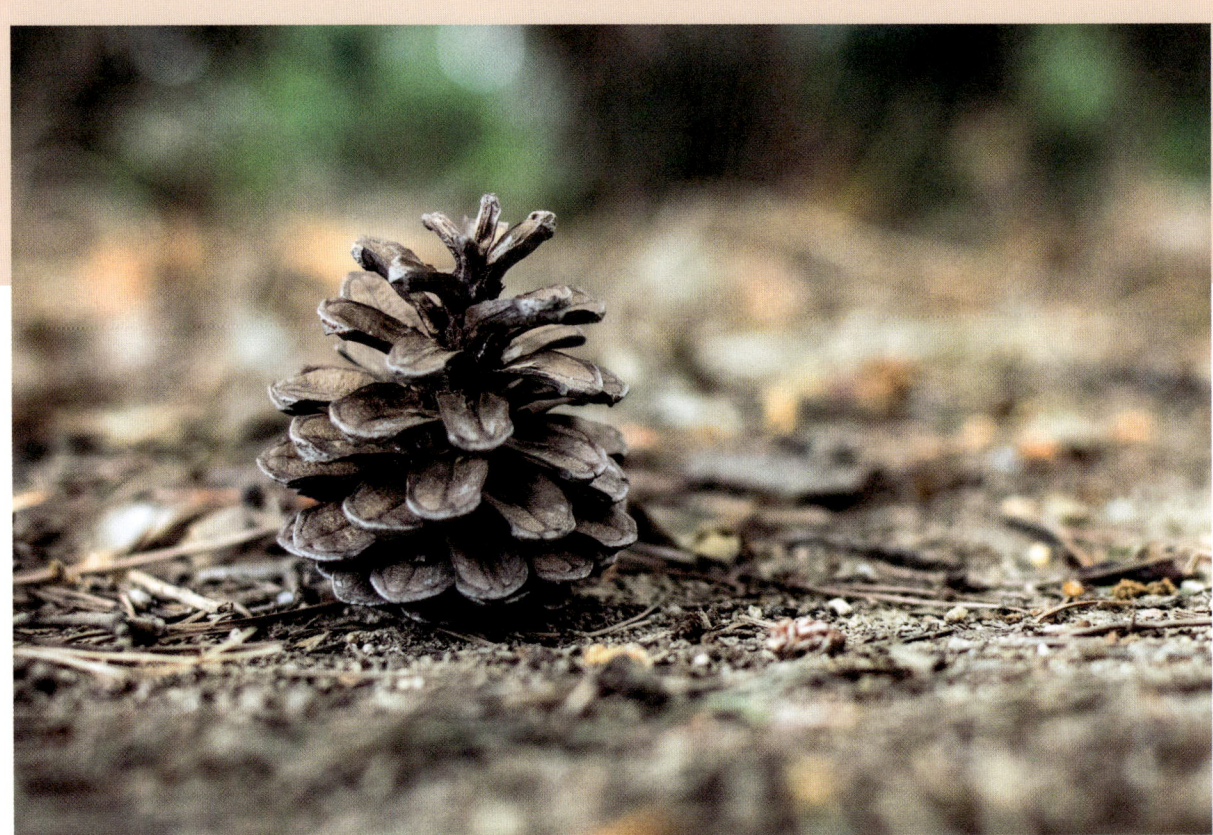

Method

1 Take a photograph or sketch your chosen object. For this project, on my computer I converted the photograph of my pine cone to greyscale then adjusted the contrast for more dramatic light and dark areas. If you are making sketches, be sure to make boldly contrasting lines and areas of shading. This will make it easier to decide which areas to carve out of your stamps (the white areas) and which to leave in (the black areas).

2 Trace off your photograph or sketch, as explained on page 52. Lift your tracing off the image and flip it over, so the design is now mirror-image.

3 Place the tracing onto your piece of lino, so the pencil tracing is in contact with the surface of the lino. As before, secure the tracing with two small pieces of masking tape.

4 Now you need to rub firmly over all the lines on your tracing so they transfer onto the lino. You could use the end of a ballpoint pen, a stylus, a spoon, or any similar hard object. If you are using traditional linoleum, which is harder than the PVC substitutes, you may need to trace firmly over the lines with a hard pencil or ballpoint pen for them to transfer successfully.

5 Once you have rubbed over the entire image, lift the bottom of the tracing paper carefully and check you haven't missed out any lines. When you're happy that your image is sufficiently traced, you can remove the tracing paper and put it to one side.

Continued...

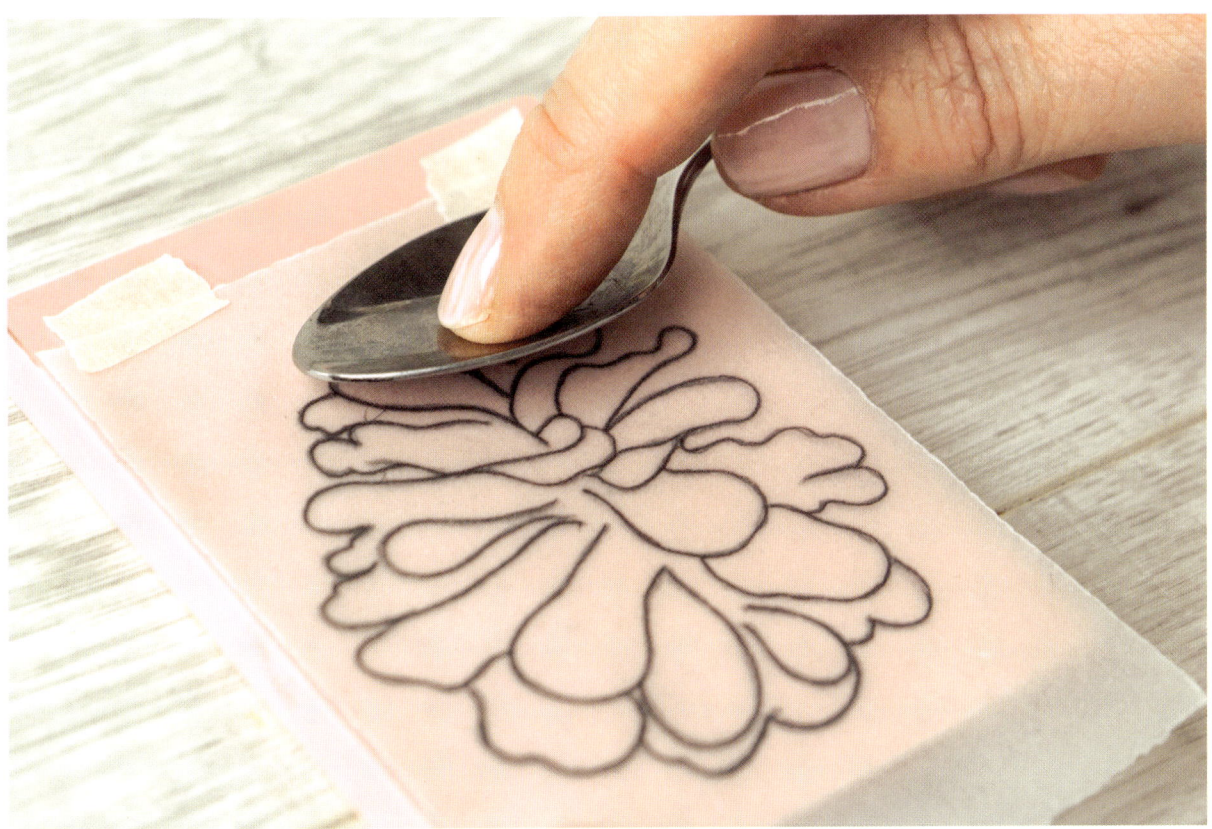

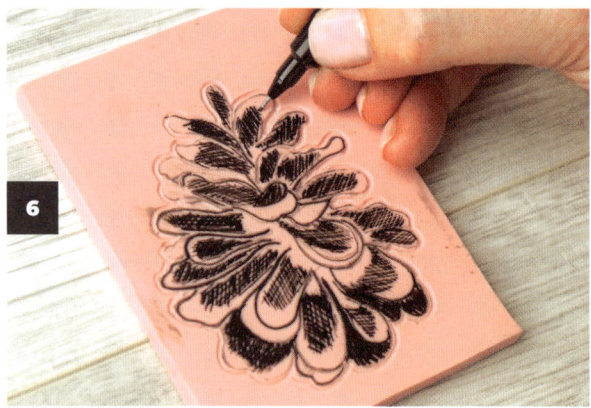

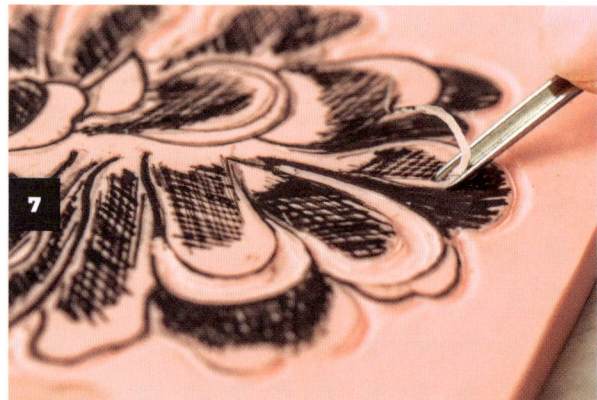

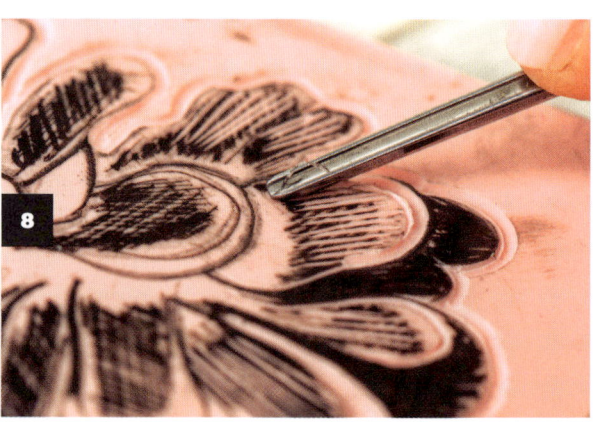

6 Carve out the main outline of the shape with a small V-shaped tool, then widen it slightly by carving along it again with the small U-shaped tool. At this stage, you will most likely need to add some more details to your image to guide your carving – mainly the shadows.

Referring to your original sketch or photograph, with the fine-liner pen cross-hatch any grey/mid-shadow areas and fill in black areas that are completely in shadow. In the steps, you will carve cross-hatched markings over the drawn cross-hatched lines, then leave the black areas uncarved. Remember: you will only be carving out the light/unshaded areas of your object.

7 Now you can start carving in earnest! Work slowly and carefully to start with, carving out the unshaded areas of your image. For me, these are the ends of the pine cone scales. I alternated between a small V-shaped tool and a small U-shaped tool, depending on the size of the area to be carved.

8 Using a small V-shaped tool, carve out the cross-hatched lines in the grey/mid-shadow areas.

CARVING TIPS

— Make sure your tool is not too large for the type of mark you want to carve. It's better to start with a small tool and then swap it for a larger one if you need to. Only use the largest U-shaped tools for clearing the larger areas of background lino. Please revisit pages 46–48 if necessary.

— As you carve, you will find that the small pieces of lino you're removing may congregate on your stamp and obscure your view of the image. Use an ordinary paintbrush from a DIY or art store to brush away these tiny pieces regularly, and keep the surface of your stamp clear of detritus.

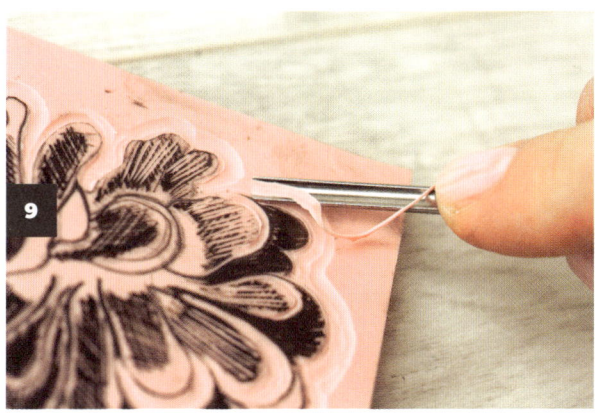

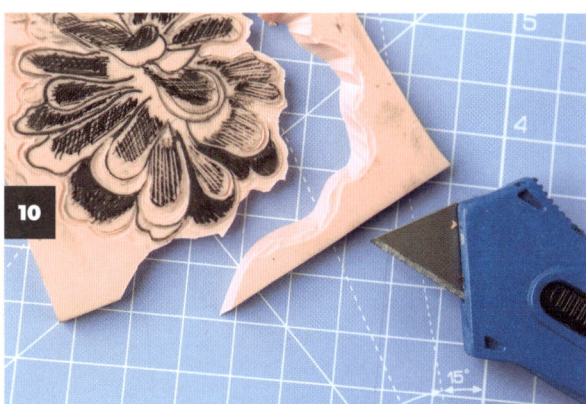

9 Once you've carved your lino where necessary, carve a thicker outline round the whole motif, over and around the first outline carved in step 6, using the large U-shaped tool. You should now have a carved-out outline around your shape that's approximately 2–3mm (⅛in) wide.

10 As this is a stamp, cut out the motif on a cutting mat with a craft knife. Make sure you cut only in the 'groove' you've carved out around your image.

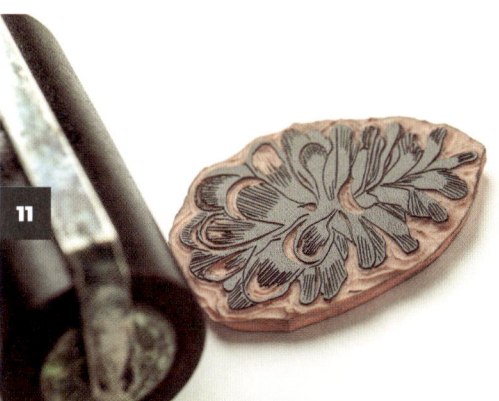

11 Now, you can ink up the stamp you've carved and make some prints. The first inking of a carved lino block or stamp is always exciting – you can see the results of all your hard work coming to life as you roll a thin layer of printing ink over the surface of the lino! Follow the steps on page 58 to apply ink to your stamp. Remember to start with a very small amount of ink, only adding more when required. These tiny stamps do not need a lot of ink – using too much will result in over-inking and problems with printing.

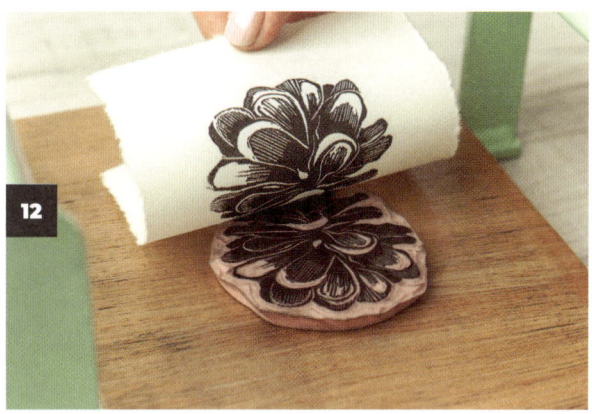

12 Following the guidance on pages 59–62, print your stamp onto your chosen surface with your preferred printing method. I used my little A5 (148 x 210mm/Junior Legal) Woodzilla press. When you lift your printed surface, be careful not to move it sideways or drop it back down, which will result in unwanted smudged areas of ink on the print. A good tip is to hold down the top end of the paper with one hand, while using the other hand to lift up the bottom end carefully.

NO. 2

PLANT THERAPY

Project brief

Building on skills gained in 'First Carves' on pages 74–79, design a print that uses a variety of marks to create 'stylized' (more decorative than realistic) leaves. Explore mark-making and shapes, and make use of both positive and negative spaces. You can print your design onto blank postcards, which are widely available online or from art and craft stores. These little postcard prints are so satisfying to make, and are wonderful to give to friends and family!

YOU WILL NEED

— A sketch you've made, and/or a photograph you've taken, for reference

— Tracing paper and pencil

— Stylus or ballpoint pen, for transferring the tracing onto lino

— Masking tape

— Scrap lino, to practise on and test markings

— A6 (105 x 148mm/4 x 6in) size piece of lino – I have chosen Speedy-Carve™ lino

— A selection of at least three carving tools, including a small V-shaped tool, a small U-shaped tool and a medium U-shaped tool for clearing the larger areas of lino

— Relief printing ink in black or a dark colour – I'm using an oil-based ink

— Scrap paper for making test prints

— A6 (105 x 148mm/4 x 6in) pieces of 300gsm (140lb) card, or blank postcards to print on; preferably they should be fairly thick and white or off-white in colour

— Your chosen equipment for printing (a spoon, baren or printing press)

— Optional: the template on page 153, for transferring

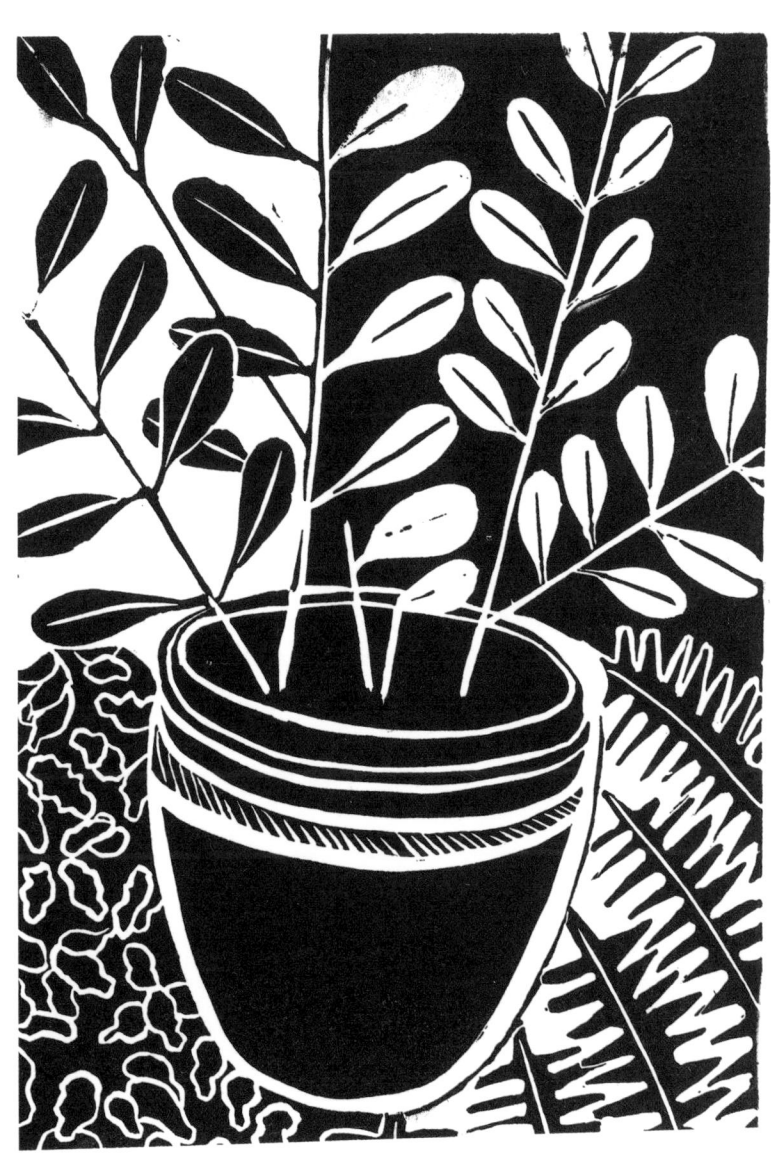

My starting point

I live in a town centre and have a tiny garden, which brings me great joy – not least because it is positively bursting with plants. Many of them are in pots, and these were the starting point for this project. I took rather a busy photograph of my potted hydrangea, which is encroached upon from all sides by other plants. So, the challenge was to create a much-simplified design for a linocut print.

I converted the photograph to black and white on my computer, to give me a better idea of how the image could work as a print. I wanted the design to have a stylized, almost 'decorative' feel to it. In my final design, the potted plant is no longer a hydrangea – just a potted plant with ultra-simplified leaf shapes that make up the top part of the composition. The minimalist pot has the addition of stylized ferns growing to the right of it, and the bold, abstract leaf-outline shapes to the left give the design a mid-century feel.

DEALING WITH NEGATIVE SPACES

Bear in mind one half of the print is white on black, and the other is black on white. The stem in the middle is the divider. This could cause confusion when you start to carve.

I like to take a picture on my camera phone of the finished design in my sketchbook then flip it; this makes it face the same direction as the traced image on the lino, and ensures that I carve out the right sections.

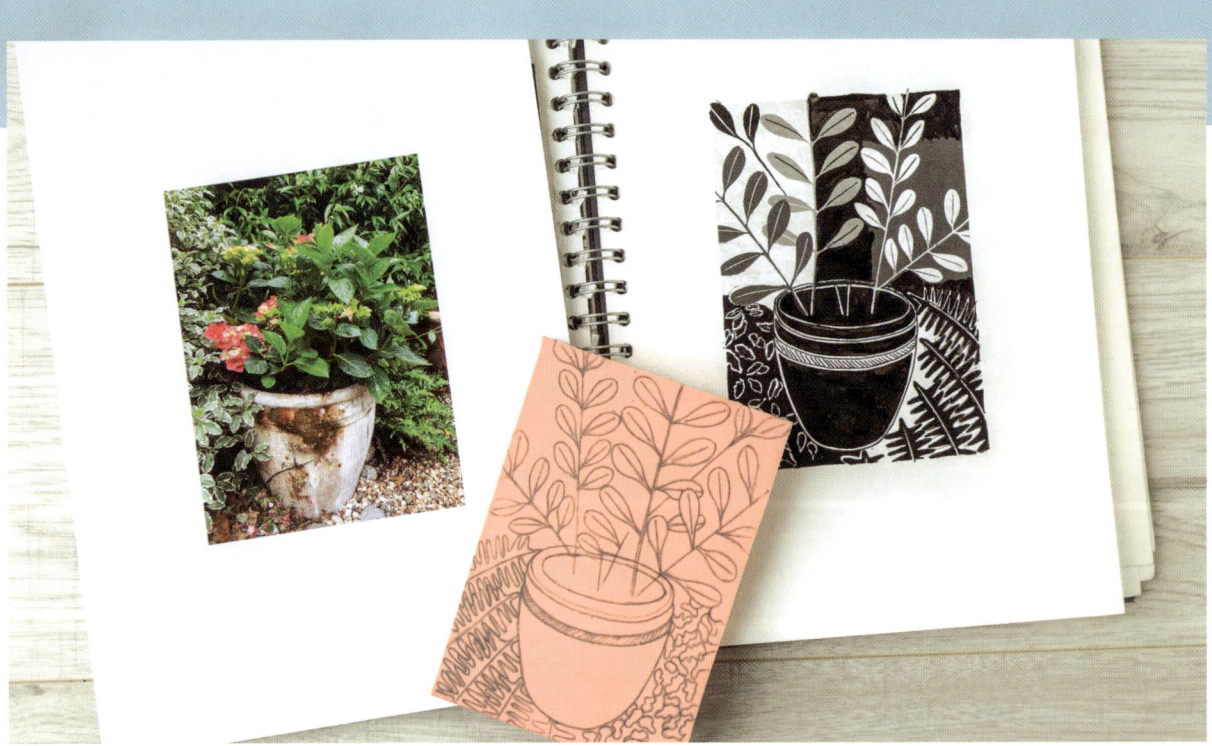

Method

1 Trace off the plant-pot design then transfer it to your lino, as described on pages 52 and 53.

2 Carve out the main outlines in the design with a small V-shaped tool. For me, this was around the pot and leaves, and along each of the stems.

3 Now to carve out the leaves in the black-background area. Using the V-shaped tools, I carved out the main body of each leaf, leaving the veins uncarved.

4 For the leaves in the white-background area, I carved along the veins only. Then, around the leaves, I cut away the background using a combination of the small V-shaped tool and the small U-shape tool, depending on how large the area was and if there were lots of awkward shapes to carve around.

5 The fern leaves on the left-hand side were carved out with a small U-shaped tool.

Continued...

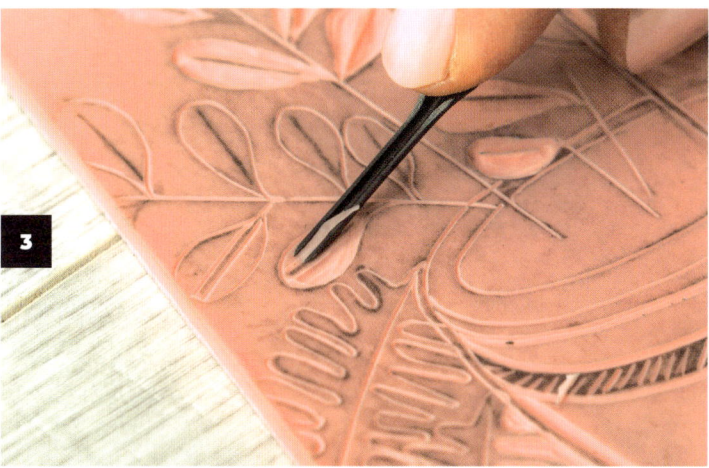

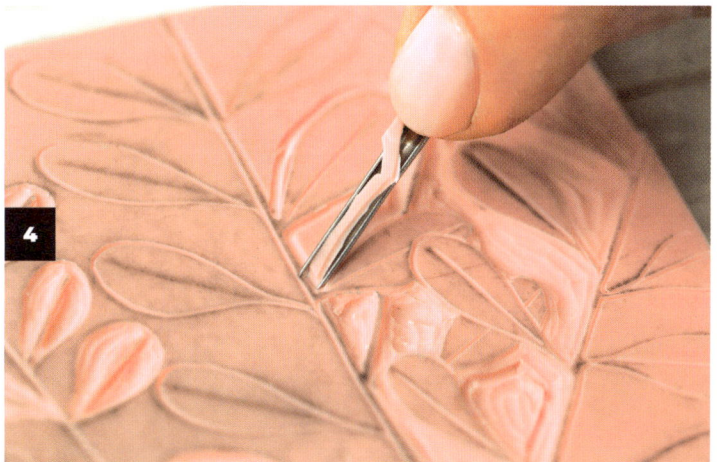

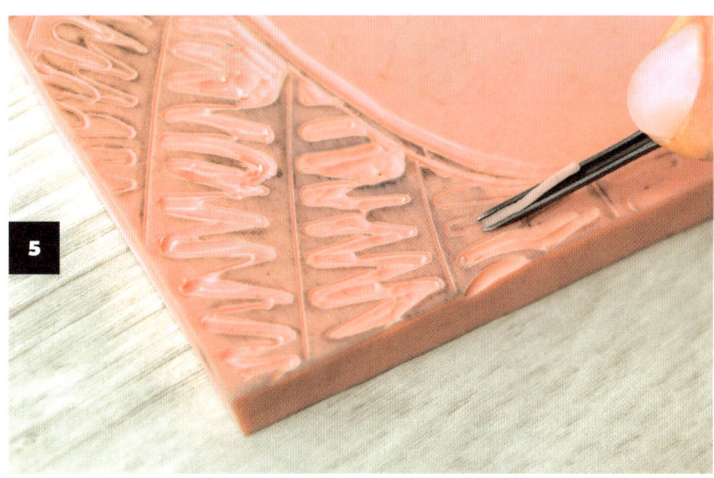

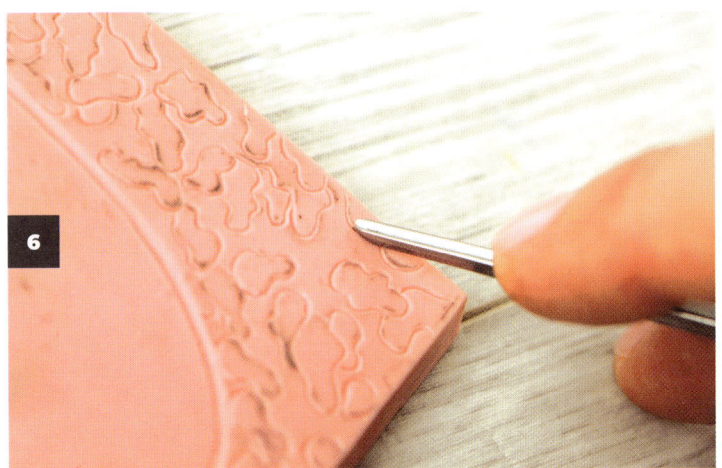

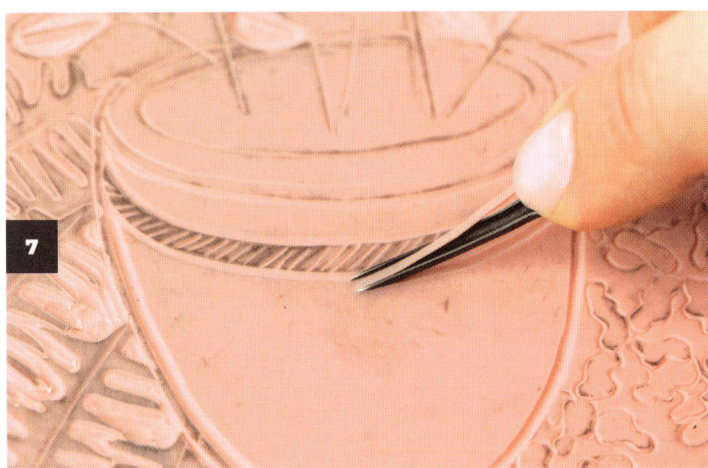

6 The outlines of the leaf shapes in the bottom right were emphasized with the small V-shaped tool. (These will be in the bottom left of the final print.)

7 The last few details on the plant pot were then added. Using a medium U-shaped tool, I enlarged the bottom line of the decorative band round the pot.

8 The main outline of the plant pot was then carved out further, again with a medium U-shaped tool.

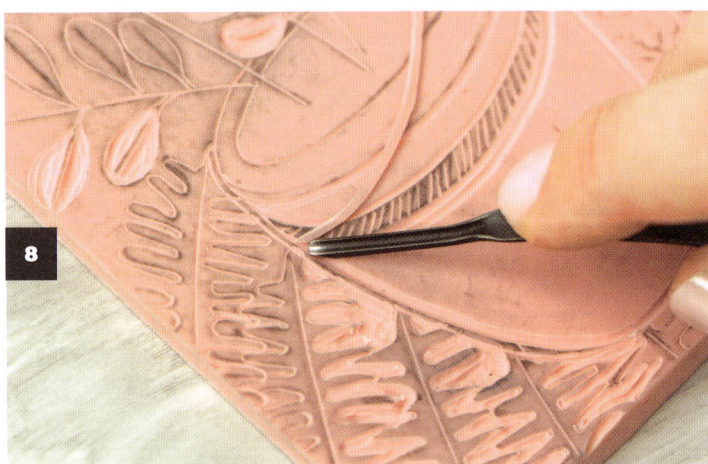

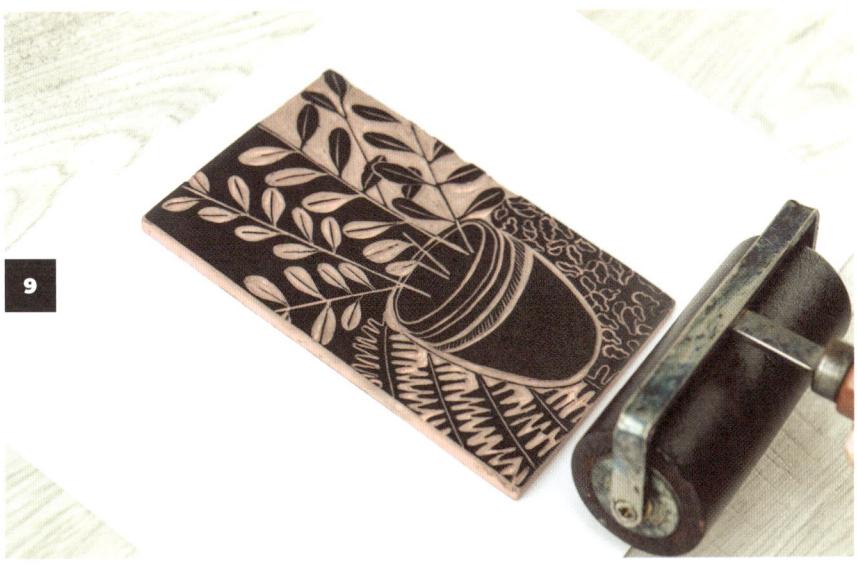

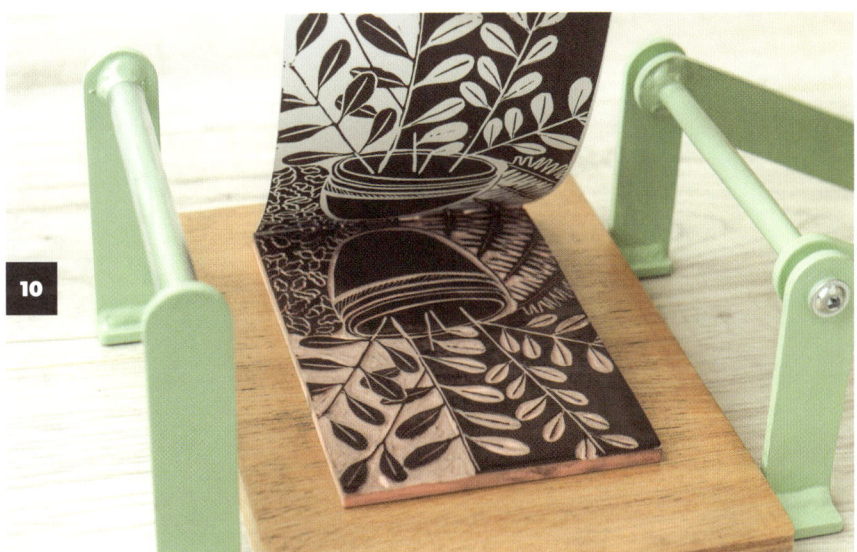

9 Ink up your lino over a protected surface, following the guidance in page 58.

10 Once you have correctly inked up your block, go ahead and start printing. If you have a number of blank postcards ready to print on, you may just start printing on those. If you have only a few cards, you might like to make a test print onto a piece of scrap or cheap paper to make sure you're happy with your carving, before committing to a more expensive surface. Print the block with your preferred printing method – see pages 59–62 if you need help deciding.

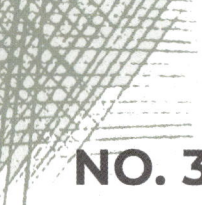

NO. 3

A STUDY IN LINO

Project brief

Design, carve and make a finished linocut print, using either a pencil/pen sketch you've made or a photograph you've taken as a reference image, of a natural subject matter close to your heart. If you are using a photograph it should ideally have a lot of tonal contrast, to make it easier to interpret as a black-and-white linocut print.

YOU WILL NEED

— A sketch you've made, and/or a photograph you've taken, for reference

— Tracing paper and pencil

— Stylus or ballpoint pen, for transferring the tracing onto lino

— Masking tape

— Scrap lino, to practise on and test markings

— A6 (105 x 148mm/4 x 6in) or A5 (148 x 210mm/Junior Legal) size piece of lino – it does not have to be exact. I have chosen Speedy-Carve™ lino

— A selection of at least three carving tools, including a small V-shaped tool, a small U-shaped tool and a larger U-shaped tool

— Relief printing ink in black or a dark colour – I'm using an oil-based ink

— Scrap paper for making test prints

— Your chosen printmaking paper, at the appropriate size for your print – if your design is an unusual size, I'd recommend opting for a larger-than-necessary size; it creates a nice border around the print, and you can always trim it down if necessary. I used Zerkall Smooth 145gsm (54lbs); Somerset Satin 300gsm (140lbs) is a good alternative

— Your chosen equipment for printing (a spoon, baren or printing press)

— Optional: the template on page 154, for transferring

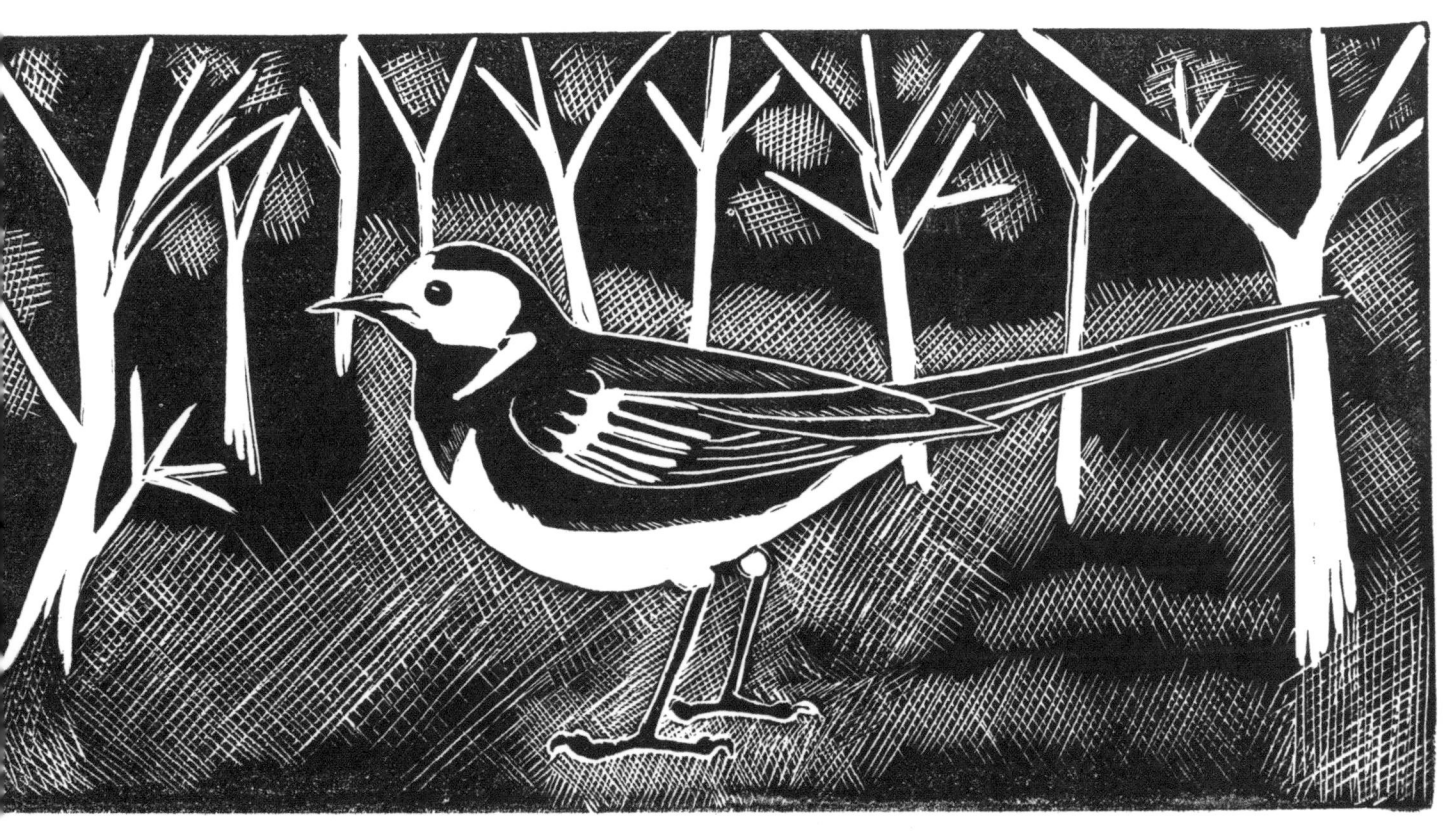

My starting point

I tend to make a large number of sketches and drawings of birds – it's something I have loved doing since childhood! So, for this project, I decided to use an image I had already made a while back. The pied wagtail is of one of my favourite bird species, and its colouring makes it an ideal subject for a black-and-white linocut print.

The sketch I had made of it had been lying in a drawer for some time, but I kept coming back to it – I liked it, but wasn't sure how I wanted to develop it into a print. This project seemed a good way to take the idea forward, with the possibility of making the design into an edition of small prints.

Before printing, I made a small study of the wagtail on a piece of scratchboard, also known as a scraper board (see below). In case you haven't come across it before, this is a sturdy white card, thickly coated on one side with black Indian ink. You 'draw' onto the surface by scratching with a sharp, pointed tool, which removes the black coating to make white lines and marks. The resulting drawings created are bold and contrasting – ideal for interpreting into a linocut print. You may have seen a similar product that reveals rainbow colours when the black coating is scratched off; this is often sold alongside children's art materials, or in hobby stores. This is not the type I would recommend you use, as the bright colours rather distract from the design. Standard, black-on-white scratchboard is widely available online and from art stores, and is a useful addition to your materials drawer. I tend to use a craft knife or scalpel rather than regular scratchboard tools, as I find a knife makes much clearer and deeper marks.

As I liked the size and orientation of my scratchboard study, which was an off-cut from a larger piece, I decided to use the dimensions for the final print. This does make the piece an irregular size, but that doesn't matter: it is important for your design to work well, and this consideration should override sticking to 'conventional' paper sizes! Just make sure the design sits nicely within the size and orientation of the paper it will be printed on.

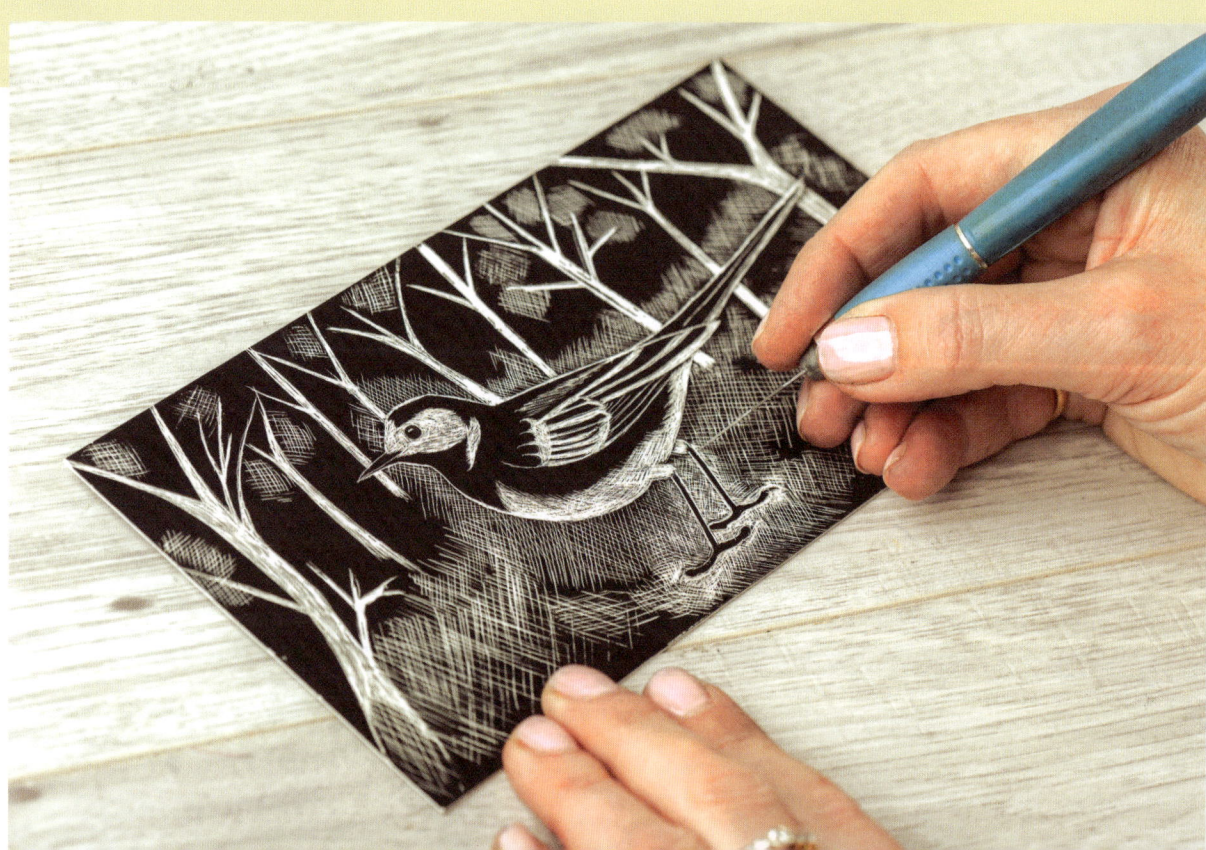

Method

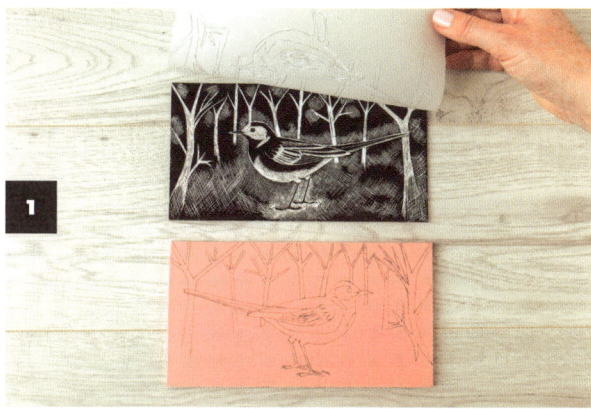

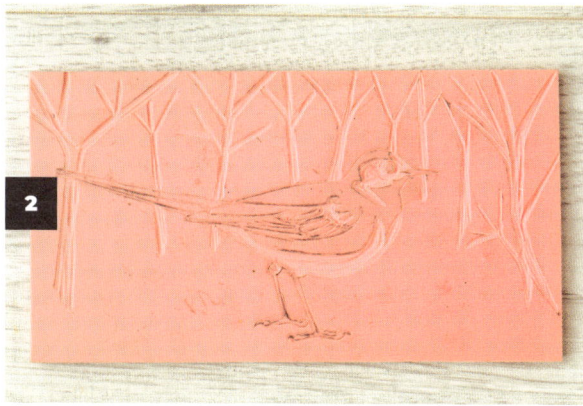

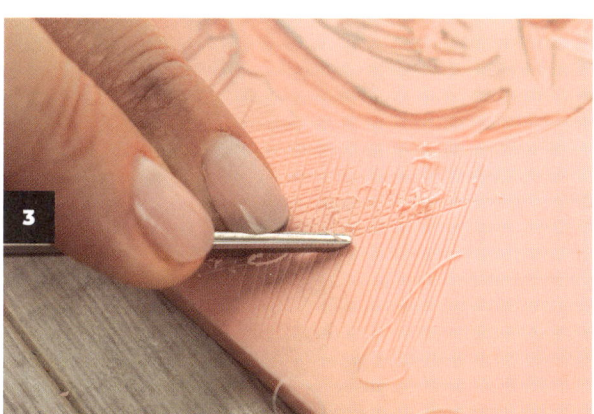

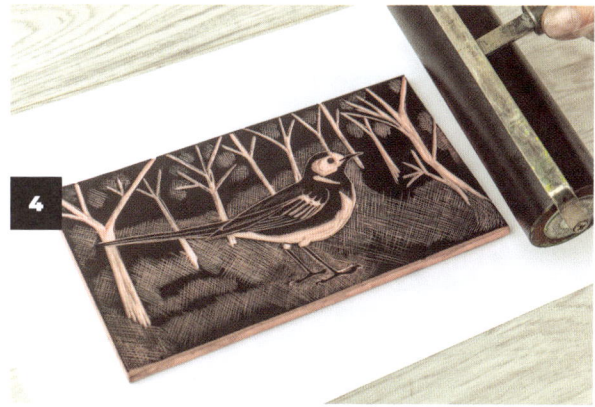

1 Trace off the key outlines in the design then transfer it to your lino, as described on pages 52 and 53. I traced directly from my scratchboard study.

2 Carve out the main outlines in the design, using a combination of your carving tools, depending on the area to carve. Then, carve in the rest of your design.

If you have already completed the previous two projects in this book, your confidence will be growing and you'll find you are becoming more fluent with your carved marks. Don't forget to keep a small scrap of lino next to you for practising any new or different marks, before committing them to your block!

When carving my designs, I tend to start with the central feature of the print – in this particular design, the wagtail – as it needs to stand out sufficiently from the background. I also like to begin carving the trickiest part

that needs to be 'right' for the print to work – in this case, it's the eye of the wagtail. For the rest of the design, you don't need to focus too much on completely recreating your reference image. Keep looking carefully at your reference image for help with placement, but otherwise be guided by the shapes and marks you see in it. Remember that every linocut print is simply a composition of shapes, marks and textures, arranged pleasingly on the sheet of paper you print it on, so this is what you are aiming for.

3 I finished off my linocut with some cross-hatched textures in the background, with patches behind the trees and around the wagtail.

4 Ink up then print your design, following the guidance on pages 58–62. I used a two-plate press for my print.

NO. 4

GETTING BOLDER

Project brief

Design, carve and make a finished linocut print that has a strong composition in black and white. This time, you'll be combining up to three different visual references to give your print a more stylized feel – similar to the 'Plant Therapy' project (see pages 80–85). It'll also be more complex compared with what you've already encountered, as you'll also be keeping in mind the overall composition throughout – from the balance of positive/ negative shapes to ensuring your markings highlight the different design elements.

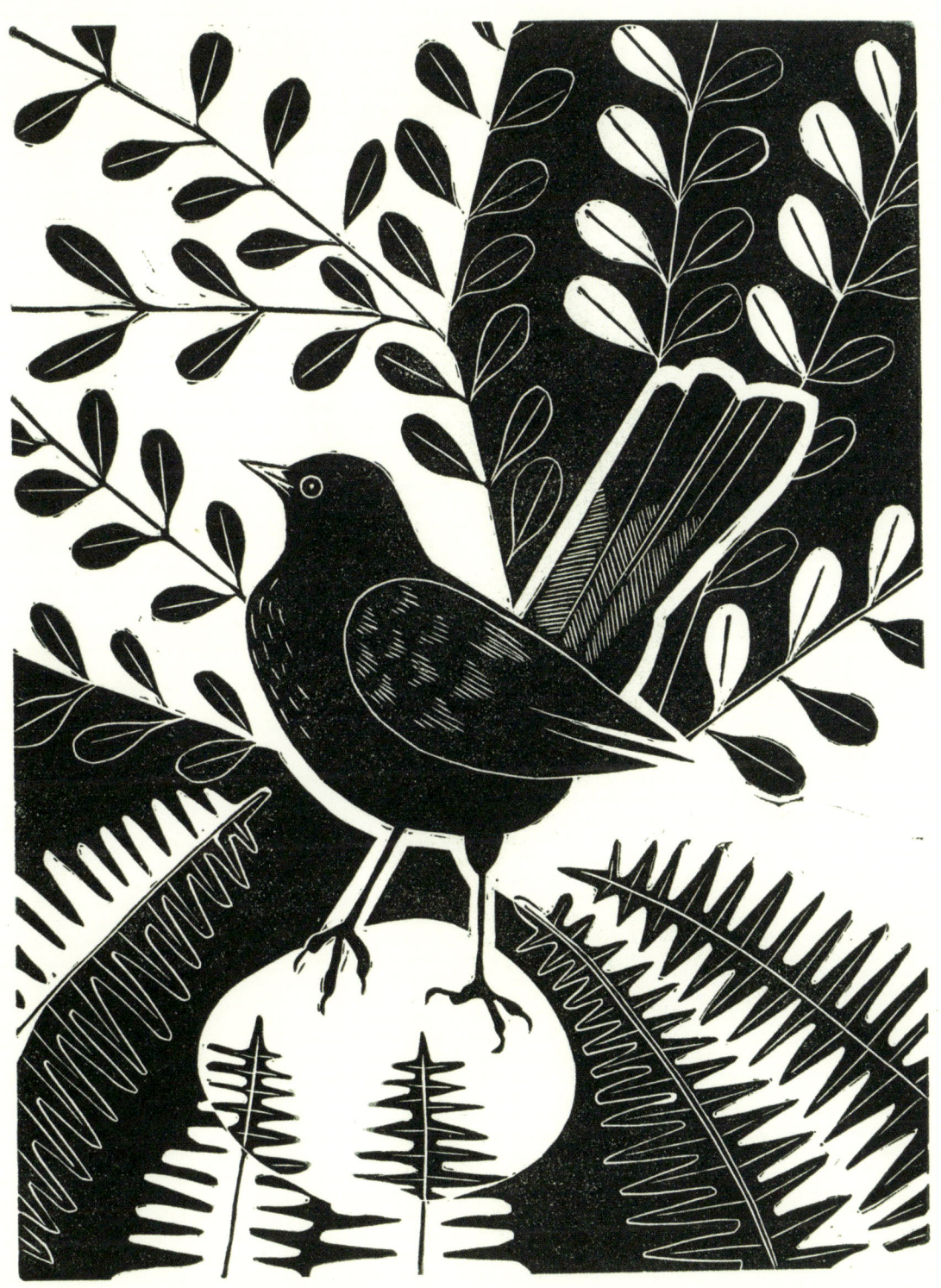

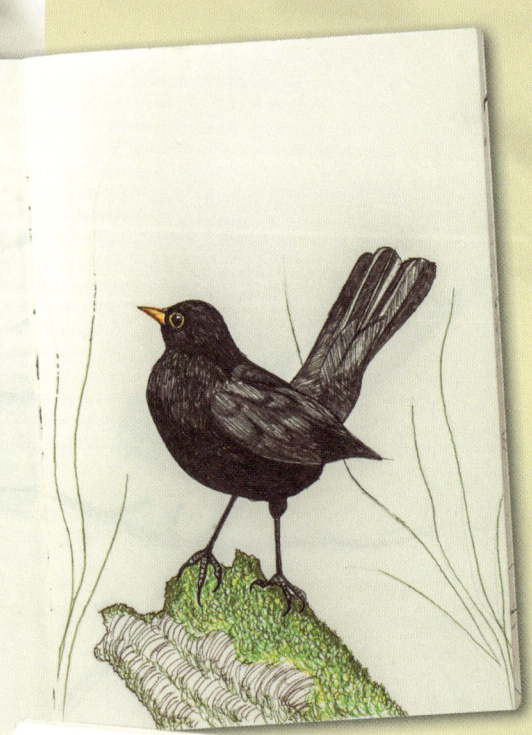

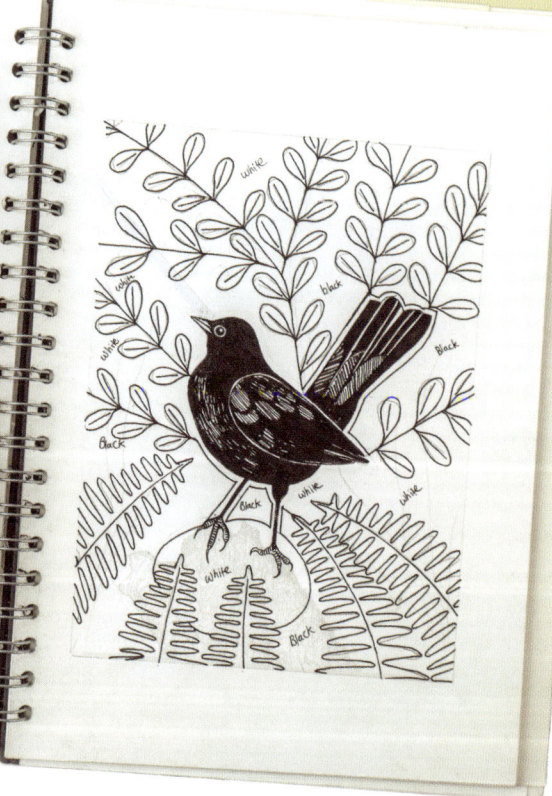

My starting point

Looking through an old sketchbook, I found a pen drawing of a blackbird made a few years ago, which I never got around to developing into an idea for a print. I love blackbirds and for me, this sketch epitomizes a male bird as he lands – looking warily around him while sounding his alarm call!

The sketch shows the bird standing on a moss-covered stump. Because I liked his pose so much, I decided to use him as a central feature of my design.

The print I was aiming for has a strong and stylized composition, and I was looking for the kind of design that had the potential for developing into a repeating pattern to print onto fabric in the future.

This meant that, unlike 'A Study in Lino' on pages 86–89, I'd need to create a new design, rather than simply interpret an existing photograph or sketch as a linocut print.

Generally, creating a new design involves combining elements from various sources – either visual or imaginary – into a brand new composition. In this case, it is the blackbird drawing, the stylized leaves (based on those in 'Plant Therapy', on pages 80–85) and a photograph of some white pebbles in my garden: a number of these surround my millstone water feature, and I have seen blackbirds hop onto the large stones after they have bathed in the water feature!

In my final reference sketch, abstract leaves frame my bird all around, and instead of the mossy stump I've had my bird land on a large, smooth, white pebble. These secondary elements lead the eye into the main, central element (the blackbird), and it's important that the positive and negative spaces I carve in the lino maintain this.

Method

1 Trace off the design then transfer it to your lino, as described on pages 52 and 53. Remember, you don't need to add a lot of detail at this stage – you can add a little but don't spend too much time; this is just the first step in developing your print.

2 For this design, and as I did for the demo project on pages 50–62, I stained my lino block with black Indian ink, to help me see my carved marks more easily. This stage is not essential.

Continued...

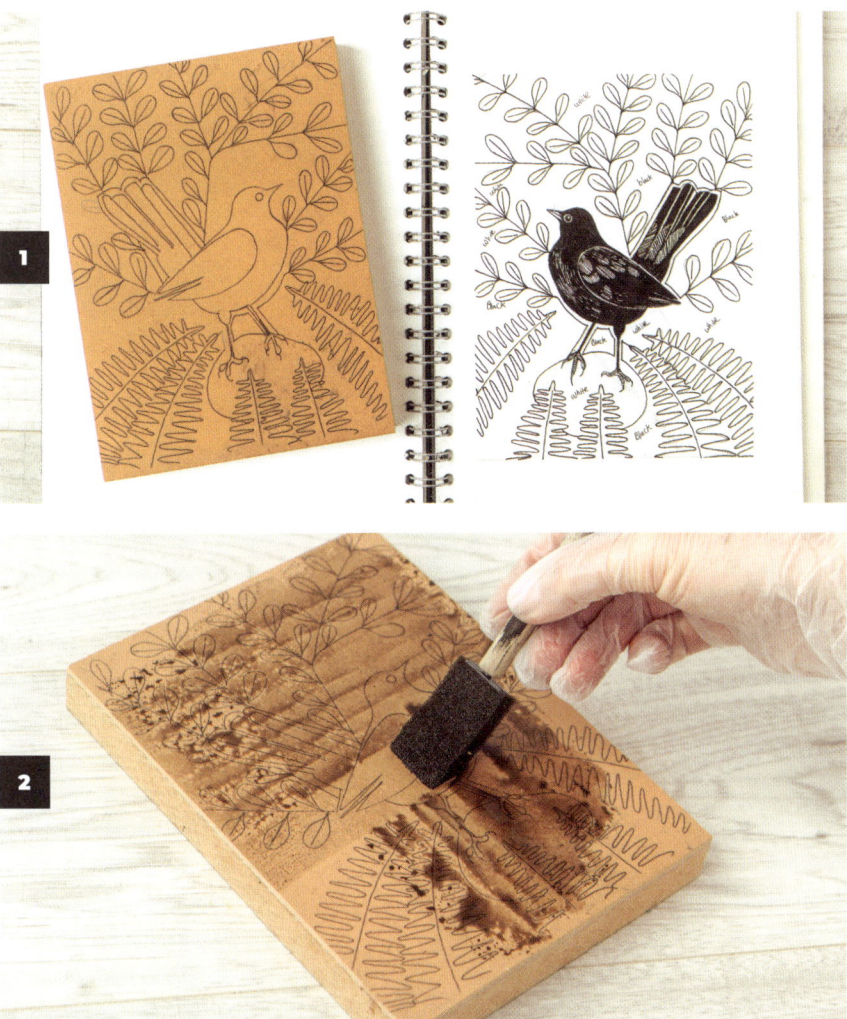

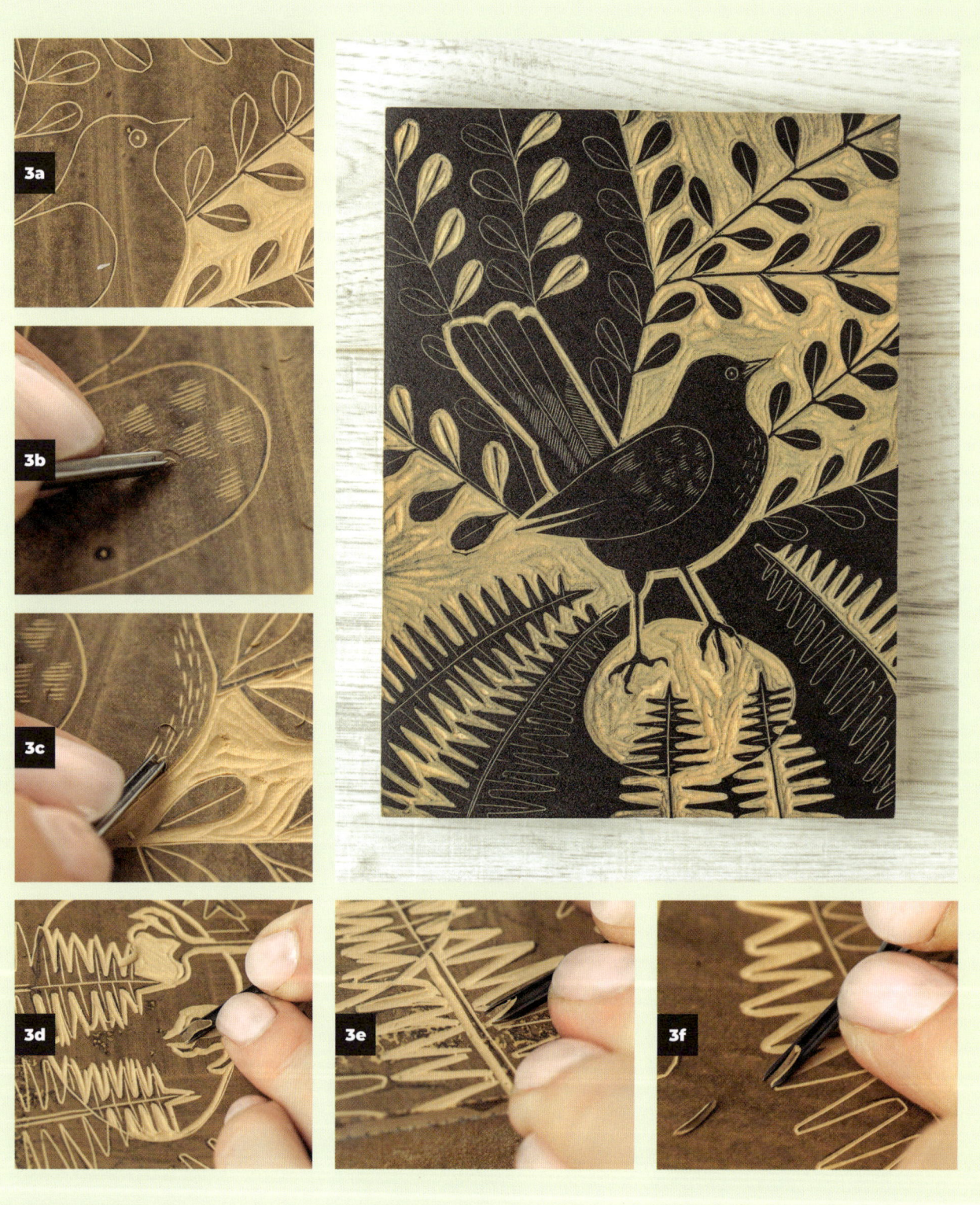

3 Let's carve! Because of the graphic, stylized nature of this design, there are very few textures or 'freestyle' marks.

— Carve out the main outlines in the design using a combination of your carving tools, depending on the size of the area to carve.

— The design relies heavily on the contrast of black-and-white areas and positive/negative shapes; therefore, it's really important to refer often to your sketch to make sure you are carving out the correct areas. A moment's lapse in concentration could lead to a carving error which would then have to be disguised or rectified in some way. Referring to my reference sketch, I carved out some of the background areas that would appear white in the final print (**3a**).

— Next, I carved the 'critical' elements of the lino – these are the details on the blackbird. I carved around the eye and then carved out the centre of the pupil with the small V-shaped tool (**3a**). The beak details were carved with the same tool. The feathers on the wings (**3b**) and breast (**3c**) were then carved out with the small V-shaped tool.

— Once the details on the bird are established, I carved a wider outline around the bird with a medium U-shaped tool; this gives the bird more prominence in the print, and pushes it into the foreground.

— The pebble on which the blackbird stands can be carved out next, around the bird's feet and the overlapping ferns, with a small U-shaped tool (**3d**).

— The remaining plant details can be carved out. The top leaves that are reminiscent of the 'Plant Therapy' leaves can be treated the same way: where the leaves sit on a black background, leave the veins but carve out the inside of each leaf. For the leaves on the white backgrounds, carve around the leaves and stems, and carve out the veins, but leave the insides of the leaves untouched. For the ferns on black backgrounds, you can either leave them simply outlined or carve out the insides of the ferns completely (**3e**). For the ferns on the white backgrounds, carve around them (**3f**).

4 Ink up your carved block for printing, following the guidance on page 58. To achieve a 'border' around the print, your paper needs to be larger than your block. You can use a press to print if you have one, but if not you can hand burnish, as I am doing here.

Place your block on a protected surface (the inked side facing up), then create a 'frame' or 'jig' around the block that's the same height as the lino block – you can use pieces of the same lino for this. Make sure that whole area of the block, including the jig, is larger than the paper you're printing on. Carefully centre your printing paper over the block then rub the baren on top, with a circular motion and pressing down quite hard at the same time. You can use a wooden spoon, or professional baren – I have ones made from glass, like the one shown.

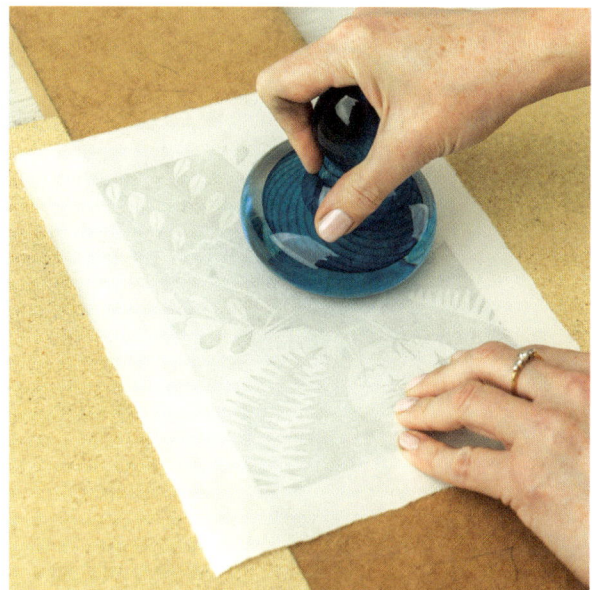

NO. 5

IT'S ALL IN THE DETAILS

Project brief

Now that you're becoming more confident in your carving skills, it's time to practise creating those small details!

This will be a print that celebrates the different textures and patterns you can find in natural subject matter. For a starting point, use either a photograph or an observational sketch featuring a subject close-up which has multiple textures and markings – for example, tree bark, fungi, feathers, fur or shell indentations. Make sure your subject choice offers plenty of scope for a wide variety of lino mark-making.

YOU WILL NEED

— A sketch you've made, and/or a photograph you've taken, for reference

— Tracing paper and pencil

— Stylus or ballpoint pen, for transferring the tracing onto lino

— Masking tape

— Scrap lino, to practise on and test markings

— A6 (105 x 148mm/4 x 6in) size piece of lino – I have chosen a traditional hessian-backed linoleum block

— A selection of at least four carving tools, including a very small V-shaped and U-shaped tools to carve out intricate details

— Relief printing ink in black or a dark colour – I'm using an oil-based ink

— Scrap paper for making test prints

— Your chosen printmaking paper, at least A6 (105 x 148mm/ 4 x 6in) in size – I used Japanese Okawara Select

— Your chosen equipment for printing (a spoon, baren or printing press)

— Optional: yellow archival pigment inkpad and a cotton bud/ swab, to add a yellow 'spot colour' (see the tip box on page 108) – I'm using Versafine colours by Tsukineko

— Optional: the template on page 160, for transferring

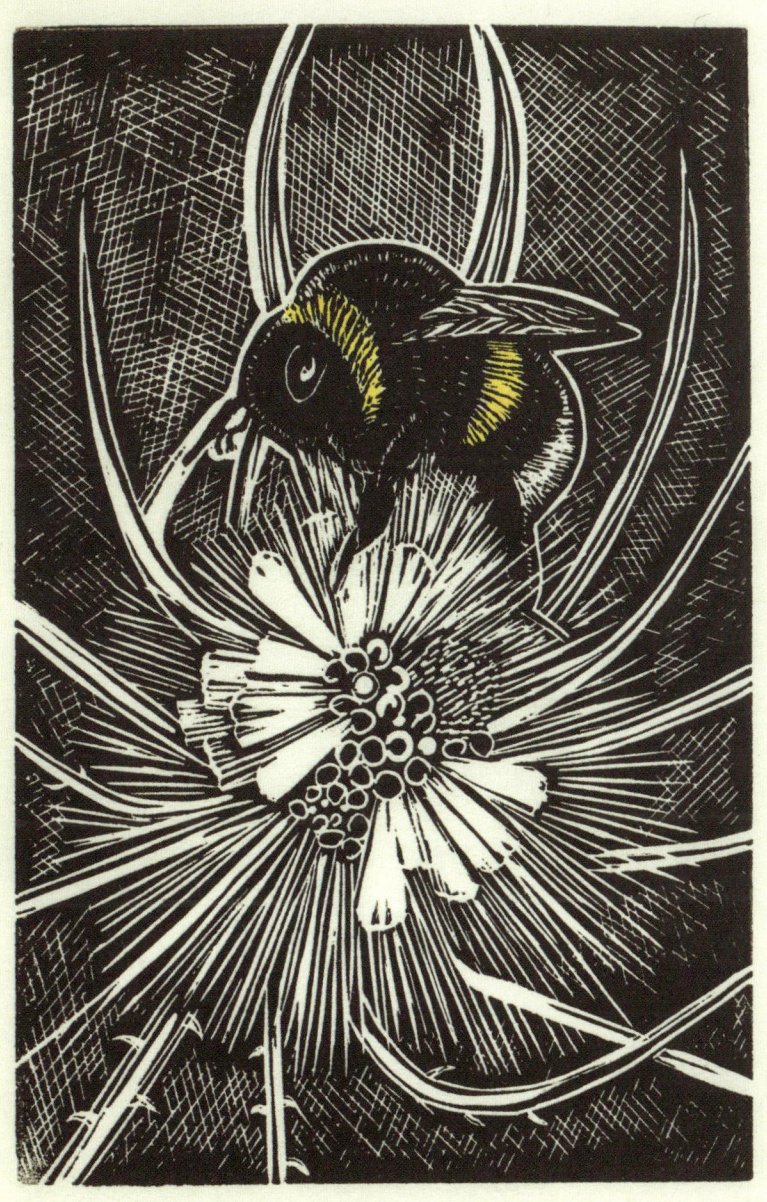

My starting point

For this print, I wanted to focus on the close-up details of an insect on a leaf or flower – what better candidate for this than a bumblebee? I had a photograph I took in the summer, of a white-tailed bumblebee feasting on a teasel flower (see right). Like most people, I adore bumblebees and their wonderful furry bodies; combining this texture with the spikiness of the flower seemed perfect for this print.

Although the photograph of the bee lacked high definition (i.e., it was a little blurry), I felt happier with the image after zooming in on the main subject and cropping off a lot of unnecessary background area.

As I've done in previous projects, I converted the photograph to black and white and increased the contrast a little, in order to make it easier to visualize how the image might work as a linocut print. Finally, I altered the scale of the image so it was A6 (105 x 148mm/4 x 6in) in size, to fit the lino block, then printed off the image, ready for tracing.

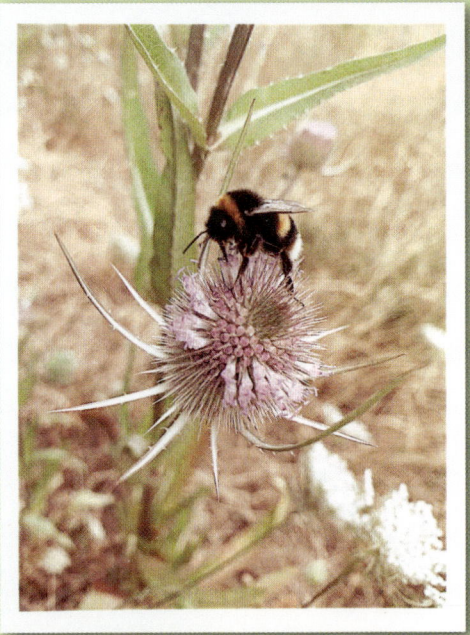

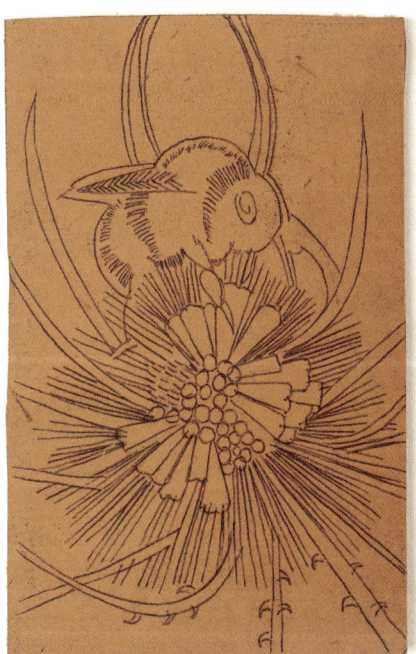

Method

1 For this print, I am bypassing the sketching stage as I have a perfectly good reference image in my photograph alone. Whether you work from a sketch or photograph is an entirely personal choice, but either way, try to use a reference image that is original and personal to you!

Trace off the design then transfer it to your lino, as described on pages 52 and 53. Again, just add the bare minimum of details at this stage.

Once the main design was on the lino, I did *ad lib* a little with the original image: to balance the composition and make it more decorative, I added one or two extra spikes to the teasel flower then extended them off the edges of the lino. Always remember that you are the artist in control of your design and it's perfectly OK to adapt it as you wish, right the way through the process!

2 After transferring my design, I stained the lino with a diluted black Indian ink, to help make my marks more visible as I carved (see page 52). I then allowed the lino to dry thoroughly before carving.

3 Let's carve! Although this is a small block, it will take longer to carve than some of the earlier projects due to the extra details included – but it will be worth it. Being able to achieve small, complex details in your work takes some practice, but is greatly satisfying!

The majority of the marks that make up this design are straight lines of various lengths and thicknesses, seen in the cross-hatched background and the spiky teasel flower. With practice, straight lines are a lot easier to carve than you might imagine. Make use of your scrap of lino to try out your lines before carving onto your block, and hold the tool firmly at all times.

Also refer back to the mark-making section for guidance on hatching and cross-hatching (see pages 46–49). You will actually find that carving a straight line in lino is easier than drawing a line on paper, due to the fact that the tool digs into the surface of the lino as you push it, which makes it harder for it to go 'off course'.

Because of the small, detailed nature of this design, I did make extensive use of my 1mm V-shaped tool for outlining and cross-hatching, and also the 1mm and 2mm U-shaped tools to carve the spikes and petals of the teasel flower.

- All the main outlines were carved initially with a small V-shaped tool.

- Next, I carved the bee, as this was the focal point of the print (**3a**). Most of the bee's details are lines that vary in length and distance; only the eye and the bee's proboscis are curves. To suggest the stripes on the bee, I carved only the 'hairs' where the yellow and white stripes would sit.

- Once the bee was established, I worked on the teasel. The spines all around the outer edge of the teasel were lines carved with a 1mm V-shaped tool (**3b**).

- The 'petals' were then carved out with a large U-shaped tool (**3c**).

Continued...

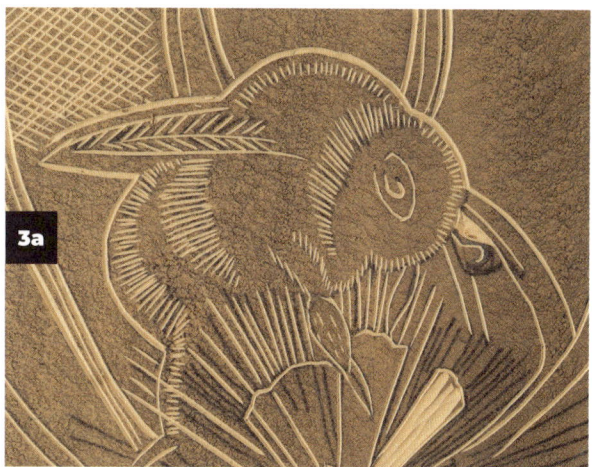

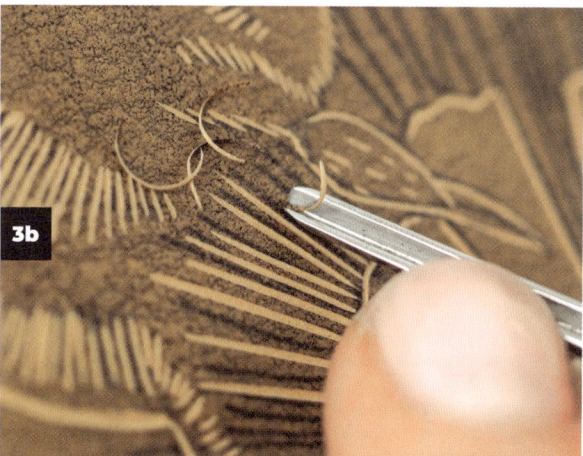

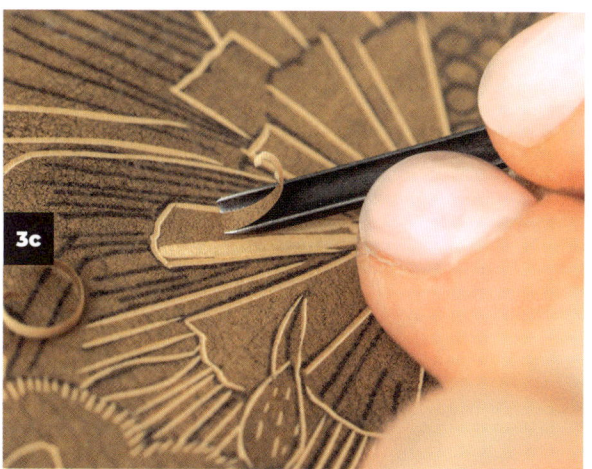

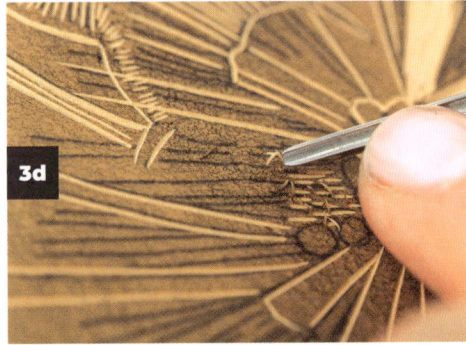

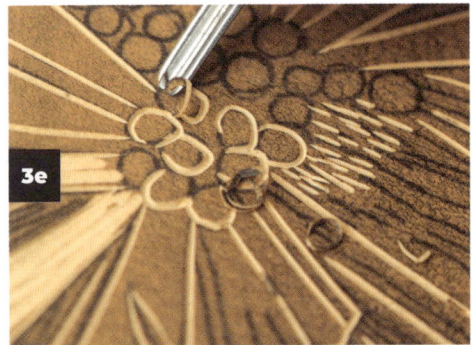

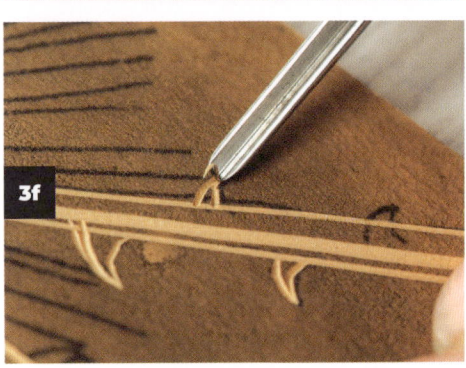

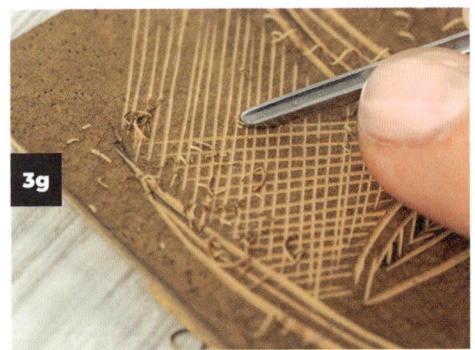

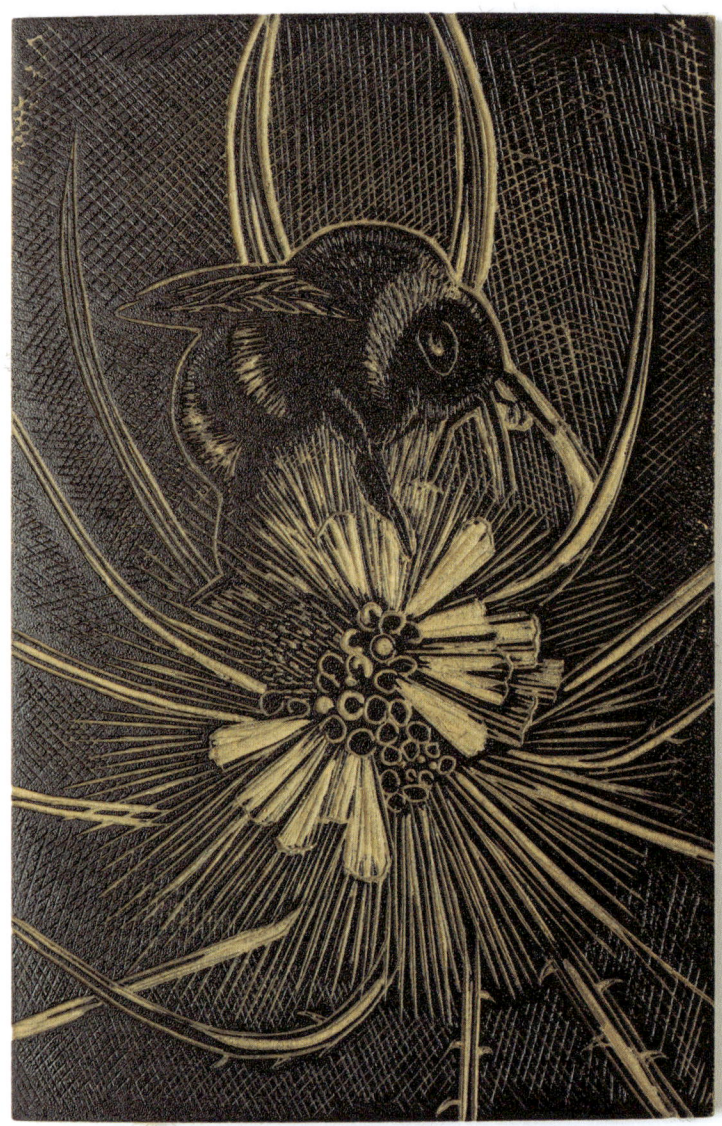

— For the tiny spikes towards the middle of the teasel, I carved 'flecks' of lines with the 1mm V-shaped tool (**3d**).

— The little flowers at the centre of the teasel were simply outlined with a small U-shaped tool (**3e**).

— The details in the teasel's spikes were carved in, including the thorns, using a mix of tools (**3f**).

— Finally, the background was filled with cross-hatched markings using the small V-shaped tool. (**3g**).

4 Once your block is carved, apply ink to get it ready for printing, as per page 58. With a design such as this, which features fine lines and small details, the most important thing is to apply your ink gradually, building up thin layers until the block is sufficiently inked up. Failure to do this will result in over-inking and a disappointing print. It is harder to rectify an over-inked block than an under-inked one, so remember, 'less is more'.

As you apply the thin layers of ink, all of your carved marks should become clearly visible. If any of your lines 'disappear' at this stage, carefully blot off the ink with some newsprint paper or kitchen paper and use your tools to carve out and define the lines little more, before applying any more ink (see also the tip box, right).

5 For a design like this, I recommend making a test print before committing to your final chosen surface. Then print with your chosen method, using the guidance on pages 59–62. For this print, I used a two-plate press.

6 This is an optional final touch: for my print, I wanted to emphasize the fact that my white-tailed bumblebee actually has a 'white tail', so I used a cotton bud/swab to apply some yellow ink to his top two stripes, leaving the third white. The ink I'm using to do this is an archival pigment colour ink pad. It's useful to have a small stash of ink pads in your printmaking supplies cupboard for additions like this – please revisit page 35 for more details on ink pads.

CARVING DEEP FOR DETAILS

When carving this block, remember that your lines, although fine and detailed, will also need to be sufficiently deep and defined enough so as to show up after you've applied your ink to the block prior to printing. Bearing this in mind, keep your carving as bold and confident as you can, and practise frequently on your scrap lino.

When you run your fingers over the surface of the carved block, you should feel the textures of the marks you have created. If you can't, the chances are that they won't print clearly enough – if at all.

If you feel that the lines aren't deep enough, carefully carve into them with your tools until they look and feel clearer. Continue working in this way until you are happy with how your carved block looks.

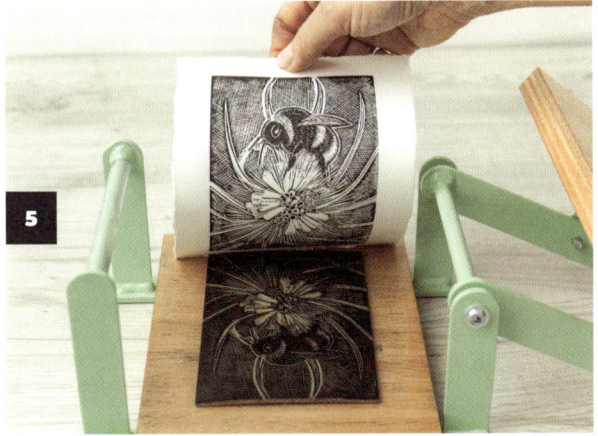

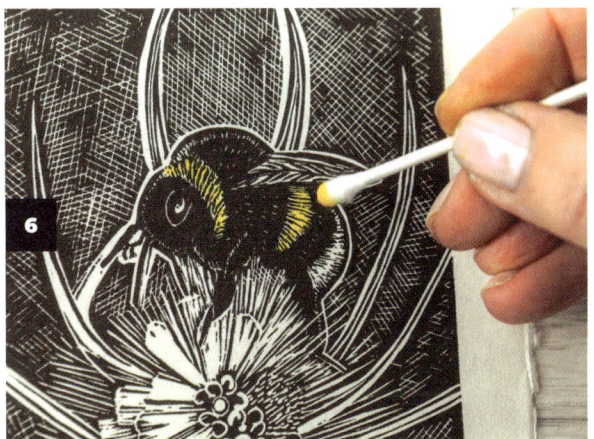

NO. 6

LET'S ADD COLOUR

Project brief

This project will use a simple technique to add a second colour of ink to the print, without having to worry about complicated registration (i.e. lining up) of multiple blocks. Using either a sketch or a photograph you've taken as a starting-point and reference, design, carve then print an A6 (105 x 148mm/4 x 6in) print. You'll then choose a specific area of your design, and cut out a separate stamp shape to fit this area of your printed image. This stamp will add a 'spot colour' to your otherwise monochrome print.

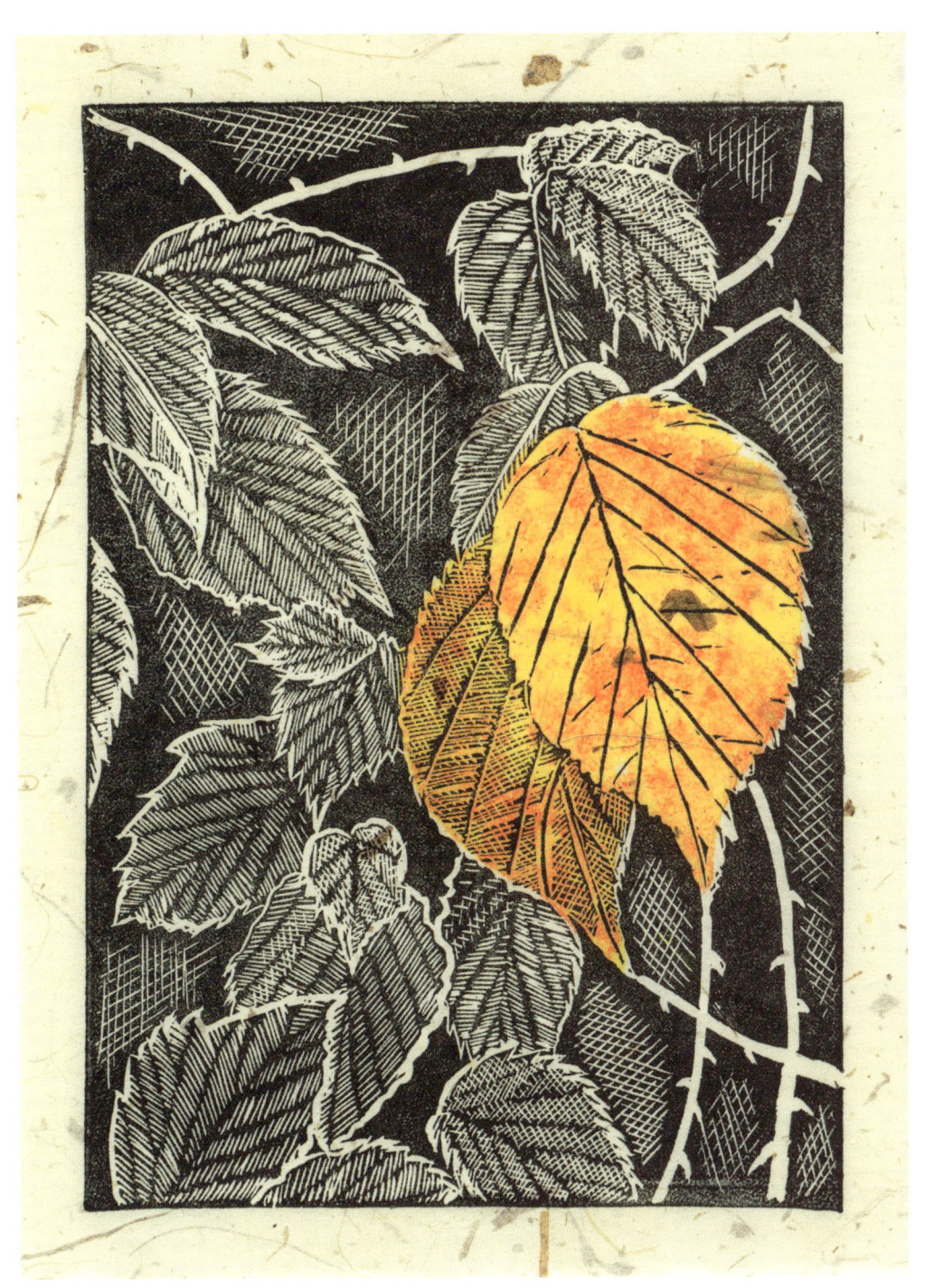

My starting point

My inspiration for this design came from a photograph I took of some bramble leaves while out on one of my daily walks. Autumn/Fall was almost upon us, and some of the leaves were already turning into rich reds and yellows. I loved how the two golden-yellow leaves in this shot stood out from the rest of the leaves in the photograph, and decided to capture this in a linocut print.

As in 'It's All in the Details' (see pages 96–101), for this project I'm using the image directly as the source for my print, without making any sketches. In order to see better how the image might work as a mostly monochrome linocut print, I converted the photograph seen right into black-and-white on my computer in photo-editing software; I also boosted the contrast to gauge where to place the lights, mid-tones and darks in the design. Once I was happy, I re-scaled the image so it was A6 (105 x 148mm/4 x 6in) in size then printed it out, ready to trace and transfer.

If you don't want to use a photograph, it's fine to use a sketch you've made instead.

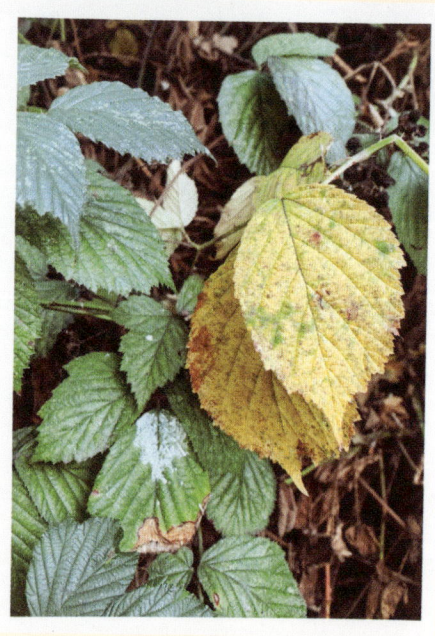

A NOTE ON ADDING COLOUR

There are no guidelines on how you apply colour in your prints, or what kind of colour you should use.

Some artists like to use watercolours or gouache to work on top of their prints, whereas others take a more 'purist' approach: because the work is a print, all areas that make up the piece should be made with printing techniques.

I like to think the archival inks I use are a kind of halfway house – as the colour applied is technically a printing ink, it's fine to dab or stamp them onto my prints!

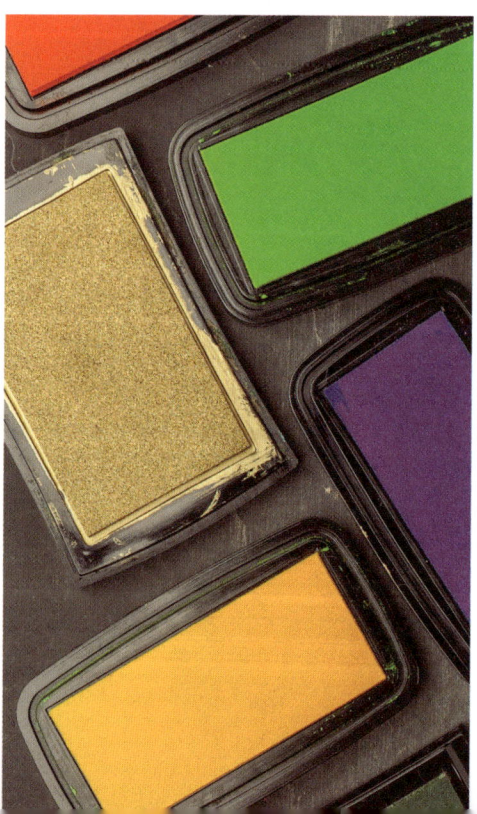

104

Method

1 Trace off the design then transfer it to your lino, as described on pages 52 and 53. Again, the design you trace off should be a simple outline of your source image, and need only include the minimum details at this stage.

2 Let's carve! As with 'It's All in the Details', I *ad libbed* the design slightly by adding some thorny bramble stems to the upper and lower left of the composition. Always be prepared to adapt your ideas as you work – this is all part of being an artist and actually creating a unique work of art, rather than simply reproducing an image as a linocut print!

— Carve all the main outlines initially with a small V-shaped tool.

— Since the two leaves in the foreground were going to be the focus of the design, and eventually stamped with my spot colour, I started with them. Firstly, I outlined the leaves with my 1mm V-shaped tool. In order for the additional colour to show up clearly once it was stamped on, much of the lino within the larger front leaf shape needed to be carved out (**2a**).

— The leaf behind it appeared slightly darker in the reference photograph; therefore, I wanted to leave more of the lino intact, but using cross-hatched marks to suggest the mid-tones in this leaf, and contrast sufficiently with the paler tone of the front leaf (**2b**).

— Alternating between the 1mm and the small V-shaped tools, the remaining leaves were carved with hatched and/or cross-hatched lines, depending on their placement in the reference image. Cross-hatched lines were carved into the areas between veins, suggesting lighter tones (**2c**); hatched areas push those parts of the leaves more into the background, and suggest they were in shadow (**2d**).

— The thorny bramble stems were carved out with a combination of the small V-shaped and the small U-shaped tools (**2e**).

— To finish, I added a bit of texture and a suggestion of shading to the darker areas of the background with a few cross-hatched marks (**2f**).

Continued...

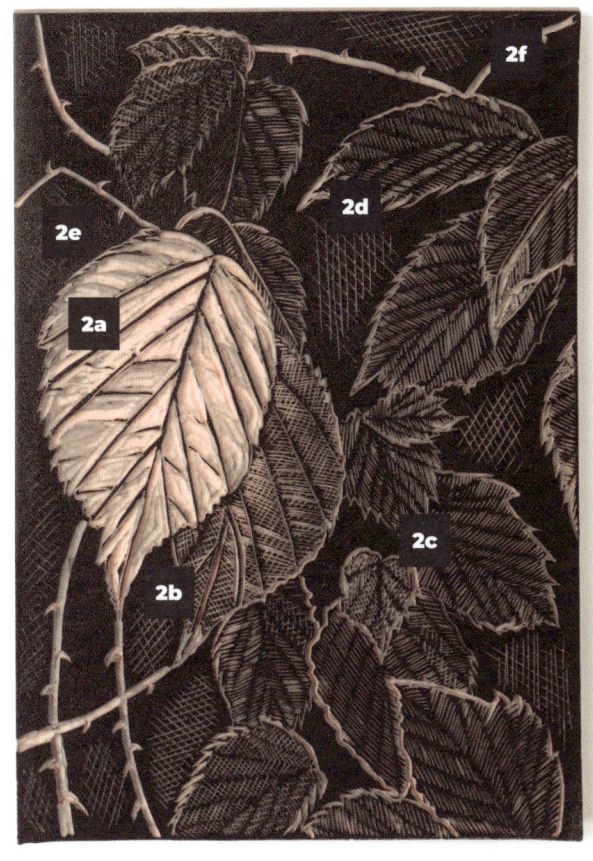

BRUSHING

As you're carving, brush away the tiny lino particles that gather with a regular paint brush. This keeps the surface of the lino clear, so you can see what has or hasn't been carved, and also prevents the particles sticking to the surface and eventually getting mixed up with the ink at the printing stage.

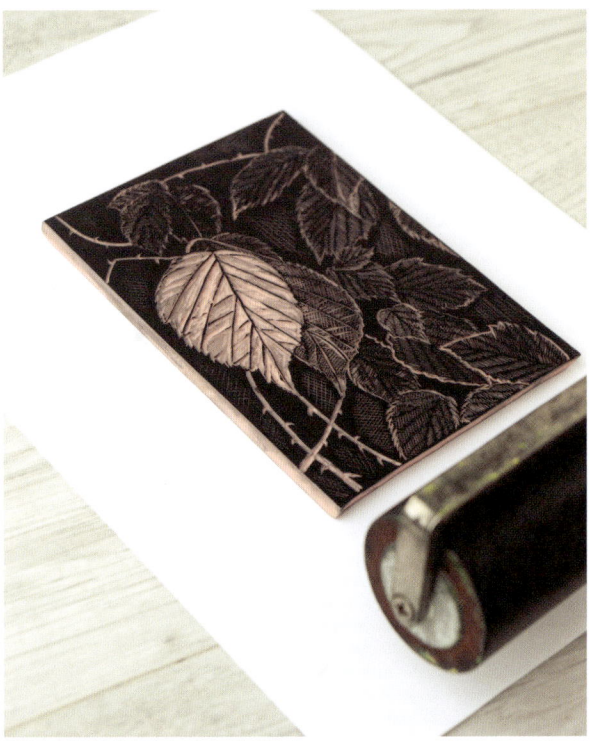

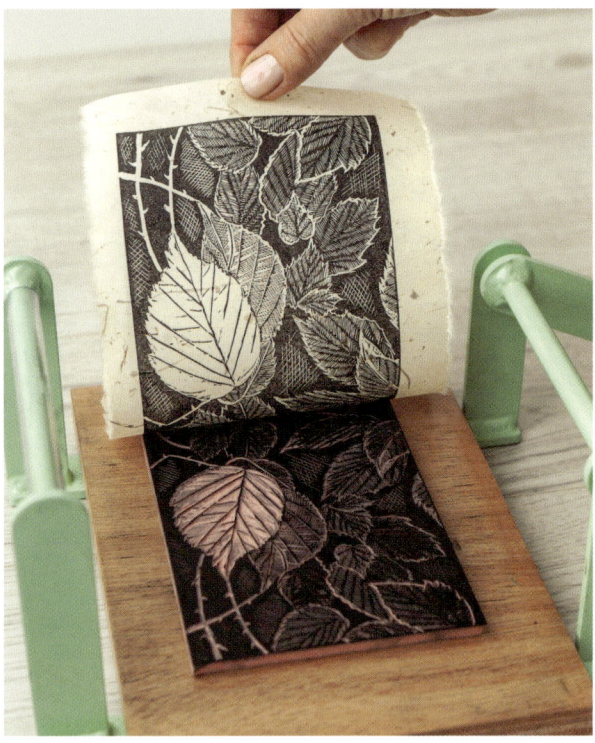

3 Once you feel you have finished carving your design, you are ready to ink up your block, ready for printing. Refer to the guidance on page 58, if you need a reminder.

As always, the first inking of your block is a magical experience which brings all of your hard work to life. It will also help to give you an idea of what your design will be like when it's printed. If you've missed carving anything out, it will show up at this point. As before, start off with thin layers of ink and build up gradually, to avoid over-inking the block.

4 When your lino block is inked up sufficiently, print it with your preferred printing method, referring to the guidance on pages 59–62. You may want to make a test print onto cheap paper first – in fact, you could use the image on the test print later on, to trace off the shapes needed for your spot-colour stamping. For my final printing surface, I chose to print onto hand-made Thai mulberry paper: the flecks of embedded banana-tree bark add a wonderful texture to this paper, and perfectly complement the subject matter of the print!

The final print(s) will look wonderful at this stage, printed in just one (dark) colour, with all of the details and marks you added during the carving stage showing in all their glory. If you decide you're happy with the black-and-white finish, you could stop here. However, if you'd like to add a spot colour, continue to step 5 onwards. Please note the print needs to be completely dry before adding any spot colours, which may take several days.

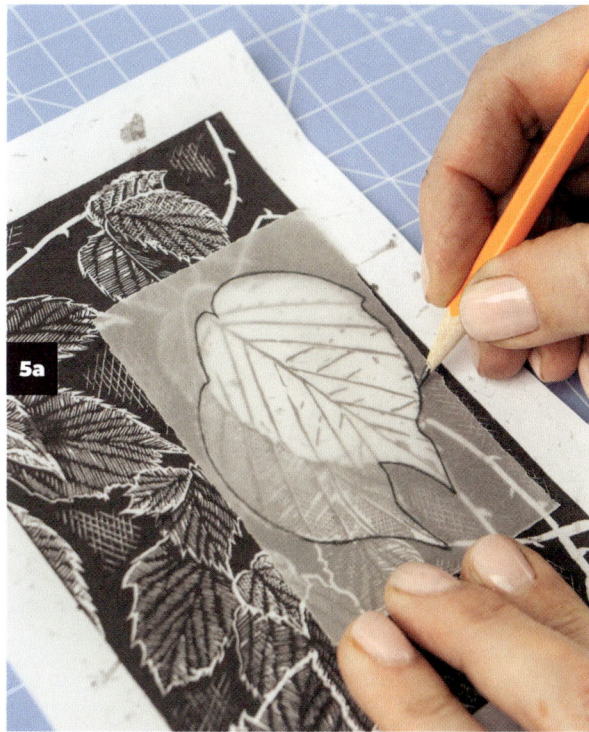

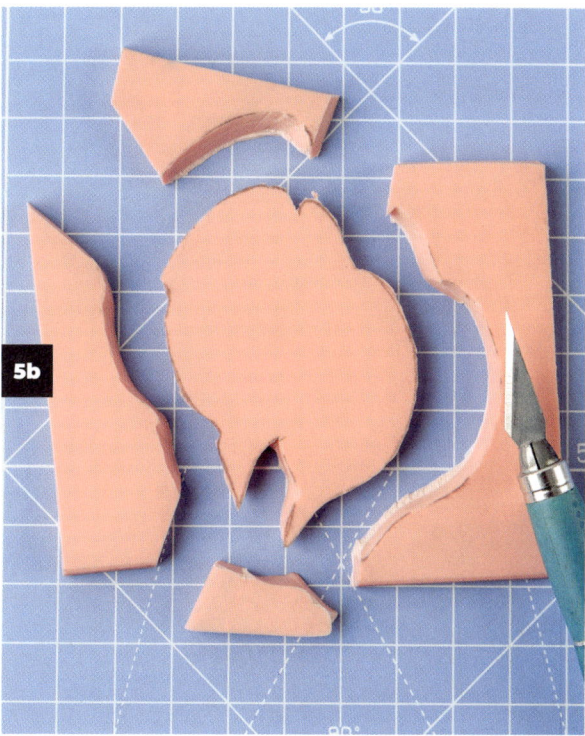

5 For this design, you'll make a stamp of an element in your print to add a spot colour (see the tip box on page 108). The stamp is simply a piece of lino cut into the shape of your element, and has no carved details. I decided to make a stamp for the two larger leaves in the foreground, based on the leaves in my reference photograph that were turning orange.

It's important to use transparent colours for stamping, so all of your carving details will be nicely visible after you've stamped the spot colour. Pigment ink pads are translucent; if you don't have any ink pads, you can combine your chosen relief print ink colour then mix in some extender medium – see step 8 on page 125 of the 'More Blocks, Please' project, for details on mixing relief print ink and the extender medium.

– Trace the shape of your chosen element – I traced the shape of the two leaves (**5a**).

– Transfer the tracing onto a small piece of lino, and cut it to shape with a craft knife (**5b**). Remember to make sure the lino mirrors the shape in the print!

Continued...

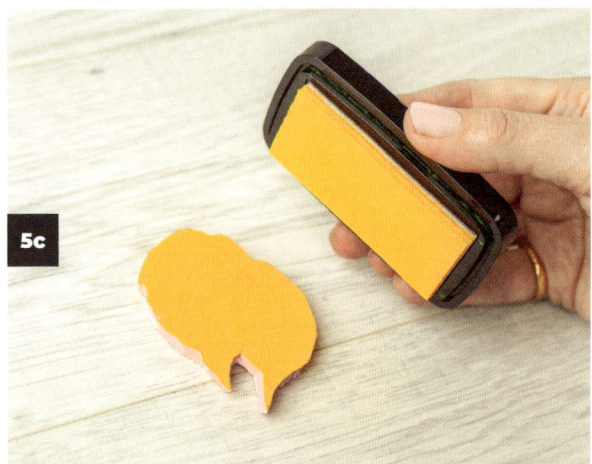

I actually applied two colours to my print, so they could blend together and create a subtle, autumnal colour effect. (This blend can only be achieved by using translucent colours.) If you wish to do the same, start off applying your palest spot colour to the stamp – I dabbed on a yellow shade of archival pigment ink (**5c**).

Stamp the colour onto the print, over the area to which you wish to apply colour (**5d**). The stamp should more or less print perfectly over your chosen spot-colour area, although if it's a little out it won't be a problem: translucent colours are always quite forgiving, when it comes to slightly inaccurate registration!

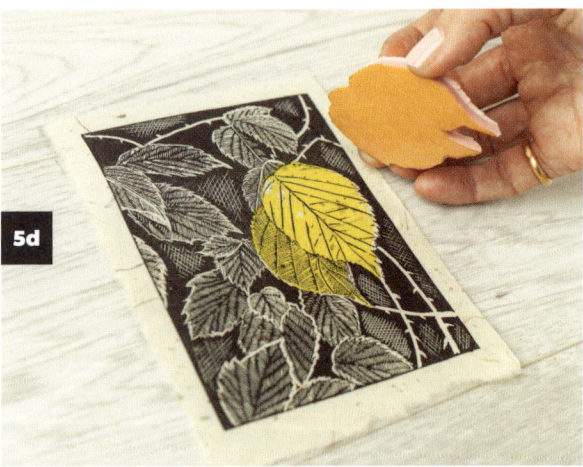

Now to over-stamp the pale shade with the darker shade – I used red. This time though, I didn't want a dense covering of ink all over the stamp, as this would overpower the yellow. So, after dabbing the stamp with the red shade, I placed the stamp onto a scrap piece of paper (without pushing it down) and then carefully lifted up the stamp. By doing this, I removed a lot of the red ink from the stamp, leaving a light, slightly uneven covering on the surface. Press the stamp with your second, darker colour over the yellow spot colour (**5e**); this added spots of red here and there, which blended with the yellow to create subtle orange flecks.

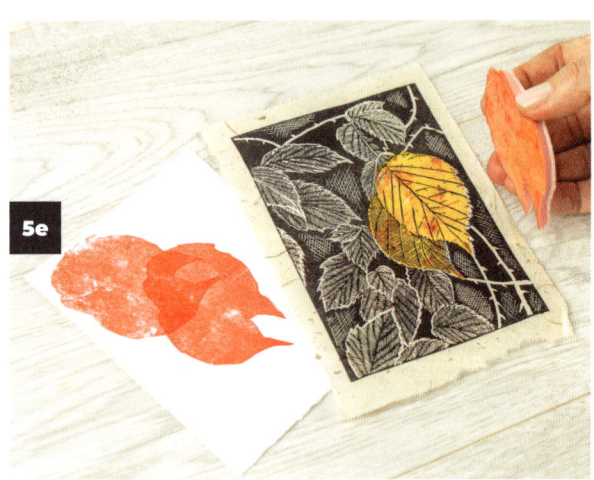

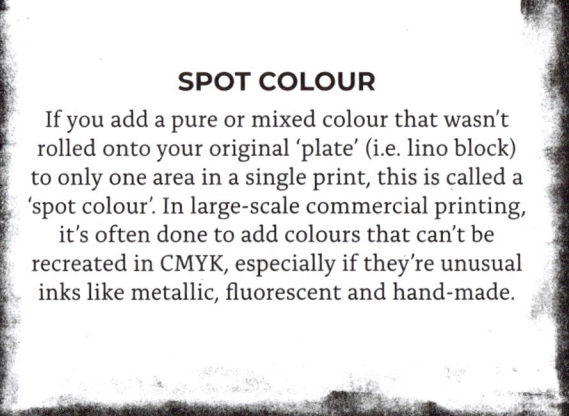

SPOT COLOUR

If you add a pure or mixed colour that wasn't rolled onto your original 'plate' (i.e. lino block) to only one area in a single print, this is called a 'spot colour'. In large-scale commercial printing, it's often done to add colours that can't be recreated in CMYK, especially if they're unusual inks like metallic, fluorescent and hand-made.

MY WALK TODAY

Project brief

We'll be creating an A5 (148 x 210mm/Junior Legal) print that is inspired by a walk in a beautiful place. This may be a place close to your home where you walk every day, or maybe a memorable walk you once took on a holiday or trip. The subject for your print can either be purely landscape, or you may wish to include animals and/or birds in a natural setting.

This print will be more complex in composition than the previous projects, and will also include finer details and more markings too.

YOU WILL NEED

— A sketch you've made, and/or a photograph you've taken, for reference

— Tracing paper and pencil

— Stylus or ballpoint pen, for transferring the tracing onto lino

— Masking tape

— Small pieces of lino, to test markings

— A5 (148 x 210mm/Junior Legal) size piece of lino – I have chosen a traditional ready-mounted linoleum block from Speedball®

— A selection of at least three carving tools, including a fine V-shaped tool for intricate details and a small U-shaped tool

— Relief printing ink in black or a darker colour – I'm using an oil-based ink

— Scrap paper, for making test prints

— Your chosen printmaking paper, larger than A5 (148 x 210mm/Junior Legal) in size – I used Somerset Satin 300gsm (140lbs)

— Your chosen equipment for printing (a spoon, baren or printing press)

— Optional: the template on page 156, for transferring

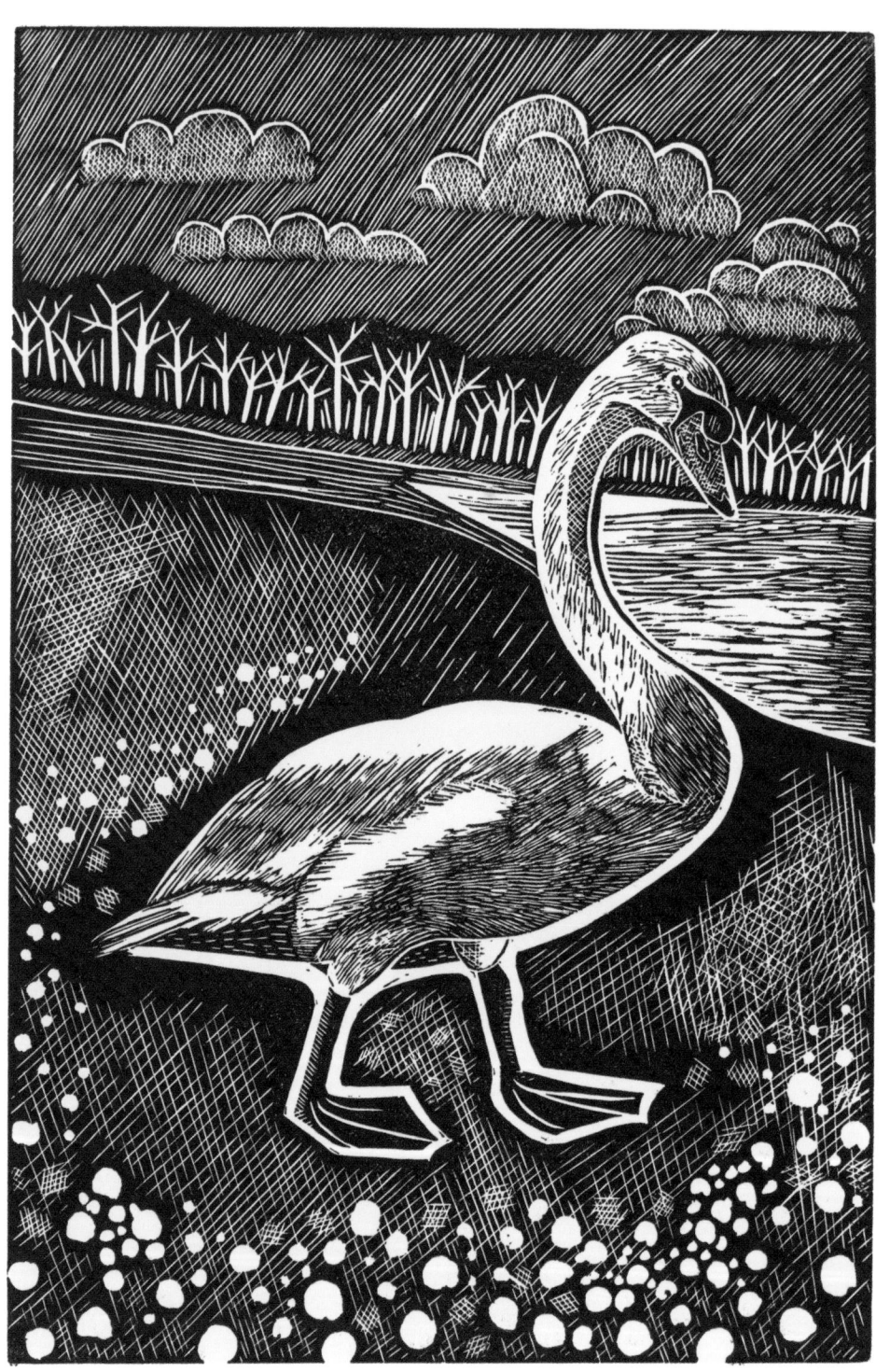

My starting point

Hullbridge in Essex, UK, is a small village just a few miles from my home, and lies alongside the River Crouch. The path that flanks the river is a favourite summer walk of mine, as there are plenty of wading birds to spot, sifting the edges of the river in search of food. There are mute swans aplenty who are always willing to pose for the camera – and it's one such photograph that I used as the starting point for this project.

I liked how the shape of the swan was central to the composition of the image, and how the S-shape of the bird connected the furthest point in the image (the sky) to the closest point (the shingle on the beach).

I started by making a mixed-media sketch of the image, stylizing the elements in the photograph and playing with printed textures on the shingle beach in the foreground. I then followed the process of transforming the image into one that would make a suitable linocut print, by increasing the contrast between light and dark areas.

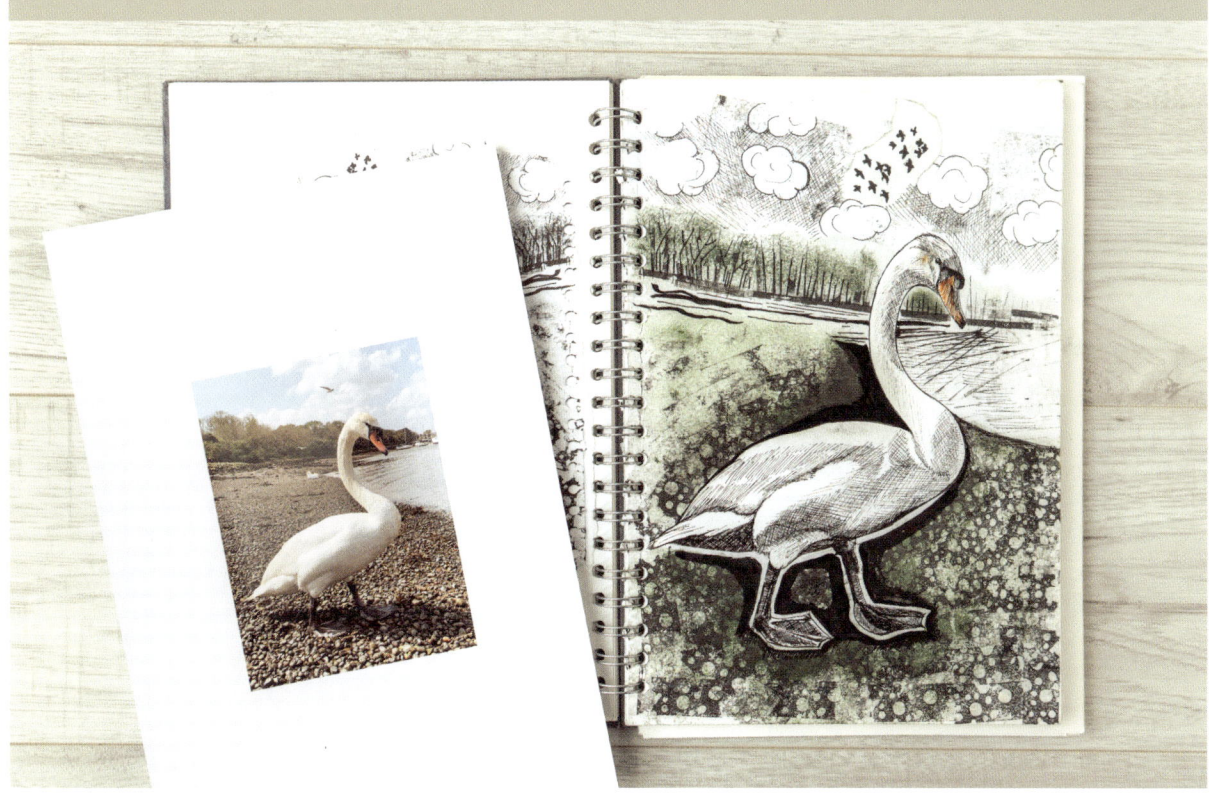

Method

1 Trace off the design then transfer it to the lino, as described on pages 52 and 53. As always, just add the bare minimum of details at this stage. Mine were the outline of the swan and key elements in the background – the clouds, trees and where the beach meets the river. I changed and simplified the original photograph and reference sketch (see page 111) by taking away the flying birds and having fewer clouds.

2 After transferring my design, I stained the lino with a diluted black Indian ink, to help make my marks more visible as I carved. I then allowed the lino to dry thoroughly before carving.

3 Let's carve! This project has scope for a large variety of mark-making compared to the previous projects, due to the fact it features an actual landscape behind the central subject (swan). Therefore, we have to find ways of indicating not only feathers, but shingle, water, trees, sky and clouds with carved marks on lino – quite a challenge!

All of your fully carved elements will need to stand out and be visible when the block is printed in a single, dark colour. In order for this to happen, adjacent elements will need to be carved differently (either carved out, left in, or with textured marks, to differentiate them from the next area). The areas of your design that are similar in tone (for instance, the swan's white neck and the pale water) can be separated by leaving an 'outline' – either solid (which will print black) or carved-out (which will print white), depending on the tonal areas you need to separate. As always, when carving, constantly refer back to your reference image(s).

— Outline the key shapes in the piece, using the fine V-shaped tool (**3a**). For me, these were the tops of the clouds, the shorelines and the swan.

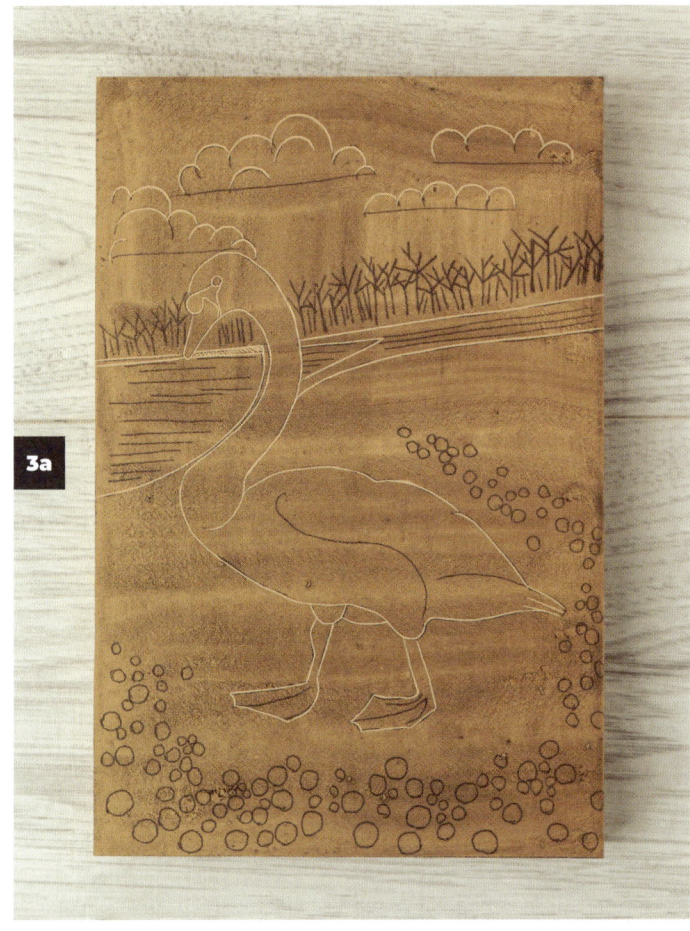

3a

TACKLING A MORE COMPLEX SCENE

The best way to approach a piece with lots of elements is not to think of them as 'shingle', 'water', 'trees', etc., but simply as shapes and textures. After all, this is what they will actually be in the artwork you create – a collection of forms and pattern that work together to give the illusion of a landscape. These elements are greatly simplified and stylized in the print, and the focus is on how well they actually work together within the composition of the piece.

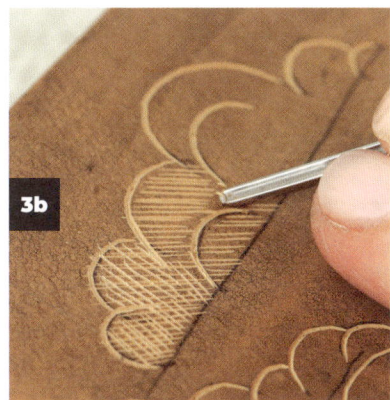

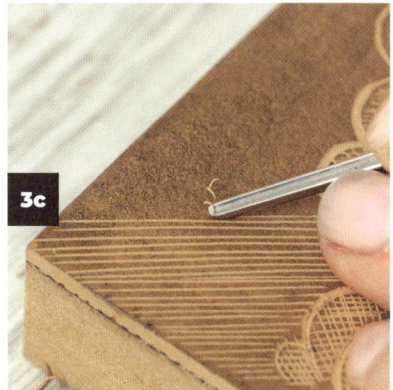

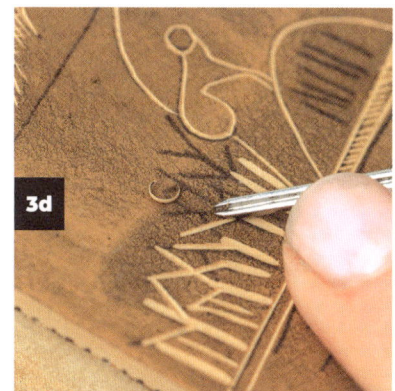

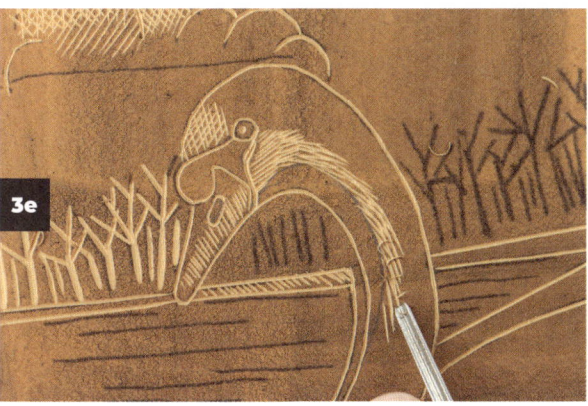

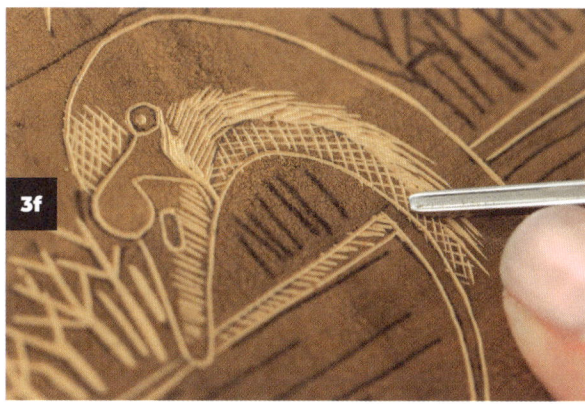

While the tops of the clouds were outlined, to suggest highlights, the rest of the clouds were carved with a mix of hatched and cross-hatched lines, using the fine V-shaped tool (**3b**) – the cross-hatched lines indicate areas in light, and the hatched lines suggest slightly darker tones.

The sky needs to be lighter than black, so I hatched the area with fine lines, very close together to create the lighter tone, using the same fine V-shaped tool (**3c**).

The line of trees that separate the land from the sky were great fun to carve. Tree shapes are easy to simplify and stylize and because they vary so much in shape and size, they are very forgiving to carve! I used a small U-shaped tool for all the trees (**3d**).

My swan was carved with lots of different markings, to indicate not only the different lights and shadows but also the different textures too (**3e**). Once the highlight of the eye was carved out with a fine U-shaped tool, the underside of the bill was marked with hatched lines using a small V-shaped tool. The top of the head is slightly in shadow, so I carved it with cross-hatched lines using the same small V-shaped tool. The rest of the head and the upper neck are made up of dense areas of small lines – time-consuming to carve, but well worth the effort!

The underside of the neck, as it's in shadow, was also carved with cross-hatched lines using the small V-shaped tool (**3f**).

Continued...

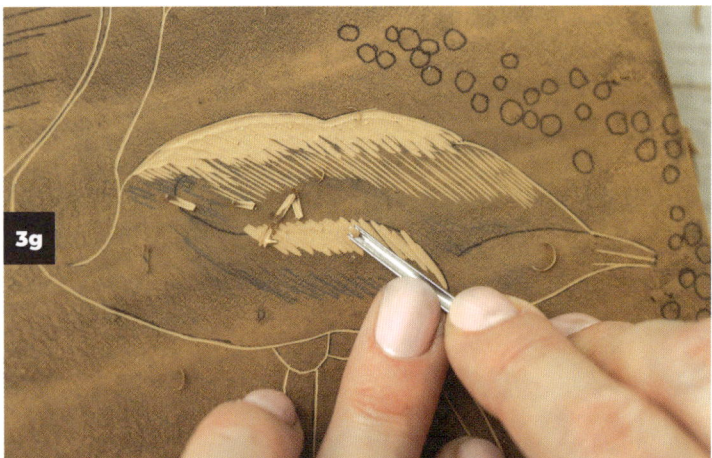

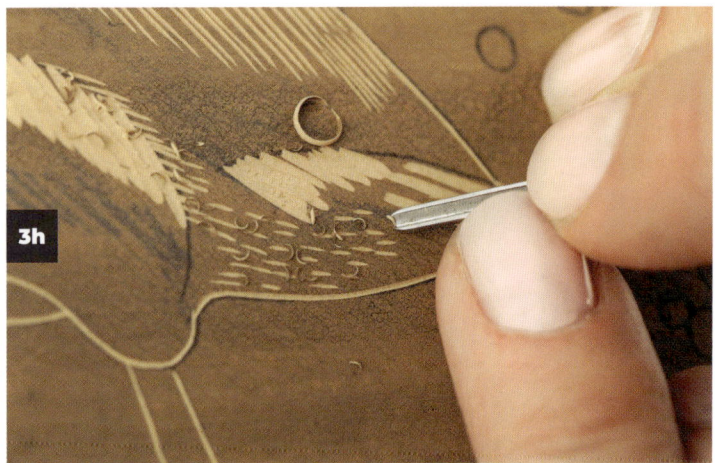

The wing of the swan not only needed to be outlined, to push it into the foreground, but also required the textures and shading seen elsewhere (**3g**). The feathers were a series of hatched lines; and areas with lots of highlights were carved out completely. A mix of fine and small V-shaped and U-shaped tools were used throughout.

Little scattered lines were marked under the tail using the small V-shaped tool (**3h**).

The 'thighs' were, again, densely packed hatched lines, but the legs and feet were left relatively untouched, with just a few outlines and hatched lines (**3i**). As with the wing, a mix of sizes of V-shaped and U-shaped tool were used.

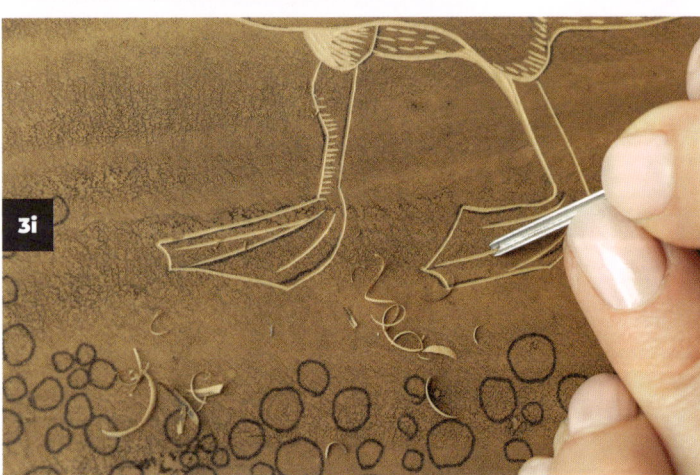

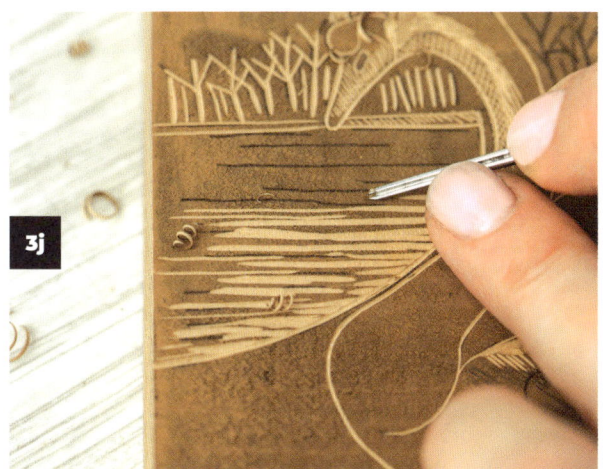

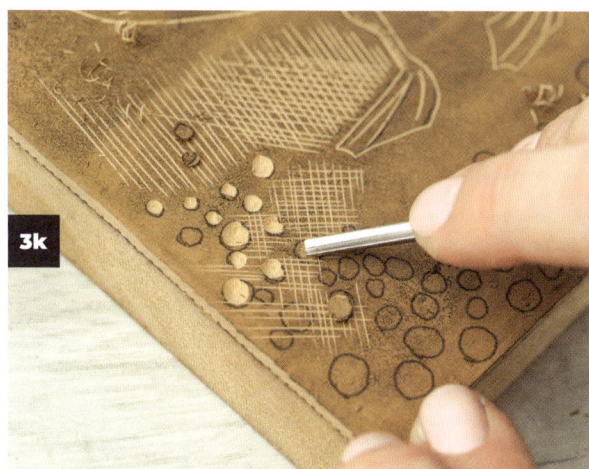

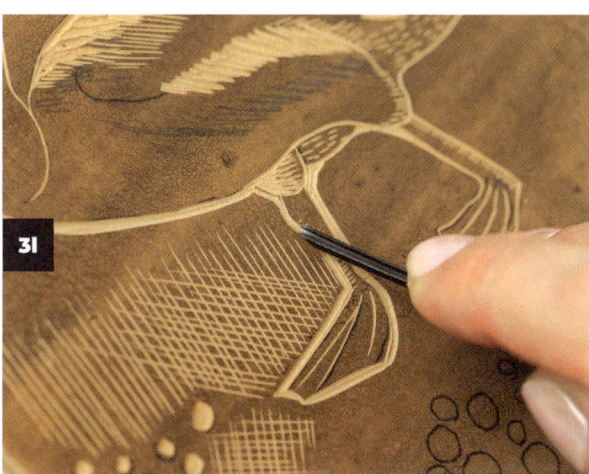

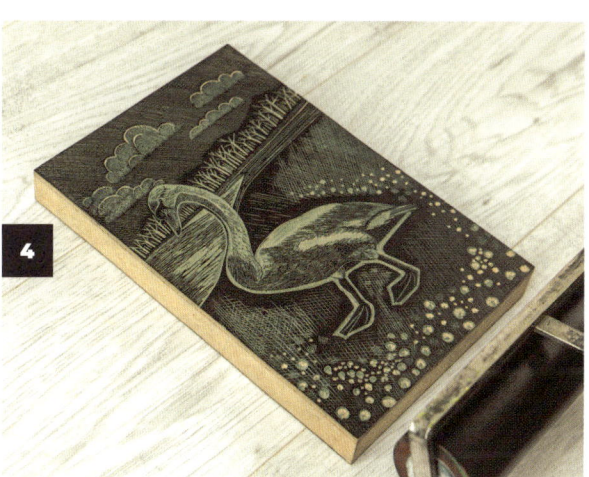

— The ripples in the water were varying lengths of thick lines, carved from the shore outwards using a small U-shaped tool (**3j**).

— For the distant shore, I worked horizontal lines with the small V-shaped tool, but I marked the near shoreline around the swan with cross-hatched lines. To help the swan stand proud, I left a border around it and didn't carve my cross-hatched lines too closely. Circles of 'pebbles' were carved away in the near foreground with a mix of small, medium and large U-shaped tools (**3k**).

— To finish, I strengthened the outline around the swan by carving over the original outline with a thicker U-shaped too (**3l**).

4 Ink up then print your design, following the guidance on pages 58–62. Remember to build up thin layers of ink, to avoid over-inking – you do not want to obliterate all your painstakingly carved details when inking up this block! I'd also recommend test printing, especially if you've explored anything new in your design.

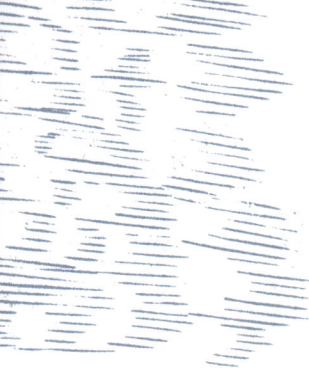

NO. 8

MORE BLOCKS, PLEASE

Project brief

Make an A5 (148 x 210mm/Junior Legal) sized print that involves simple registration (lining up) of two identical-sized blocks, achieved by making a jig. The second block is lined up and printed over the print made by the first block, resulting in a multi-coloured print. This is ideal for edition printing (see the box on page 124). For your subject, choose a favourite nature-inspired sketch you've made, or photograph you have taken.

YOU WILL NEED

— A sketch you've made, and/or a photograph you've taken, for reference

— Two sheets of tracing paper and a pencil

— Stylus or ballpoint pen, for transferring the tracing onto lino

— Masking tape

— Small pieces of lino, to test markings

— Two A5 (148 x 210mm/Junior Legal) size pieces of lino – I have chosen traditional hessian-backed linoleum blocks

— A selection of at least three carving tools, including small V-shaped and U-shaped tools and one large U-shaped tool

— Relief printing ink in two colours – one light/bright colour and one that's more dark/sobre. There needs to be enough contrast between the two inks so that they show up well against each other. You can either buy ready-mixed colours, or you can mix your own. I have used oil-based inks for this project

— Extender medium, to mix in with the lighter coloured ink to create a more translucent shade that will print nicely under the darker colour – my extender medium is by Cranfield, as this is the brand I used for the relief ink

— Cheap paper, for making test prints

— Five to ten sheets of your chosen printmaking paper, larger than A5 (148 x 210mm/Junior Legal) in size to accommodate a border – I used Somerset Satin 300gsm (140lbs)

— One sheet of thick (at least 1000 micron thickness) A4 (210 x 297mm/US Letter) sized cardboard for the registration jig

— Ternes Burton pins and stripping tabs, for paper registration

— Craft knife and cutting mat

— Your chosen equipment for printing (a spoon, baren or printing press)

— Optional: the template on page 157, for transferring

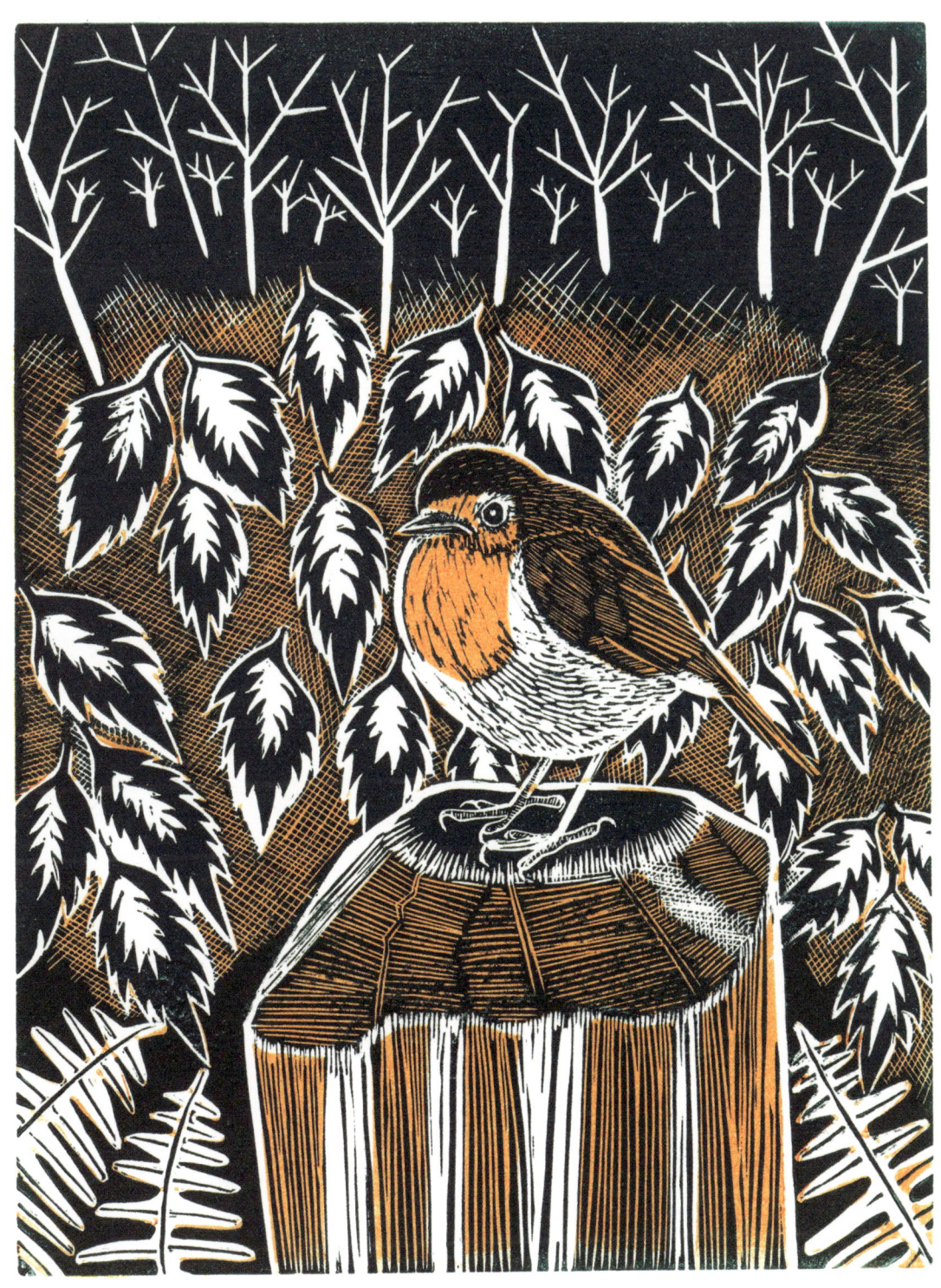

My starting point

I take literally hundreds of photographs with my camera phone on my daily walks, but rarely manage to capture birds sufficiently clearly to use as reference sources for my prints. This was one occasion when I managed a decent shot – thanks to a very obliging robin!

From this photograph I took of a robin on a fence post, I created a sketch for my print. When making the sketch, I stylized and simplified the leaves; I also added trees in the distant background and ferns in the foreground – either side of the post – to enhance the composition, while adding interest and a decorative element. (It's always the artist's licence to change things around!)

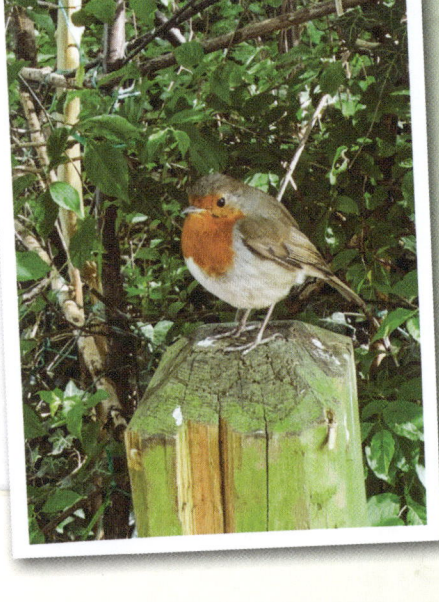

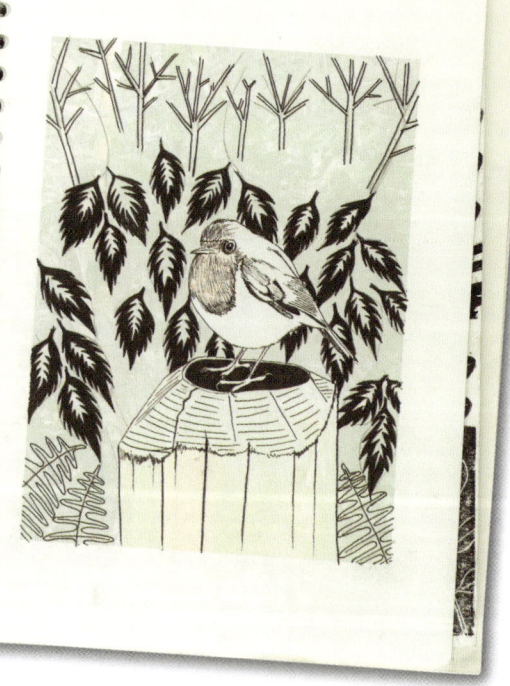

PROCESS OF MAKING A TWO-COLOUR PRINT

The important difference between this print and the ones in the previous projects is that we are required to plan and carve two lino blocks, then line up and print one block over the print of the other to create a multi-coloured print. This is a more complex print to create (hence why it is the eighth project!).

When making a two-colour block print, we start by creating the 'key' block: this is the primary block that provides the main details in a print, and pulls everything together. It's also always the darkest colour in the print. We make a print with the key block, and this helps the printmaker decide where the second colour – always the lighter colour – should appear in the image. A 'secondary block' is then made, and carved appropriately so the block only prints the second colour in the areas decided.

Method

1 Let's start with the key block, which includes all the details in the print. Trace off the design then transfer it to the lino, as described on pages 52 and 53. I didn't draw in all the textures in the robin, just the key outlines.

2 After transferring my design, I stained the lino with a diluted black Indian ink, to help make my marks more visible as I carved. I then allowed the lino to dry thoroughly before carving.

3 Let's carve! For my key block, I'll be carving in most of the details in the print, which include the robin and its many textures, the background trees, the background leaves, the log and the foreground ferns.
   If you need a reminder of the different kinds of textures you can achieve with your carved marks, see page 48.

— Outline the key shapes in the piece using the fine V-shaped tool.

— As with the tree shapes in 'My Walk Today', I've given the trees a minimalist treatment, carving them with simple lines using a small U-shaped tool (**3a**).

— Once the eye of the robin was carved with a fine U-shaped tool, I carved out the rest of his details (**3b**). The top of his head and back are small scattered lines, carved with a fine V-shaped tool; the forehead and shaping around the chest and wing are little parallel lines, again marked with the fine V-shaped tool; the wing and tail are a series of broken parallel lines that get longer and thicker towards the tail, and these were carved with varying sizes of V-shaped tool.

— I completed the robin by carving his chest and stomach (**3c**). His stomach was a series of layered marks that flowed downwards, carved with a fine U-shaped tool. I carved out the whole chest area with the small U-shaped tool.

Continued...

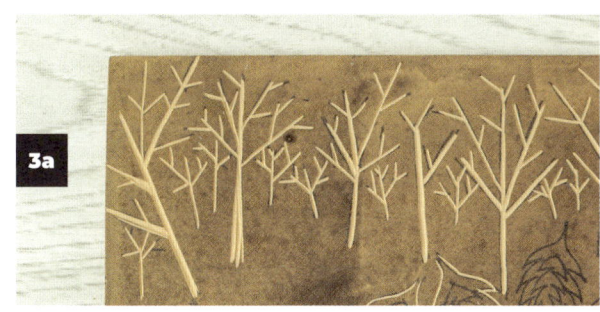

3a

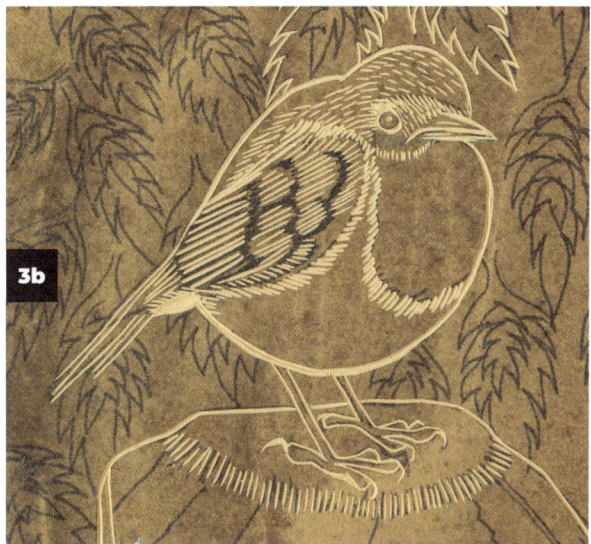

3b

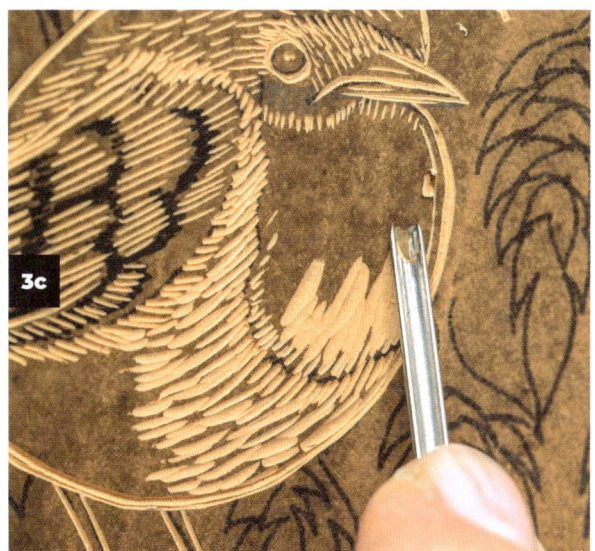

3c

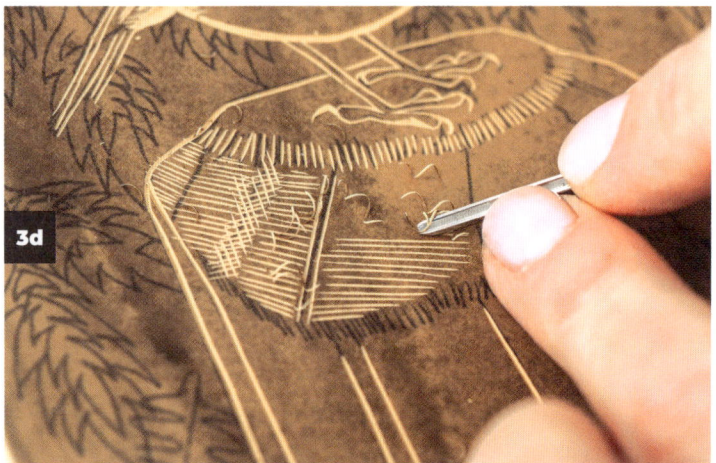

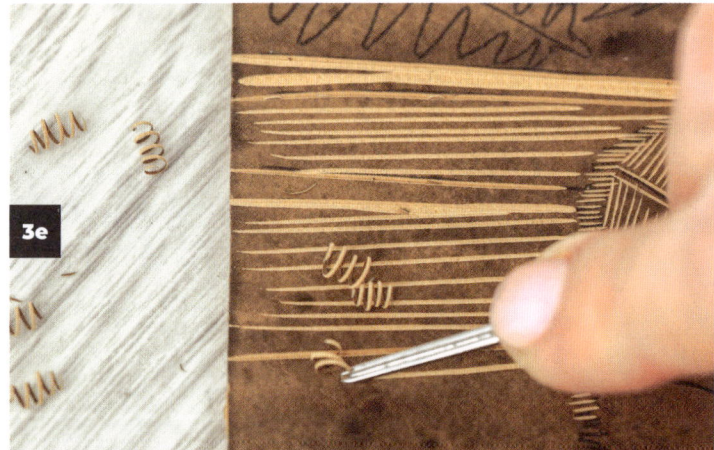

The wood textures of the post the robin is perched on were simply carved lines of varying thicknesses, and were really fun to carve (**3d** and **3e**)! I recommend keeping your test scrap of lino next to you for areas like this, to test out marks and tools before you commit anything new to your block.

In this design, I surrounded the robin with stylized leaves – these are simple, yet decorative and effective. Leaving little 'veins' uncarved along the middle of each leaf, the rest of the inside areas of the foreground ferns were carved out with a small U-shaped tool. For the background leaves, I carved out the inner areas only, and left the rest of the leaves uncarved (**3f**).

To finish, I carved cross-hatched markings around the robin – in among the background leaves, and just below the trees – with a small V-shaped tool. Cross-hatched areas in between the leaves provide tonal variations without looking too 'busy' and overpowering the main element of the print (the robin).

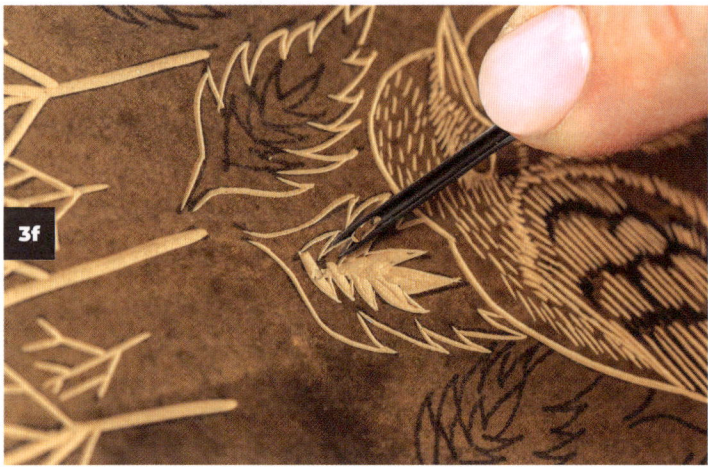

4 When you are happy with how the carving looks on your key block (**4a**), make a test print to inform your second colour. Using a small amount of black or dark-coloured oil-based printing ink (I've used some of the dark green I'll mix in a larger quantity, to use in the finished print) and a roller, ink up and then print your design onto your cheap paper, following the guidance on pages 59–62 (**4b**). Use this print as an opportunity to make any adjustments to your lino before proceeding to the next stage.

Then, when it has dried, colour and draw over your test print to work out where you'll put your second colour. As I wanted to make the robin's famous red chest prominent in the print, I decided to use burnt orange for the secondary colour, and then use this colour for other colourful elements in the print to give the piece harmony – the feathers in the robin's body, areas of the post he's perched on, and the cross-hatched background – pushing the robin more into the foreground.

5 Transfer the design from the key block onto your secondary block: ink up your key block with black oil-based ink (this won't work with water-based ink!), then print it onto your sheet of tracing paper. While the image is wet and newly printed, carefully flip it over and place the tracing paper – ink side facing down – onto your second lino block. It's very important that you line up the edges of the printed image with the edges of the block (which should be exactly the same size) – this is why you use tracing paper to perform this task!

Once the print is in the correct position, and ensuring that it doesn't move, apply pressure all over the back of the printed area of the tracing paper to transfer it to the block – I used a baren for this (**5a**). Peel off the tracing paper to reveal a lightly printed lino block (**5b**). Note this method flips the design, so that when you print with the carved secondary block it will print the correct way.

Leave the printed block to dry as much as possible, before starting to carve into it.

Continued...

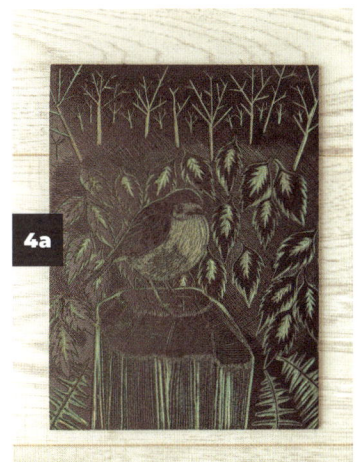

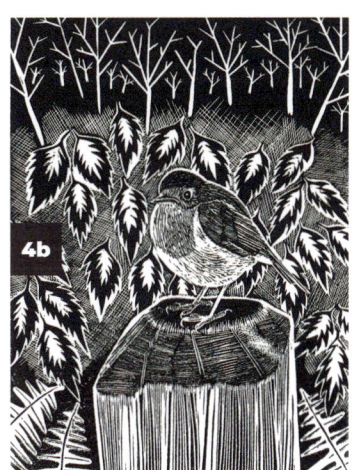

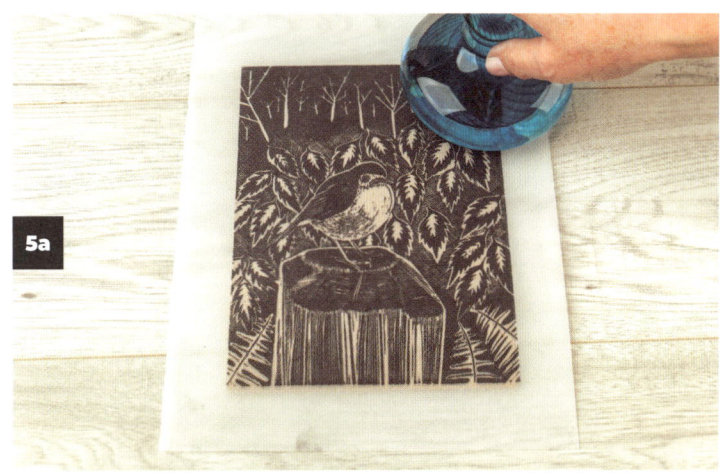

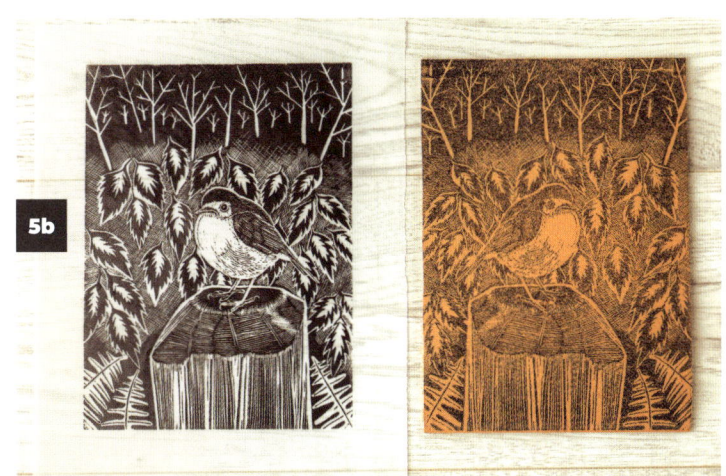

6 Using your annotated test print from step 4 (see previous page) as a reference, begin carving out the areas that *won't* be printed in the second colour. The carving of this block is actually pretty simple, as there are no small details to carve – it is simply a matter of leaving areas of the image where we want the second colour to be printed uncarved.

As the ink on your block may still be slightly tacky, I recommend wearing gloves to avoid getting smudges on your hands. I also suggest working from the bottom of the lino upwards, to avoid smudging the ink on the lino and therefore losing the details that will guide your carving.

I carved out the following areas:

— the background leaves and foreground ferns

— the eye and belly of the robin

— the top round area and some of the vertical lines in the post the robin is perched on

— along the bottom of the treeline, I carved out some more cross-hatched lines to create a neat transition between the burnt orange background behind the leaves and the dark treeline

— the treeline.

After I finished carving, I cleaned away the ink with non-toxic solvent (such as Zest-it), wiped the whole block with a cloth damp with soapy warm water, then dried it with a towel or dry cloth.

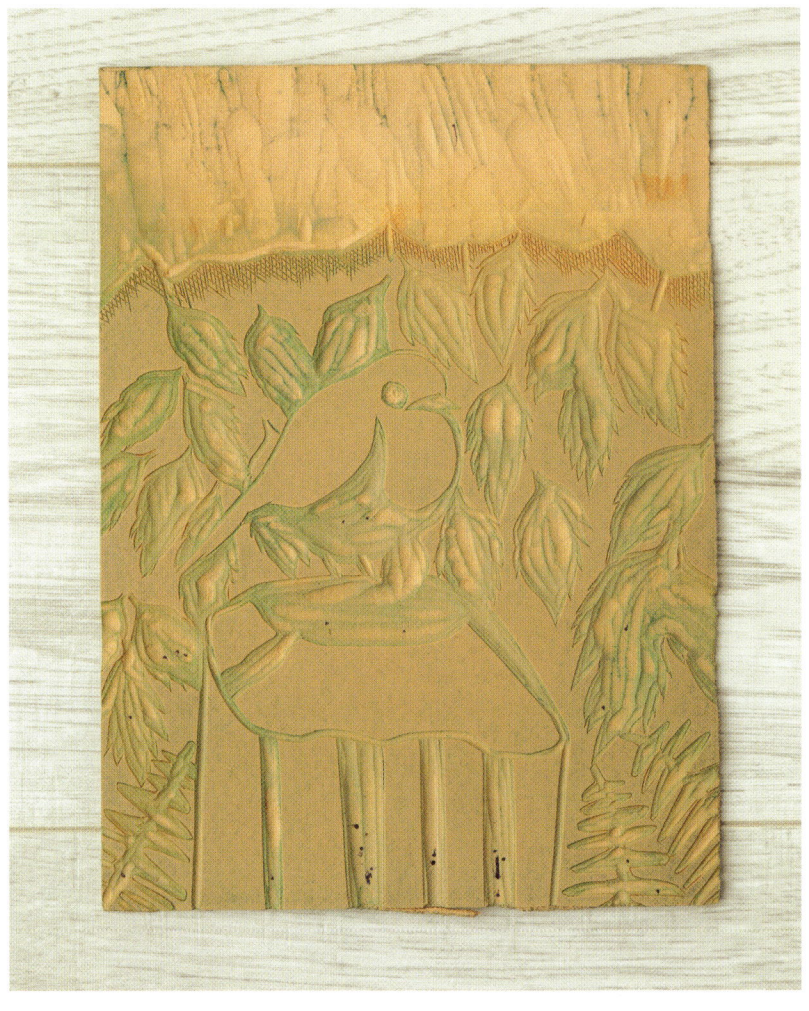

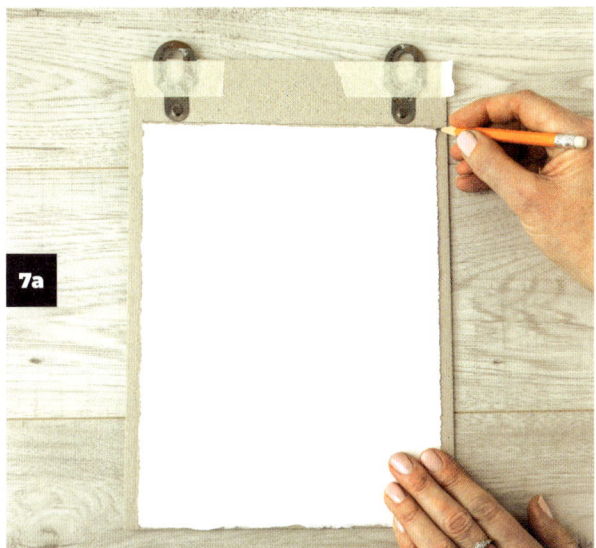

7a

7 Now both your two-colour blocks are carved, you can set up the registration.

— Decide on the size of your paper. I wanted to keep a fairly large border around my print – approximately 2–3cm (¾–1¼in) all around the printed image. Therefore, I have hand-torn my paper to a size that's slightly smaller than A4 (210 x 297mm/US Letter). This makes the paper a custom size. If you do this yourself, note that you need to make sure that all of your sheets of paper are trimmed or hand-torn to the same size.

— You'll then need to set up a registration frame or 'jig', to make sure your lino blocks are placed in exactly the same position before you print them. There are different methods of making a jig, but for this project I'll keep things simple with a frame jig. Take the thick cardboard sheet, making sure it's at least 5cm (2in) taller than your chosen printmaking paper. Place a sheet of your trimmed (or hand-torn) paper centrally between the two side edges of the cardboard, ensuring that the printing side of your paper is facing down and also making sure the bottom edge doesn't overhang the bottom edge of the cardboard.

— To ensure that the paper is placed in exactly the same position for both colours, I'm using the 'clip and fasten' system. I use Ternes Burton pins and stripping tabs, which are used by printmakers the world over. They are cheap to purchase from specialist printmaking suppliers and are an invaluable part of your printmaking kit – particularly if you plan to make multi-block prints on a regular basis. Lay a Ternes Burton pin in each top corner of the paper, about 2cm (¾in) in from the sides and so the round, stud ends are just above the top of the paper. Tape them firmly to the card with masking tape or a stronger tape if you wish. It's important these pins are securely attached to the cardboard jig: if they shift during the printing process, you'll spoil your registration.

— On the card, draw around your chosen printmaking paper, so you have its outline on the jig (**7a**).

Continued...

WHAT IS REGISTRATION?

In printmaking terms, registration simply means lining up the multiple blocks correctly, so that when you print them the colour layers will be printed in the correct position.

Good registration means that the colours you print will appear in the correct parts of your image.

Registration tends to be a somewhat contentious issue among printmakers: some place the utmost importance on perfect registration, while others worry less about precise registration of the blocks and are happy to achieve a 'looser' style with their prints.

My personal advice would be to aim for 'perfect' registration, but not to worry unduly about slight colour misplacement. Remember, you are creating a hand-made print, with all the quirks and charms resulting from this process!

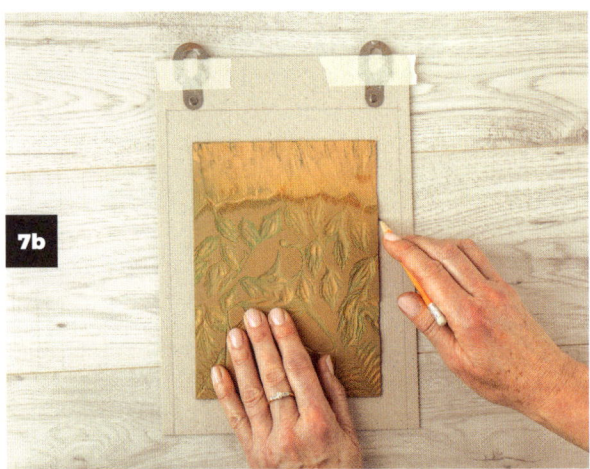

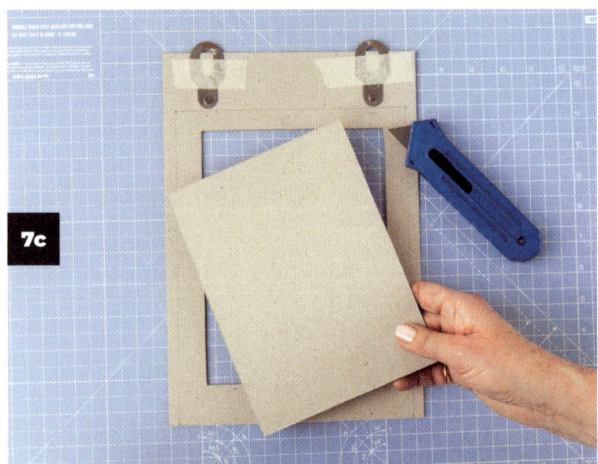

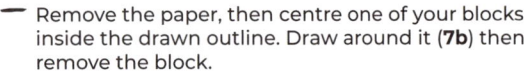

- Remove the paper, then centre one of your blocks inside the drawn outline. Draw around it (**7b**) then remove the block.

- Over a cutting mat and using a craft knife or scalpel, cut out the small block outline. Your block will sit in this gap (**7c**). Your jig is complete.

- Prepare your printmaking paper. Place the trimmed or hand-torn paper over the jig, the front facing down, and line it up with your drawn outline. Take two Ternes Burton stripping tabs and clip the top circular holes onto the studs of the Ternes Burton pins; they should snap firmly into place. Lay the other ends of the tabs on top of the paper, then tape in place (**7d**). The tabs should be fixed firmly enough to stay in place, but bear in mind you will need to remove the masking tape after printing without damaging the back of your paper. Carefully lift the tabbed paper off the studs.
  Since we are making a small edition (see the tip box, below right), repeat this step with the rest of your printmaking paper.

WHAT IS AN EDITION?

This is making a set of prints (i.e. more than one print) that are as similar to each other as we can possibly achieve, using a hand-made process. You can have as many prints as you wish in an edition, and several editions can be made of one design – although most printmakers will want each edition to vary slightly from the last (e.g., printed onto different paper, in a different coloured ink, etc.).

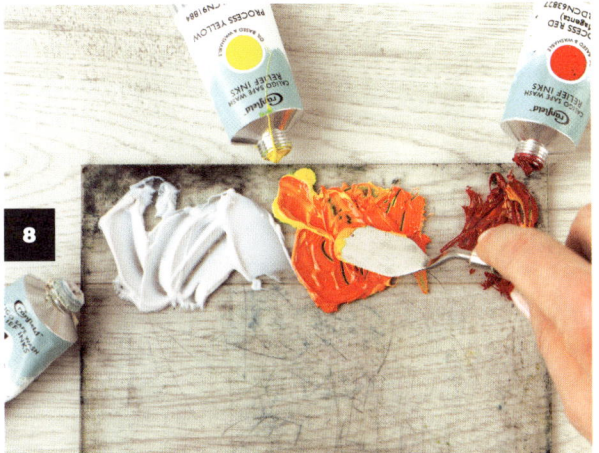

8 Contrary to what you may expect, the secondary block is actually printed first, with the key block containing the detailed design printed in a darker colour on top afterwards. This means the first colour to prepare is the one for your secondary block.

For my secondary block colour, I mixed up a burnt orange colour, which is sufficiently bright without being too garish, using pure (process) yellow and pure (process) red oil-based relief inks.

Once I achieved my desired colour, I mixed in some extender medium. This is a special colourless medium (it appears white when squeezed out) that makes the colour its mixed into a little translucent, making it perfect for building up layers of colour in a print.

9 Ink up the secondary block with your first colour. Then, carefully place the block in the hole in the cardboard jig, the inked side facing up.

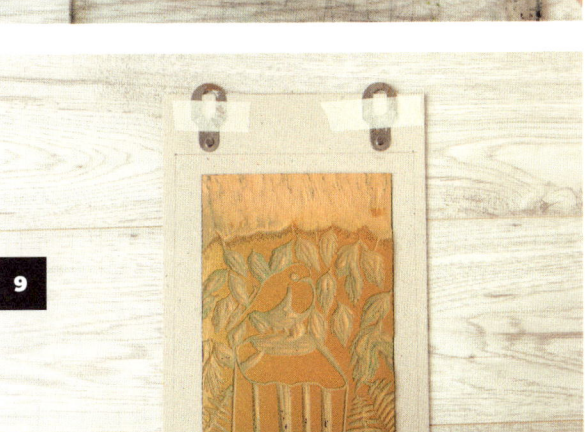

MIXING RELIEF INKS

Relief inks can be mixed together, like paint, to make tailored colours and shades. You can use colours straight from the tube, if you'd rather not mix your own, but I would definitely recommend having a try – it gives you a lot more control over how your print will look, and makes it more personal to you.

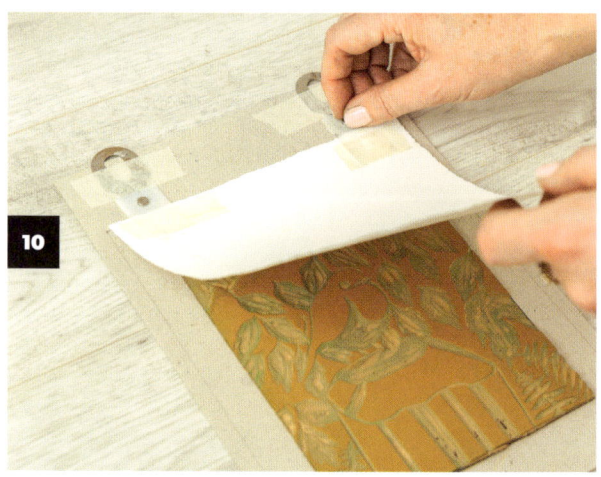

10 Take your first sheet of printmaking paper, making sure that the right side is facing down. Carefully slot the tabs onto the studs of the pins with one hand, while holding the paper up clear of the inked block with the other hand. Make sure the tabs click firmly onto the metal pins before you drop the paper down onto the block, ready for printing.

11 Once the tabs have clicked onto the studs, you simply let the other end of the paper fall down on top of the block. You can go ahead and print, either by hand-burnishing with a spoon or baren (**11a**), or using your printing press (see pages 59–62).

When you're finished, pull the paper up from the bottom end and hold it clear of the block, while carefully releasing the tabs from the metal studs at the top. Here's the secondary block printed with the first colour, in **11b**.

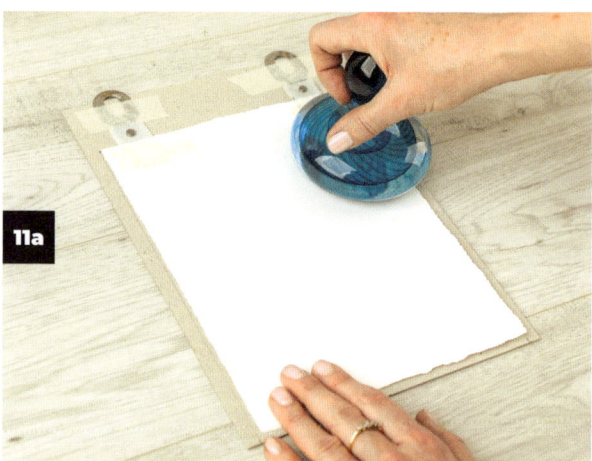

12 Make a print onto each sheet of paper you have prepared for your edition – I had five sheets for mine. You will now have a print (or a set of prints) with a semi-abstract image, made up of simple, flat blocks of colour – but possibly with the subject matter already being recognizable!

At this stage, I'm always excited and impatient to print the top layer and see how the final print will turn out, but it is very important to wait for the ink to dry completely before printing on top of it! This may take anything from two to five days, depending on the room temperature in which the prints are left to dry, so do be patient!

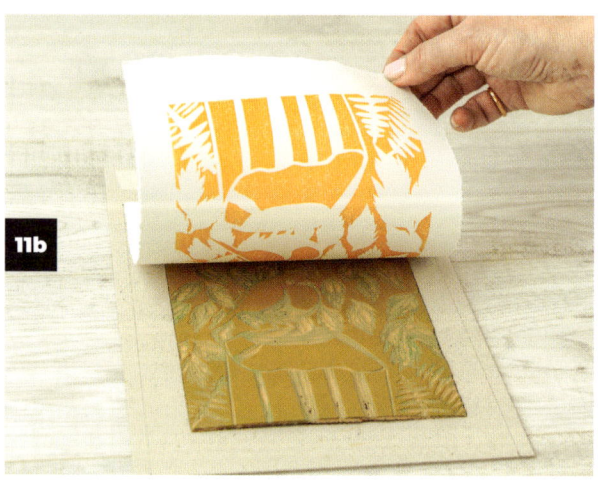

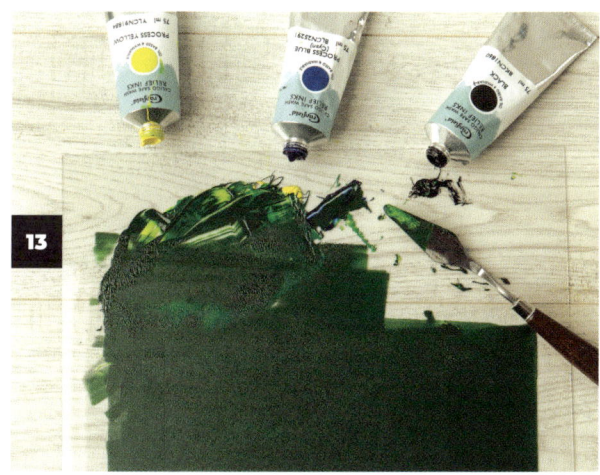

13 Once your prints are bone-dry, you are ready to print your top colour with the key block. Mix up the second, darker colour – for my design I mixed a very dark, petrol green, which I find a little less harsh than simply using black straight from the tube. I didn't add extender medium to this colour as I wanted it to be sufficiently dark enough to contrast well with the burnt orange. If you're in doubt about what colour to use, simply use black.

14 Ink up the key block with the secondary colour then carefully place it in the hole in the jig, the ink side facing up. Take one of the dried prints from step 11 and click the tabs onto the clips, holding the paper aloft throughout. Note the printed side should face down. When the tabs are secure, let the paper drop onto the block. If you have registered it correctly, it should be in exactly the same position as it was before, when you printed the previous block colour.

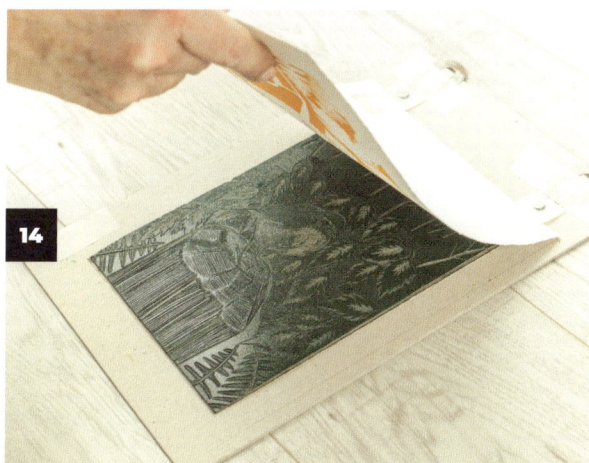

15 Print the second colour using your preferred method. If you are hand-burnishing as I did, be sure to hold the paper securely down on the block with one hand, so as not to let it move as you burnish with the other. Once you have applied sufficient pressure to print using one means or another, it's time to peel the paper back and reveal your finished print – even more exciting and possibly a little nerve-wracking with this one, as there has been a lot of work involved! Avoid letting the print drop back onto the block, and lay it down on a clean surface to dry, or put it on a drying rack if you have one.

Re-ink the key block and repeat the above printing process with the remainder of your prints, until each one is printed with the two colours.

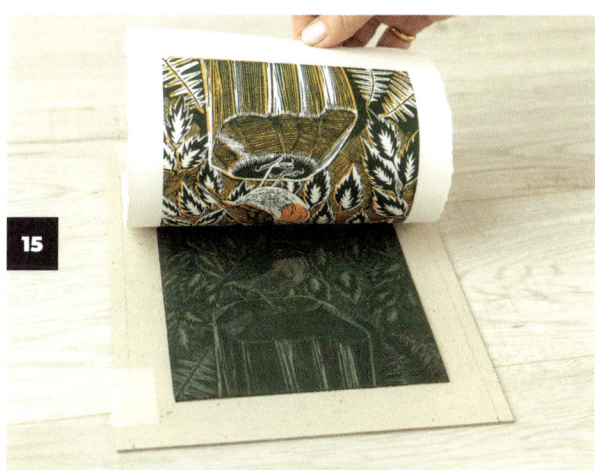

16 You have now made your first multi-coloured block linocut prints! Before you begin the arduous (but necessary!) task of cleaning up, find an ink-free surface and lay out the prints to appraise and admire. Do the colours work together as you hoped they would? Is the printing clear and sharp? How accurate is the registration? Inevitably, there will be some prints that have turned out better than others – but this is normal, even for professional printmakers. A slight overlap of one colour onto another isn't a problem if the print works well as a whole. Remember – you may spot things 'wrong' with it that noone else will ever notice!

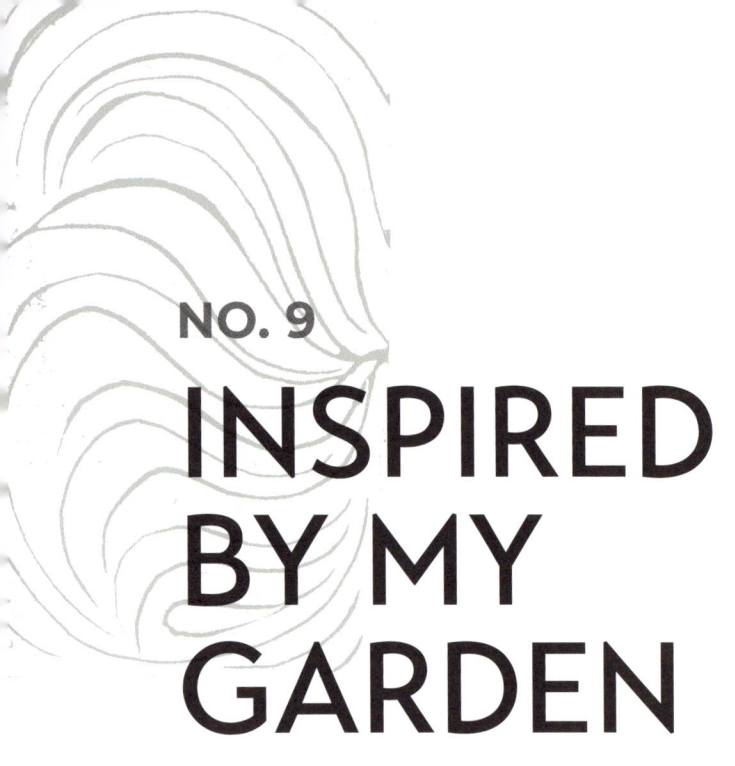

NO. 9

INSPIRED BY MY GARDEN

Project brief

You are going to be more ambitious with this print by making it larger – A4 (210 x 297mm/US Letter) in size! The composition will also be more complex compared to your previous prints, but will allow for a certain amount of free-styling. This means there will be opportunities for you to consolidate and build on the skills you've gained over the course of this book.

Your starting-point will be a garden – this can either be your own outside space, or your favourite public garden or park. Your print should be composed of multiple elements and include some areas of colour.

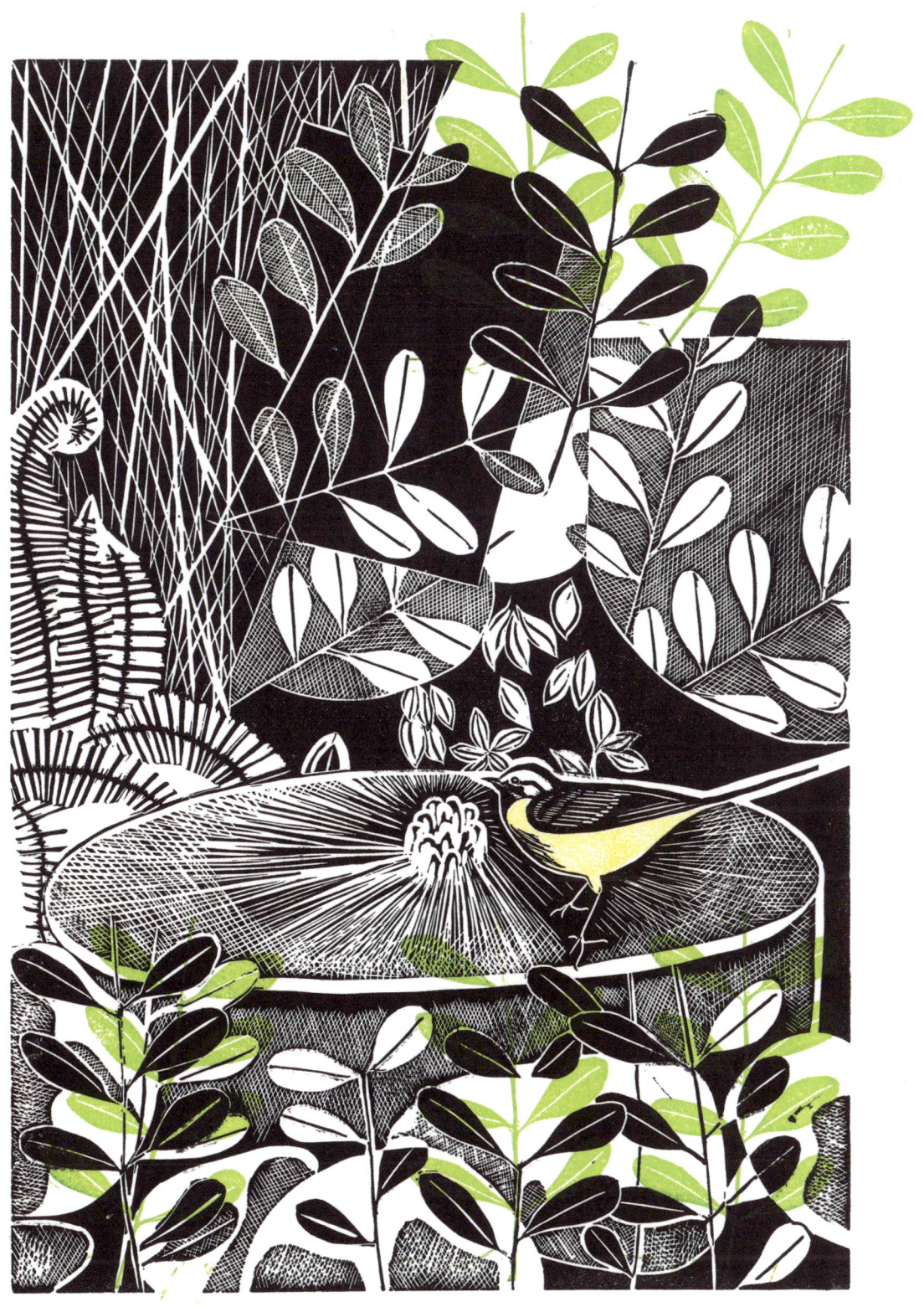

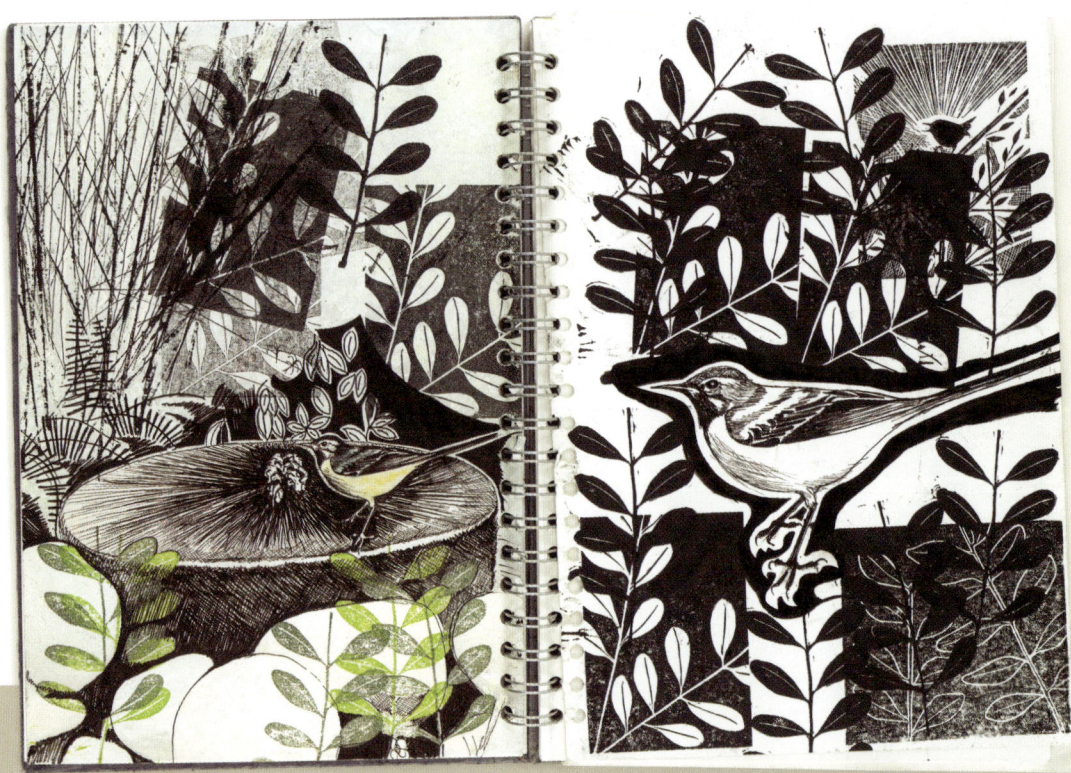

My starting point

I'm sure I've mentioned before that I love my garden!

Although it's tiny and is situated in the middle of a busy town surrounded by buildings, the garden has become a joyful sanctuary of green growth and babbling water. My reclaimed millstone water feature sits in the corner of the garden, flanked by ferns, grasses and low-growing shrubs. Large pebbles are laid around it, adding to the overall effect. Sadly, for me, the urban location and small size of the garden means the amount and variety of visiting birdlife tends to be limited – but there are the occasional gems. One such highlight is the grey wagtail that flies over now and again, making a special stop-off at the water feature! Perhaps he sees similarities to a bubbling brook, but whatever its attraction for him, I'm always thrilled when he pays us a visit.

I wanted to interpret this image I love so much as a linocut print. I began by making a sketch and then started to print on it – first with the sides of a thick piece of card dipped in ink, then with a small, stylized leaf stamp in a different colour. The sketch developed into a fun and free mixed-media exercise in textures, with some added colour.

Despite the looseness of the sketch, I decided to use the image as it was, without trying to develop it into a design, as I didn't want to lose the spontaneity of it. The very nature of the linocut process tends to be quite methodical – but I wanted to create a print that would give me the opportunity to 'freestyle' on it – even if just a little! I decided that the free styling could be done at the end, in the form of printing with extra colours on top of the main print.

Method

1 Trace off the design then transfer it to the lino, as described on pages 52 and 53. If you have a fairly complex design, you may need to use carbon paper – see the tip box below.

2 As always, you only need a simplified version of your design, with just the minimum of details included, to guide your carving. When you start to carve your block, you will be referring closely to your reference image(s) for guidance on different tones and details.

Although the transferred image is much simpler than the reference sketch, it will be a challenge (albeit a very enjoyable one!) to turn this rather riotous, busy collection of lines and shapes into a beautifully carved lino block for printing... But as you've got this far, you are well prepared for the challenge!

3 This is optional, depending on the complexity of your design: after transferring your design, you may wish to stain the lino with a diluted black Indian ink, to help make my marks more visible as you carve. Make sure to allow the lino to dry thoroughly before carving.

Continued...

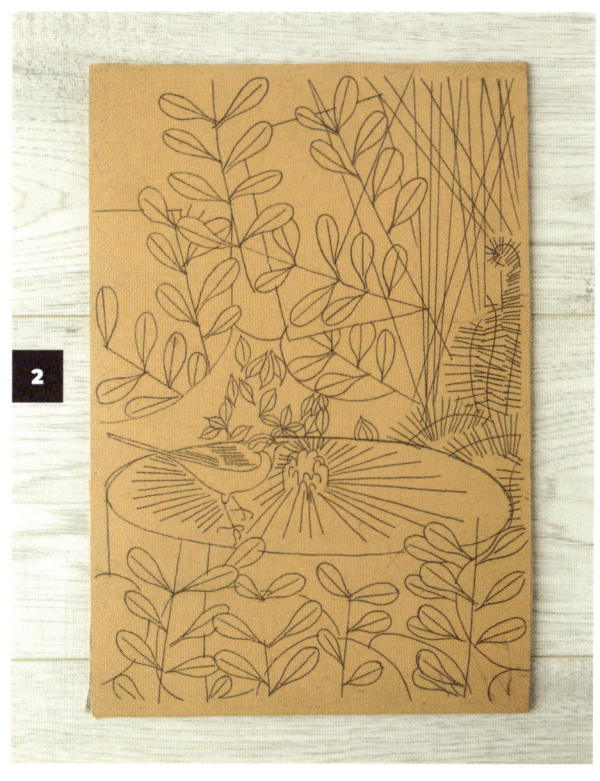

2

TRACING WITH CARBON PAPER

Carbon paper is ideal for transferring more complex designs, as it eliminates an extra drawing stage.

Place the sheet of carbon paper on top of your lino block, with the 'carbon' side facing down. Then place a photocopy of your reference image (this image will need to be 'flipped' to make sure it prints in the right direction) on top, and tape it to the carbon paper to prevent movement. Simply 'draw' over the reference image with a ballpoint pen, pressing firmly to ensure that the carbon paper underneath transfers your lines clearly onto the lino. If you use a coloured pen to press over the lines of your design, it will be easier to see if you've forgotten to trace anything!

Once you have traced off your desired outlines, remove the reference image and carbon paper from the lino block to reveal your transferred design – all flipped and ready to carve.

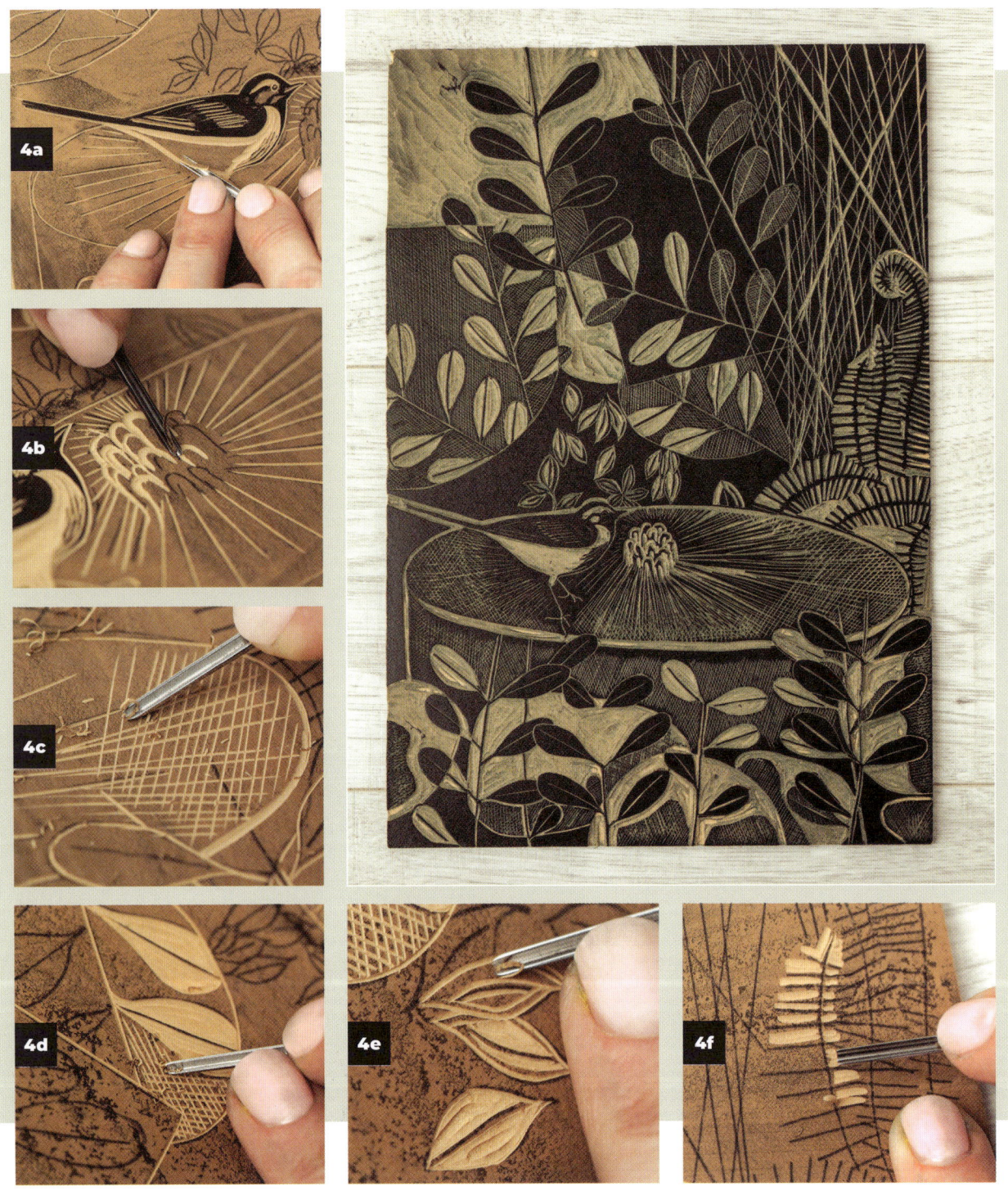

4 OK – let's start carving! Carve your block until you're happy with how it looks. Do remember to refer back to page 48 if you need any guidance with markings. Here's how I approached my design.

— The key shapes in the piece were outlined using the fine V-shaped tool.

— I then moved on to the focal point of my design – the wagtail. Although he is small, he is important.

Using my fine V-shaped tool, I started with the little bird's face before outlining the shapes inside his body. I then carved out the details on his wing using a mix of fine and small V-shaped tools; then, leaving a few lines on the front of the belly uncarved, I removed the rest of lino along his stomach (**4a**). I used a fine V-shaped tool to carve around the belly markings, then a medium V-shaped tool to remove the lino in the stomach area.

You may notice I partly coloured in the wagtail with a permanent black marker pen. When I have an element that features lots of textures and details, in addition to staining the lino I will colour in areas I want to keep black with a marker pen, to make sure I don't carve anywhere I shouldn't!

— The millstone was developed, with the bubbling water carved out with a small V-shaped tool (**4b**) then shading added all around the outside of the stone by working cross-hatched lines with the fine V-shaped tool (**4c**).

— I have two different kinds of leaves in my design – symmetrical, rounded leaves on a stem, and small pointed leaves clustered around the top of the millstone. There is a mix of solid, cross-hatched and completely carved-out shapes behind the leaves at the back of my design, an idea which came about when I used some of my carved stamps to print directly onto my initial sketch. I liked them so much that I decided to retain them in the final design!

With these shapes, the use of positive and negative space and the simplified, stylized leaves hark back to the earlier 'Plant Therapy' (see pages 80–85) and 'Getting Bolder' (see pages 90–95) projects – but, of course, this will be more challenging, to reflect your growing skills and confidence.

Depending on the background behind the rounded leaves with a stem, either I carved out the whole leaf (cross-hatched background – **4d**), cross-hatched the leaf (black background), or left the leaves untouched (completely carved out background). I used a mix of V-shaped and U-shaped tools in a mix of sizes throughout.

— I carved the little pointed leaves in a variety of different ways with the fine V-shaped tool and the small U-shaped tool: some were completely carved out with a small vein left in, some I left in 'borders' that would print, and some overlapped which meant giving them a thicker outline (**4e**).

— To finish, on the far right-hand side of the lino, I carved out the grasses with V-shaped tools in a range of sizes, as they sat over a dark background. For the ferns, which were also over the dark background, I suggested their shape and leaves by carving out the negative spaces with a small U-shaped tool (**4f**).

Continued...

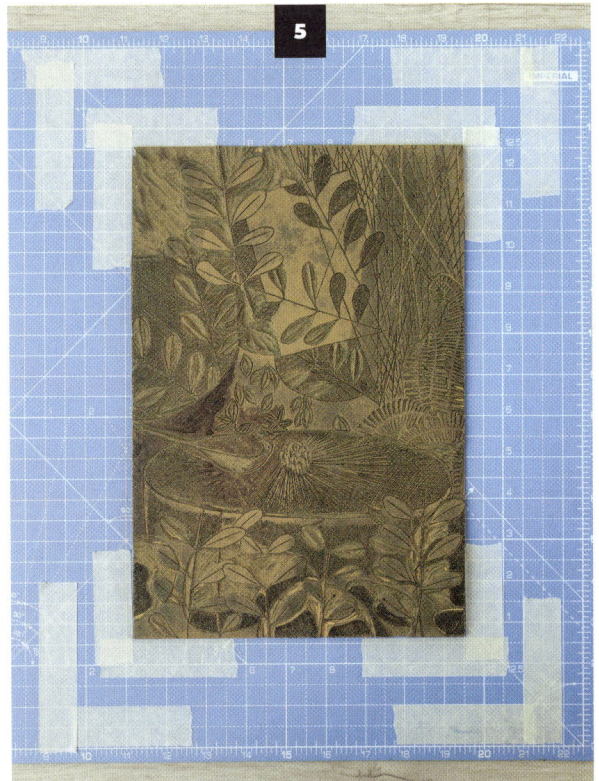

5 When I select my paper size, I also decide on the size of the borders that will be around the print.

I like to mark out the position of the lino block and the sheets of printing paper on my press or table (depending on which printing method I'm using), and for this I generally use strips of masking tape to mark the corners. I position the lino block first, and tape around the corners (see the inner taped markings), then the paper is positioned and the corners taped in the same way (see the outer taped markings).

Once you start printing, simply line up the top corners of your sheet of paper with the outer markings while holding up the bottom of the paper. Once the top corners are lined up with the taped outer markings, just drop the rest of the sheet on top of the inked block, making sure you are still holding firmly onto the top of the sheet to prevent movement. I taped a gridded surface in the photograph, left, as this helps ensure that your paper and lino are in the right position when printing, but you don't need a gridded surface necessarily.

6 It's time to ink up your block. As this is a larger block, ideally you should use a wider brayer (it should be at least the same width as the block you're inking up). However, don't worry if you don't have one: just roll over the block repeatedly in both vertical and horizontal directions, trying to eliminate any obvious 'lines' left in the ink by the ends of the brayer.

If you notice anything obvious you have forgotten to carve, it's best to correct this before printing. Blot the area(s) to recarve with an old kitchen towel or newspaper, recarve then re-ink. Before recarving, it's a good idea to lay a piece of kitchen paper on the rest of the block, so your hand (or sleeve!) doesn't make direct contact with the rest of the inked surface. Once you have made any necessary adjustments to the carving, remove the kitchen paper and carefully sweep off any small lino particles.

Print the block using your chosen method (see pages 59–62). For this print, I'm hand-burnishing. I recommend making a test print, before committing to your chosen paper. This allows for a 'proofing' stage, so you can assess the design after it's printed and make any more tweaks they're needed.

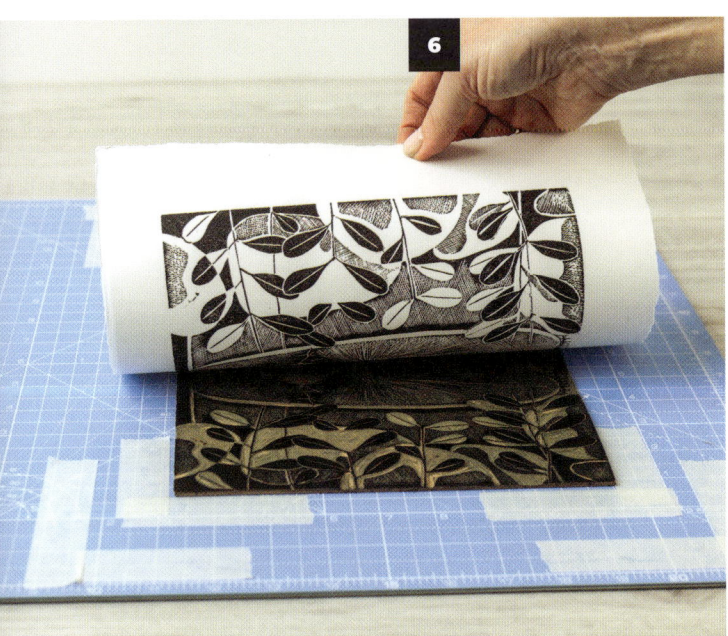

7 For me, this print wasn't quite the finished article – I wanted to add pops of colour to selected areas of the design, to create more interest. I used exactly the same technique used in 'Let's Add Colour', on pages 102–108 – spot-colouring with a stamp. I created to stamps – one for my wagtail, and one that echoed the shape of some of the foliage in the design.

When it comes to cutting out a stamp, It doesn't matter about slight discrepancies in size and shape – the ink with which you stamp (archival pigment ink) is pale and translucent, and therefore forgiving when it comes to minor misregistrations.

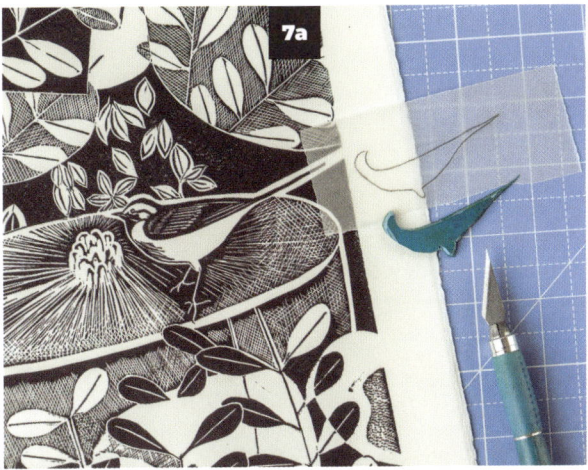

- As the star of my print is a wagtail, I wanted to bring a little more attention to him. Grey wagtails have a yellow underside, so I decided to make a point of this. Using a small off-cut of tracing paper, I traced off the bird's underside from the finished print (make sure the print is dry before you do this!). I then transferred the shape onto a small PVC lino scrap then cut it out with a craft knife on a cutting mat (**7a**). Because this shape is small, it is quite fiddly to cut out and requires care – avoid cutting towards the fingers of your other hand!

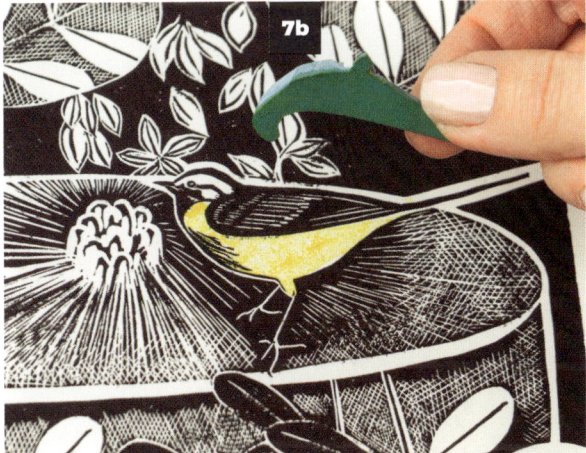

- I like to test my spot colours and stamps on a scrap of paper before committing them to my chosen surface, to test the results. By doing this, I found the yellow colour I wanted to use was too strong, so I stamped off the excess onto a piece of scrap paper with very light pressure, before stamping onto my main print. This removed some (but not all) of the ink from the stamp, resulting in a paler colour that I preferred (**7b**).

- My second stamp was similar to the round, stemmed leaves carved on the main block. As it was a freestyle element of the design, this stamp didn't need to fit onto a specific shaped element in the design, and therefore didn't need to be cut exactly to shape. Because of this, I could use a scrap of any sort of lino I had lying around – I used a small scrap of hessian-backed linoleum, cut into a rectangle shape. I traced a small section of the stylized leaves from my print, then transferred it onto the lino scrap. I then dabbed the stamp in lime green ink and pressed it multiple times in among the existing black, white and cross-hatched leaves (**7c**).

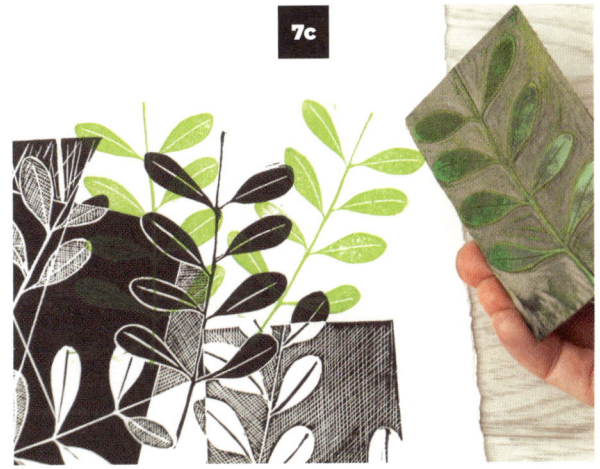

NO. 10
MIXING IT UP!

YOU WILL NEED

— Selection of linocut prints you've made in the previous projects – these can be slightly 'imperfect' ones and/or test prints

— Thick cartridge paper or card, larger than A4 (210 x 297mm/ US Letter) in size, for your collage backing

— Sharp paper scissors

— Craft knife and cutting mat or sheet of heavy-duty card to cut on (essential for this project!)

— Glue – preferably archival 'book-binding' glue, but can be PVA, craft glue or a regular glue stick

— Clean, dry printing roller for smoothing the pieces after they've been stuck down

— Optional: reference image (such as a rough sketch of your design), if you need one

Project brief

Create a nature-inspired collaged piece that is entirely made up of pieces of any of your rejected linocut prints from the previous projects. Try to incorporate elements of as many of the prints you've made as possible! The finished artwork should be larger than A4 (210 x 297mm/US Letter) in size, but it need not necessarily be rectangular or square.

You do not need to use a reference sketch or photograph for this artwork, although you can if you wish. You will find the project more enjoyable and creative if you work from your imagination, and let yourself be guided by the pieces of your prints!

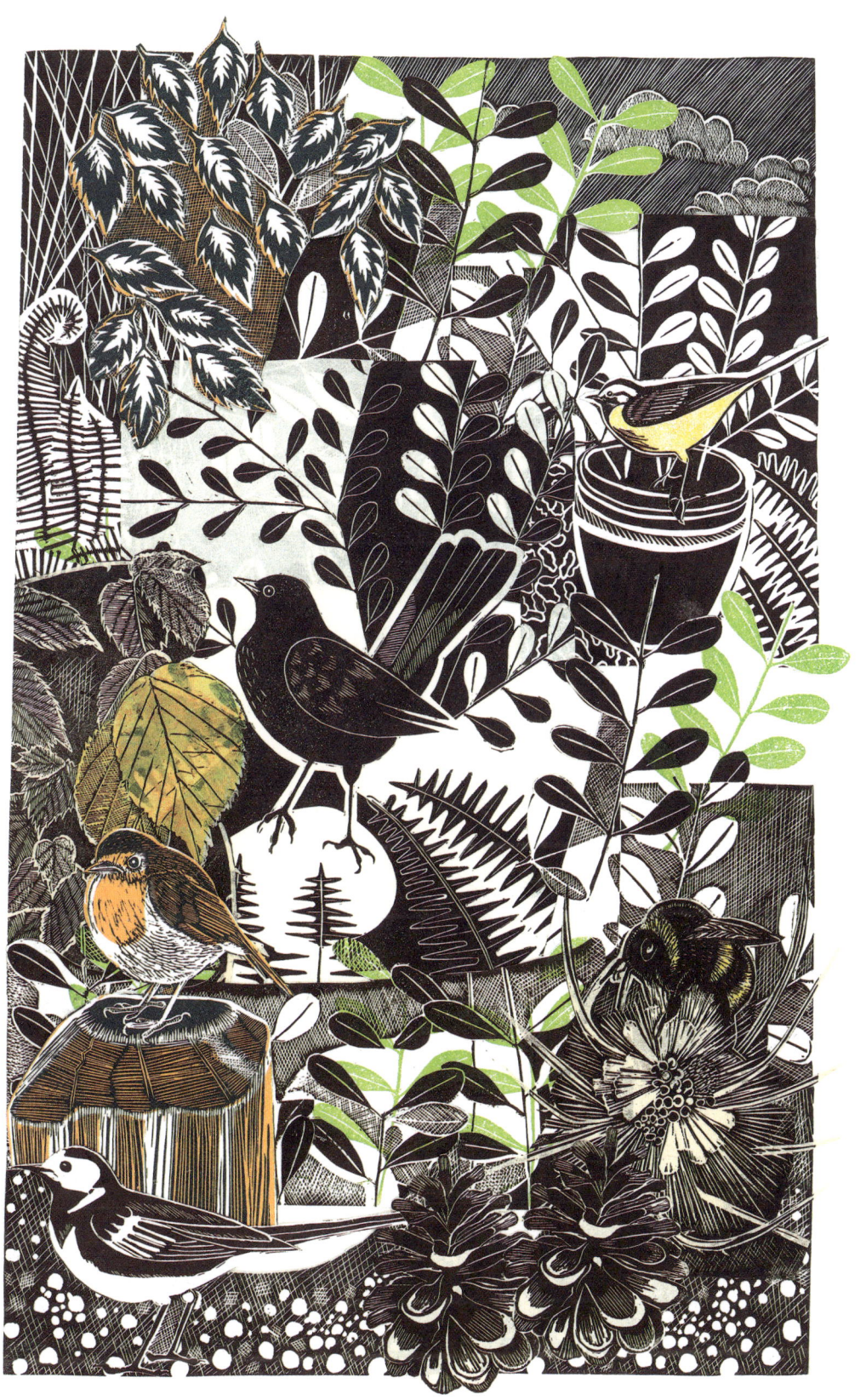

My starting point

Making a collage with your prints is wonderfully liberating, as it's possible to create incredibly complex artworks with this technique. It's also a great way of recycling test prints and prints that, for one reason or another, you have 'rejected' from the main editions.

Collaging with cut-up pieces of our hand-made prints is such good fun! After completing the other projects in this book, we have a ready array of beautiful hand-printed imagery to work with; we can cut, tear, place, layer and stick them to create literally any composition we wish. We can combine the flora, fauna and scenery from different prints

into one involved artwork – without being limited by our carving and printing skills. We can even make considerably larger pieces than our range of printing equipment would normally allow!

My starting point was literally a jumbled collection of different test prints and mis-prints. I spread them out on my table, with no particular idea for the artwork I would eventually create. I prefer to be led by the images laid out before me, which often results in new inspiration!

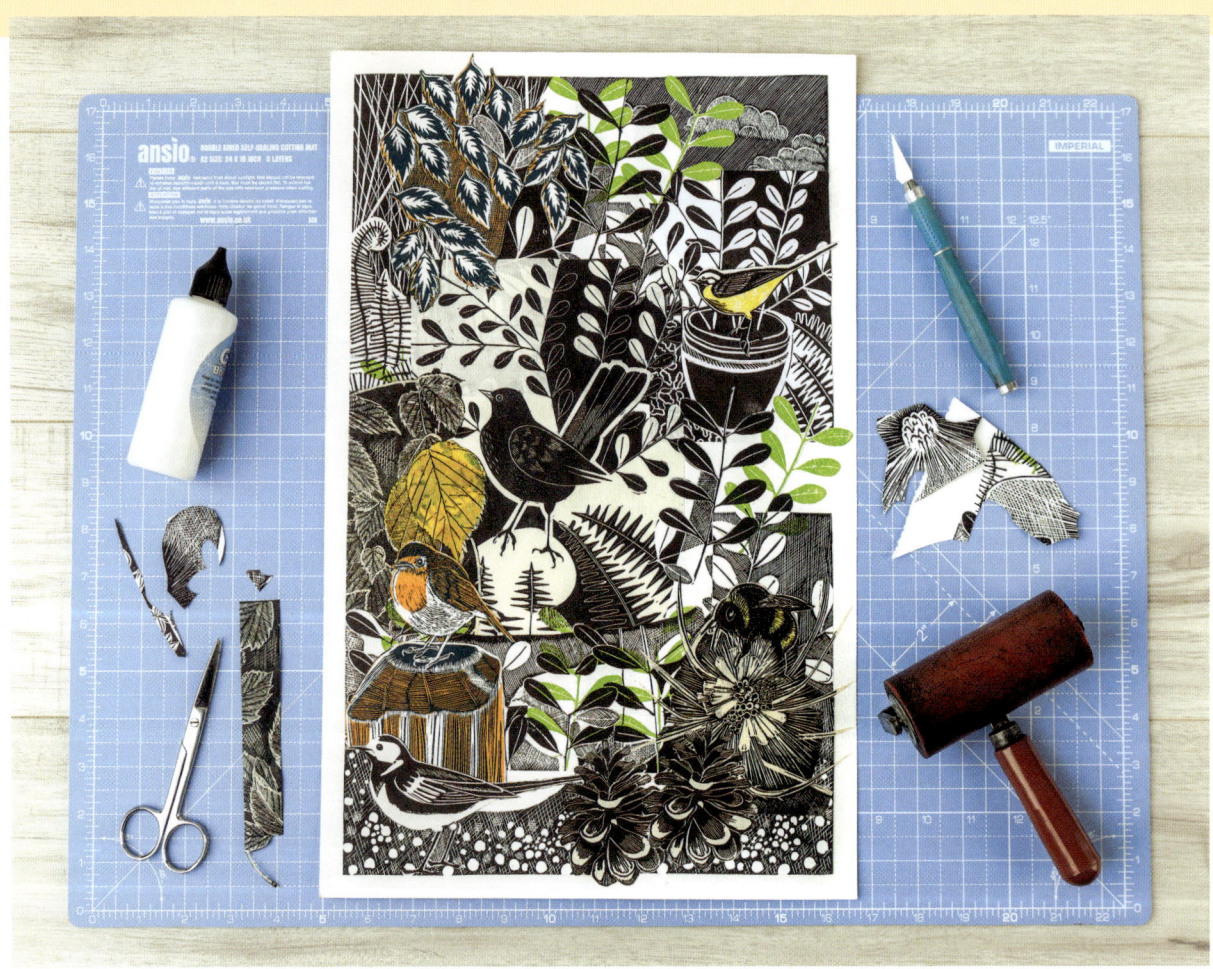

Method

1 Once you've spread out your prints and spent a few minutes considering the creative potential they offer, start cutting them up as soon as possible. Rather like the hesitancy people sometimes feel when starting to draw on a new piece of paper, we can find ourselves being 'precious' about cutting up prints. Remember, these prints are not part of any edition, and would most likely be relegated to a drawer and forgotten about!

— Use a sharp craft knife or scalpel to cut out small shapes, central characters and features that need 'precision' cutting – these might be animals, birds, insects or flowers – so that they can be cleanly removed from the rest of the print.

— Background elements or textures can then be cut with scissors, or even torn out in sections. These elements or textures will form the base of your collage, and can be layered over each other; the 'central characters' will then be layered on top.

2 As you are cutting out your prints, inspiration will kick in and you will start to form some ideas for the artwork you want to create. Imagine the 'scene' or theme you will create in your artwork.

— Start to lay the pieces out on your collage backing. Try out different combinations of printed pieces; see what the effects are of placing birds or animals against different backgrounds or textures; experiment with overlapping, or cutting around the shapes of some of the leaves, so that the colours and textures behind them are partially visible.

— If a particular combination works well, keep the pieces together and put them to one side until you decide where you want them to go in your composition. The work you are aiming to create should now slowly be emerging!

— Don't be discouraged if you're struggling to create a 'realistic' scene. You are working with a limited selection of imagery and, unless you're really lucky, you won't be able to recreate a life-like landscape with the correct scales and perspective – and nor should you! This is a piece of art, with colour, pattern and a pleasing composition being the most important criteria for its success.

— At this layering stage, it's important to refrain from sticking anything down. There will be plenty of time for this, when you are 100 per cent certain you are happy with your collage design. Once the pieces are stuck down, they're hard to remove without damaging them if you change your mind.

3 When you're completely happy with the placement of the pieces for your collage, you can start to stick them down in their final positions on your backing paper or card.

— Before removing the pieces, take a photograph of your arrangement. You will almost certainly need to refer to this for correct replacement and guidance.

— It's important to be systematic when glueing down your pieces, and remember that you will be layering and overlapping some of the pieces, too. You'll need to stick down your pieces in the right order. For my collage, I'm starting at the top and working down, placing the background pieces first and the 'central characters' on top of these.

— Because a lot of my background pieces have straight edges, I have chosen to arrange them in such a way as to leave a narrow border around the edges of my collage. I like the appearance of a white border around an artwork, and doing this will also make the finished collage appear like a linocut print!

— Aim for little to no visible wrinkles or creases, but don't worry if the odd one creeps in! Make sure that you apply the glue sparingly too, close to the edges of the piece but without 'flooding' over. Smooth the piece gently with a clean finger and then press it down firmly by rolling all over it with a clean, dry brayer until it is stuck down perfectly smoothly.

4 Congratulations – you have completed the final project in this book! When you evaluate your work, remember that this piece is a collage, not a print: the surface will not be smooth and even, and inevitably there will be some visible joins. These little 'flaws' are unavoidable in collage and to my mind, only add to the authenticity and charm of the finished piece!

TROUBLESHOOTING

If you are just starting out with linocut printing, you will very soon discover that it is not always an easy, straightforward process – and if you're already some way into your printmaking journey, you'll have found this out already!

It is often said in printmaking that 'every day's a school day', and I can honestly say that, in my own practice, never a day goes by when I don't learn something new. I can also say that I wouldn't have it any other way! The frustrations and disappointments I have experienced when things 'go wrong' are easily outweighed by the enjoyable challenge of finding solutions to problems and the outcomes achieved – not to mention those wonderful 'happy accidents' that happen along the way!

Having said this, it is always useful to have a bank of actions you can take if things are not working out for whatever reason. Listed on the following pages are some problems commonly encountered during the whole process of making a linocut print, with suggestions for either solving the issue, or minimizing and/or ameliorating the problem.

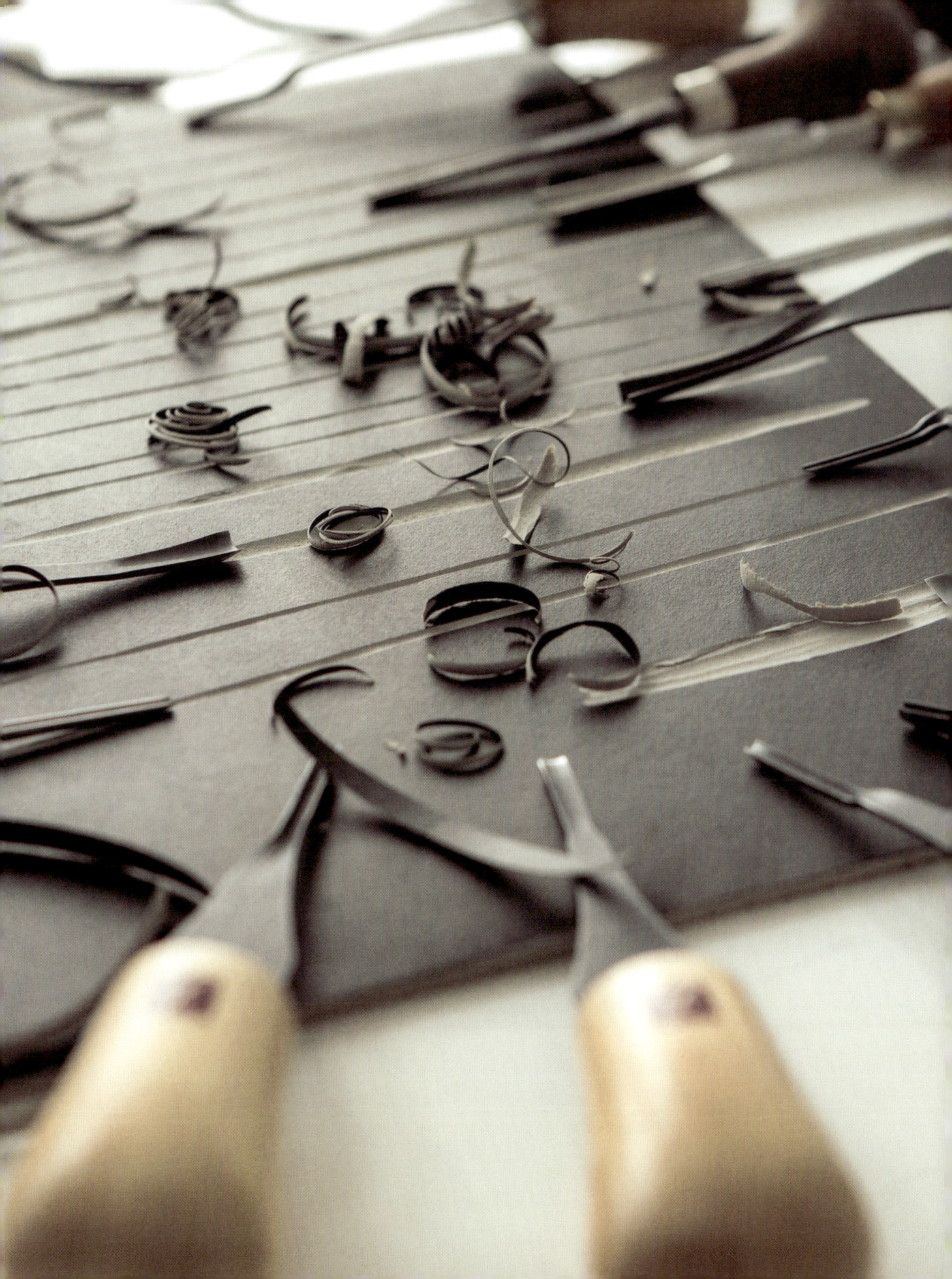

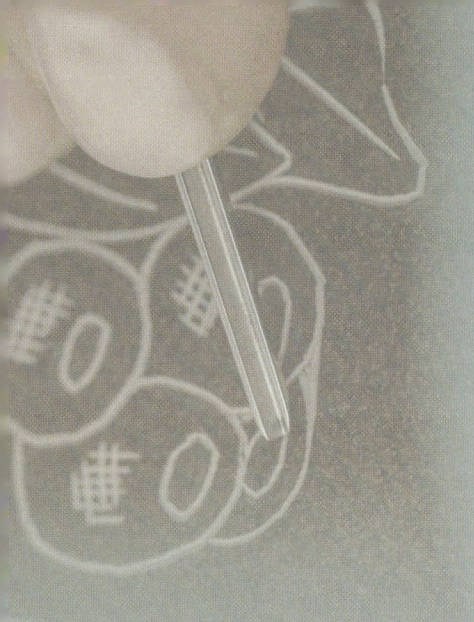

Problem 1: I've made a carving mistake!

Carved marks on lino are permanent and can't be rubbed out or painted over, so if you carve out something by mistake, particularly if it is important to the overall design, it can seem pretty catastrophic! However, this doesn't necessarily mean starting the whole thing again; there are things you can try which may sufficiently improve, if not completely eradicate the mistake. Before you throw the whole thing away, try these possible solutions.

WORK INTO IT

Often, 'mistakes' made when carving are actually quite minor, although they may be annoying when they happen. These can sometimes be improved by carving additional marks and/or lines around the 'mistake'.

For example, if you feel you've miscarved some veins on a leaf, try carefully adding more veins to branch out from them. If you're trying to carve straight lines – for instance, if your lines keep going wonky in an area with cross-hatching, it's best to ignore the occasional wonky line and just keep carving the remaining lines. It may be worth reaching for your try-out lino scrap and practising your straight lines some more, until you feel confident to return to carving your main block. You will find that a few wonky lines will not necessarily spoil your design – and other people probably won't even notice them!

Although they can be incredibly detailed, natural forms and textures do tend to be fairly forgiving of inconsistencies in our mark-making. It's the whole effect of your carved block you should focus on, rather than the tiny individual areas that make up the design.

Right
Accidental mark made at the bottom of the lowest berry.

Far right
I've turned the mark into an additional berry.

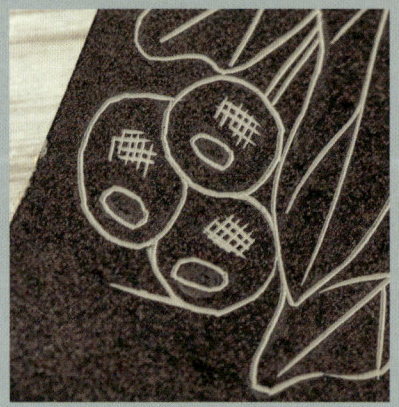
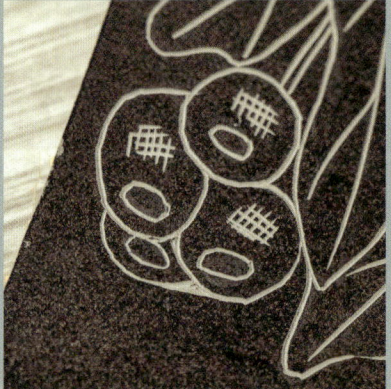

EXPERIMENT WITH WOOD FILLER

If your mistake can't be disguised with more carving – for example, if you've accidentally carved out something which you should have left in – you can fill in the accidental carving with wood filler then re-carve the area correctly.

I should point out that although using this method will give you a chance to rectify a carving error, results can vary. Depending on the size and type of the carved mark, it can work very well, acceptably well, or poorly. Therefore, I would advise you to try this only if you think it's absolutely necessary.

If I ever feel I've made a 'major' error when carving, I will usually put the block to one side and re-visit it the following day to assess the damage with fresh eyes. In doing this, I will often reach the conclusion that the error isn't as drastic as I first feared and can be disguised or minimized by further carving, as discussed above.

If you feel you do need to repair and re-carve the area, gather a repair kit of wood filler, a small palette knife and sandpaper, then follow the steps, right.

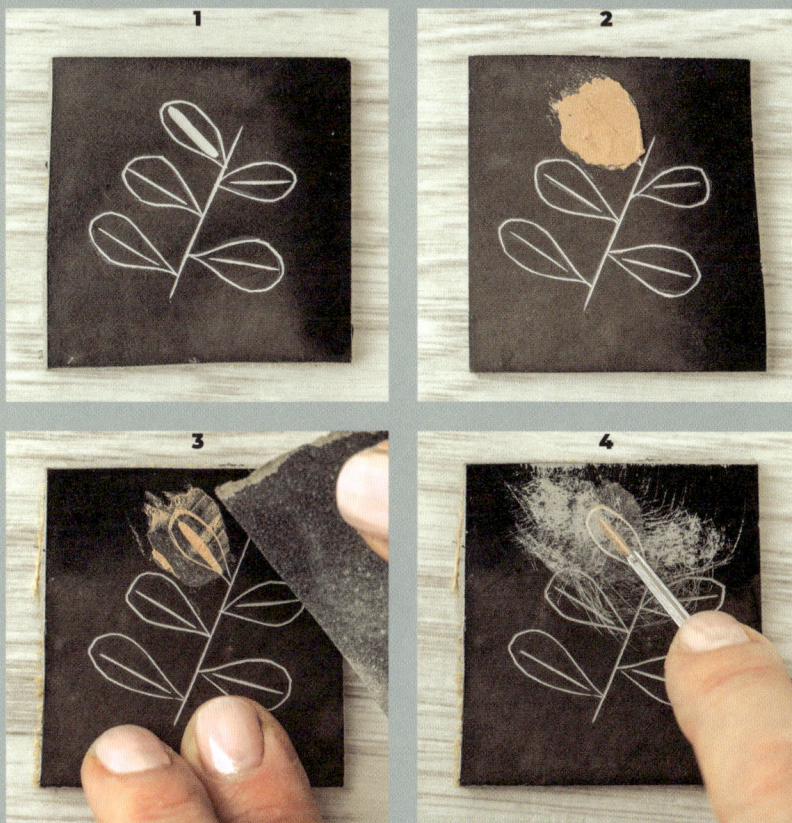

1 In this example, I used too thick a tool for the top-left leaf vein.

2 Squeeze out a small amount of the filler and use your palette knife to spread it carefully over the erroneous area, making sure it's completely filled. Level off the filler as smoothly as you can; the surface should be just slightly proud of the surrounding lino surface. Leave the filled block to dry thoroughly, preferably overnight.

3 Check the filler is bone-dry, then sand down the wood-filled area carefully with your sandpaper until it's perfectly smooth and completely level with the uncarved lino.

4 Now you can very carefully re-carve the area. It may help to draw on the detail lightly with a pencil first – but beware of pressing too hard with a sharp pencil and damaging the wood filler. Once re-carved, you can go ahead and print your block as described on the previous pages.

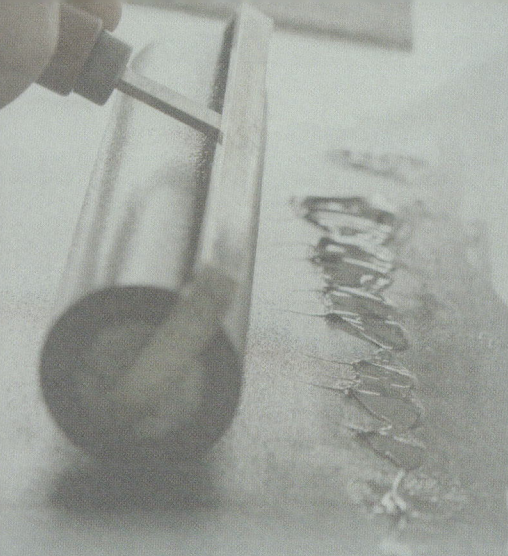

Problem 2: I'm having a bad print day!

You have carved a beautiful design and are excited to print it. You set out your printing table, prepare the paper, ink up the block and launch happily into your printing session. However, you repeatedly get (at best) unsatisfactory or (at worst) poor prints! How common is this scenario? The answer is, far more common than you might think!

OVER-INKING

This is one of the most common causes of poor printing results. As you can see from the top-right photograph, the leaves and berries in the print have lost a lot of their detail and definition. The image also looks overly black and 'heavy'.

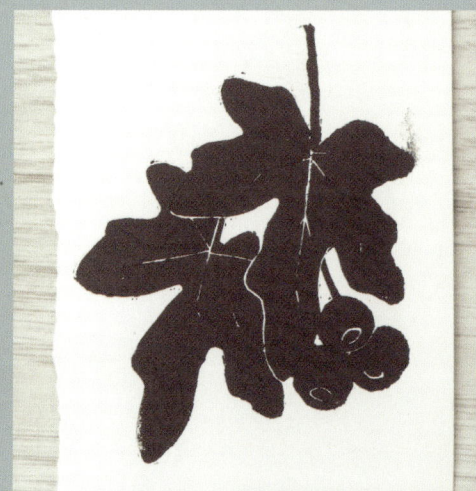

- If you have applied **too much ink to your lino block**, you will need to remove the surplus ink before making any more prints. You don't need to clean up the block completely. If you're using a press, simply run the block through the press several times, printing onto cheap paper or newsprint until the paper is coming out virtually clean. If you're not using a press, you can use newsprint or kitchen towels to blot away the excess ink.

- Always **avoid rolling out too much ink** – not only is it wasteful, but you run a greater risk of over-inking.

- Always check your brayer before rolling it onto your block – the ink coverage should be smooth, with a slight 'glisten' when the light reflects on its surface as you hold it up. You should start with just a thin covering of ink on your brayer and gradually apply it in layers to the block, until the coverage is sufficient to make a good print. It's fairly easy to tell if you have too much ink on your brayer. There will be thick 'blobs' that will transfer to the lino if you roll them on, resulting in an over-inked block, which in turn will produce an over-inked print. The brayer in the bottom-right photograph is over-inked. If there is **too much ink on your brayer**, you can easily remove the surplus by rolling it on a wipe-clean sheet or a piece of newsprint.

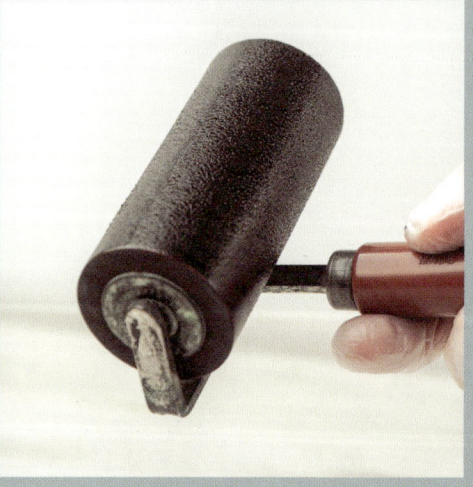